IMAGES
of America

MADRAS

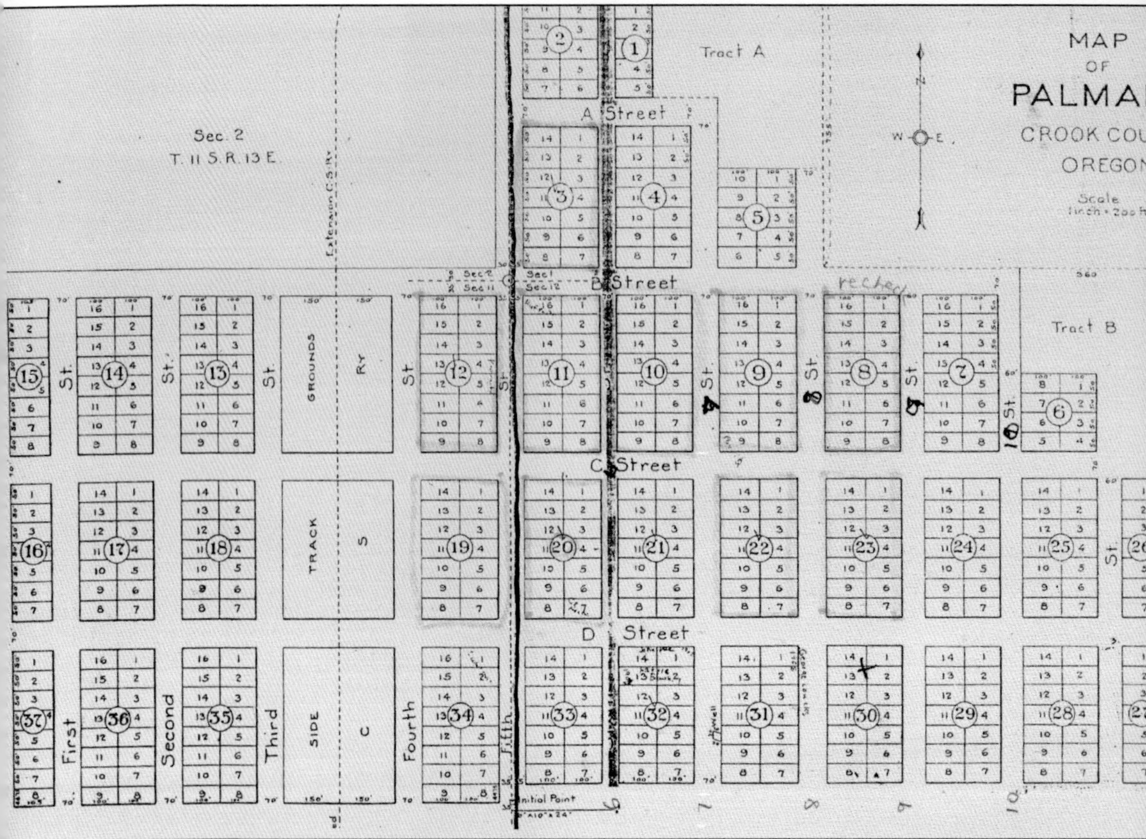

John Palmehn platted a new town on July 18, 1902. This map is the original plat for Palmain, which was the first submitted name for the community. Post office officials rejected the proposed named of Palmain, citing another post office with a similar name. The name Madras was then submitted and accepted. (Courtesy of Beth Crow.)

On the Cover: The arrival of the Oregon Trunk Railroad into Madras and central Oregon on February 15, 1911, marked the beginning of a new era in the development of the community and its surrounding area. This photograph of local dignitaries and railroad officials commemorates the arrival of the first train to central Oregon and was an occasion for celebration throughout the region. (Courtesy of Jefferson County Historical Society.)

IMAGES
of America

MADRAS

Steve Lent

ARCADIA
PUBLISHING

ISBN 978-0-7385-9325-8

Published by Arcadia Publishing
Charleston, South Carolina

Printed in the United States of America

Library of Congress Control Number: 2011943028

For all general information, please contact Arcadia Publishing:
Telephone 843-853-2070
Fax 843-853-0044
E-mail sales@arcadiapublishing.com
For customer service and orders:
Toll-Free 1-888-313-2665

Visit us on the Internet at www.arcadiapublishing.com

To Barbara, my lifelong partner.

Contents

Acknowledgments

Many hands helped in the development of this book. The Jefferson County Historical Society has been of tremendous assistance in providing most of the photographs in the book, and special aid from Phyllis Lange, the museum director, has made the search for images and information a less daunting task. County historian Beth Crow provided additional photographs and her vast knowledge of local history has contributed to the accuracy of the book, and her advice is highly cherished. Beth and Phyllis also reviewed the document for accuracy. Jefferson County Historical Society president Jarold Ramsey has provided encouragement in the completion of this project. The Juniper Branch of Family Finders also has provided much information accumulated for another book by the author on the place names of Jefferson County and was very useful in segments of this book.

Hundreds of photographs have been searched, trying to find the best way to tell the story of Madras. Unless otherwise noted, all images appear courtesy of the Jefferson County Historical Society.

The Crook County Historical Society and Bowman Museum in Prineville have also been very helpful in assisting the photograph searches and information gathering.

INTRODUCTION

Madras has a history of boom cycles and is one of the lesser-known communities of central Oregon. It had its beginnings in the early livestock industry, when cattle and sheep were introduced to the lush grazing lands. Felix Scott Jr. was the first to herd cattle to central Oregon and wintered just northeast of present Madras in the early 1860s. Large cattle operators Till and Coleman established a cattle empire on Trout Creek north of present Madras and grazed cattle in "the Basin." In the late 1870s and the 1880s, Dr. David Baldwin developed the famous Hay Creek Ranch, one of the largest sheep ranches in the United States. The Baldwin Sheep and Land Company was a significant operation and played an important role in the development of Madras by utilizing the community as a shipping point for wool and lambs. Those products were shipped from Madras to national markets via the railroad once it arrived.

The site of Madras was originally known as "the Basin" because of its location in a relatively dry bowl-like valley. The raising of livestock was the primary business in the vicinity until the homestead era began around 1900. A large influx of homesteaders came to the region to dry land farm. Water was limited and large areas of land were cleared and planted to winter wheat. Thousands of land-seekers from around the United States and some foreign countries hoped to make a living from the land. Dry land wheat did become a successful crop for some farmers, but years of drought and poor crops led many to abandon their dreams, sell their farms or homesteads, and move on to other regions.

The first big boom in the Madras vicinity occurred in 1911 when the great railroad war to central Oregon brought the arrival of the Oregon Trunk Railroad and the Deschutes Railroad, operated by major rivals James J. Hill and Edward H. Harriman, respectively. The race up the Deschutes River Canyon was one of the last major battles between railroad giants. The two railroads blasted their way up the Deschutes River on opposite banks of the river and frequent skirmishes occurred between the rival construction crews.

Madras served as a major supply source for the competing railroad construction crews and was the first community in central Oregon to host the railroads. A major celebration was held in the community to welcome the railroads on Railroad Day, February 15, 1911. Thousands of central Oregon residents attended the festivities with the hope that the railroad would soon expand south to other communities and open the interior frontier to national markets. Madras became known as the "gateway to central Oregon." Prominent local businessman and political figure Howard Turner called it the "greatest day in the history of Madras." By the end of 1911, the Oregon Trunk Railroad had arrived in Redmond and Bend.

Madras experienced a boom when livestock and farm products could be shipped to a wider market via the railroad. The region continued to grow dry land products, as irrigation was slow to arrive in the Madras vicinity. One local farmer, Tillman Reuter, gained many national awards for his outstanding dry land crops. Major irrigation developments began in Central Oregon as early as 1905, but expanded irrigation did not reach to farmland south of Madras. The Bureau of

Reclamation began development of the North Unit Project in the early 1930s, building Wickiup Dam on the upper Deschutes River to provide water storage for the expansion of irrigation into the Madras region. Eventually, the North Unit Canal was constructed to Madras and water was diverted from the Deschutes River just north of Bend and delivered to the rich farmlands surrounding Madras in 1946. The canal was known as the "Grand Furrow." The arrival of water for irrigation made the Madras region a major farming zone.

During World War II, the Army established a bomber training facility at the Madras airport and the community hosted the trainees in barracks established in the community. After the war, the City of Madras acquired the airbase facilities and agricultural aircraft used for spraying crops began operating at the airport.

Industrial operations like farming, equipment production, and lumber products industries followed the big irrigation projects. Madras, however, remained primarily an agricultural economy. A new boom began with the construction, in the mid-1950s and early 1960s, of Pelton Dam and Round Butte Dam for hydroelectric power on the Deschutes River a few miles west of Madras. Local businesses and laborers benefited from the large projects and Madras became a prosperous and active community. After construction of the dams, the reservoirs impounded by the dams became extremely popular recreation sites with boaters and fishermen.

Culturally, Madras has long had ties with the Warm Springs Indian Reservation, about 15 miles north of Madras. Additionally, the large farming operations attracted a large migrant workforce of Hispanic laborers, adding to the cultural diversity of the Madras community. Native American and Hispanic influences make Madras the "melting pot" of central Oregon.

One

The Early Settlement Years

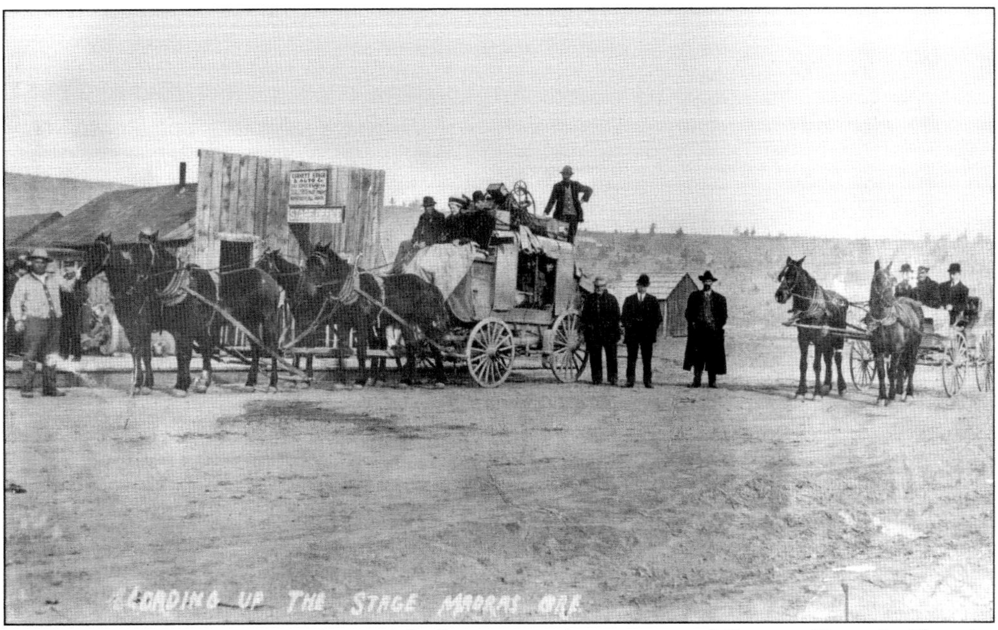

John McIntire Cornett operated one of the largest stage lines in central Oregon. Here, the Shaniko to Prineville stage waits to depart from the Madras stage depot in early 1911. The driver of the stage is Jarve "Casey" Jones and the man standing on the back of the stage is owner John Cornett. Douglas Hood is the gentleman standing third from the rear of the stage and seated in the mountain hack to the right are Charles W. Elkins, an unidentified man, and Will Wurzweiler.

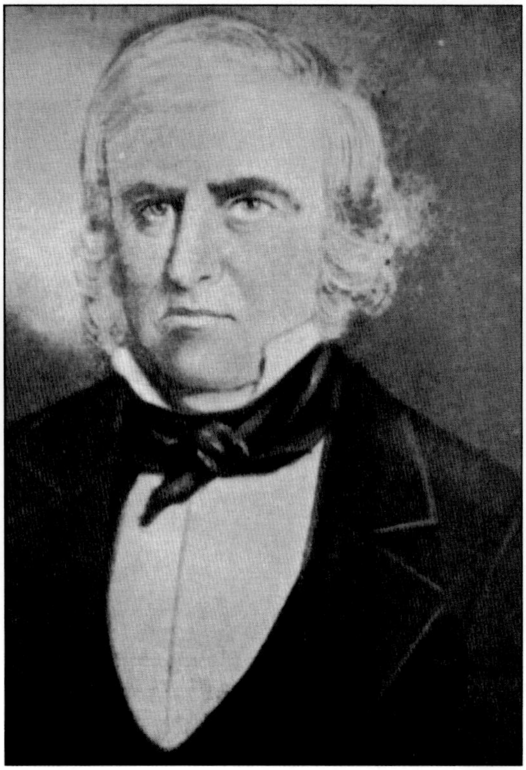

The first known non–Native American man to travel near Madras was Peter Skene Ogden, a fur brigade leader of the Hudson Bay Fur Company. He traveled up the Deschutes and Crooked Rivers just west of Madras in the winter of 1825 searching for beaver and other animal pelts on the Snake River Expedition. He also led subsequent expeditions that passed through the region in the winters of 1826 and 1827.

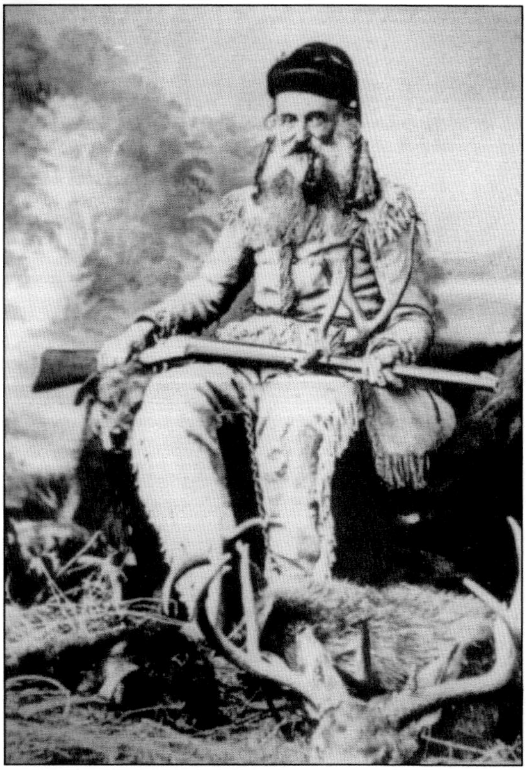

In 1845, Stephen Hall Meek convinced hundreds of people that he knew of a shortcut on the Oregon Trail to the Willamette Valley. Based on his promotion, they followed him from Fort Boise on a perilous journey through the interior of Oregon. Unfortunately, he did not know the country as well as he advertised. It became known as the Lost Meek Wagon Train. The party split up on the Oregon High Desert but came together again just north of Madras at Sagebrush Springs. Both segments had passed through the Basin where Madras is now located. It was one of the deadliest shortcuts on the Oregon Trail.

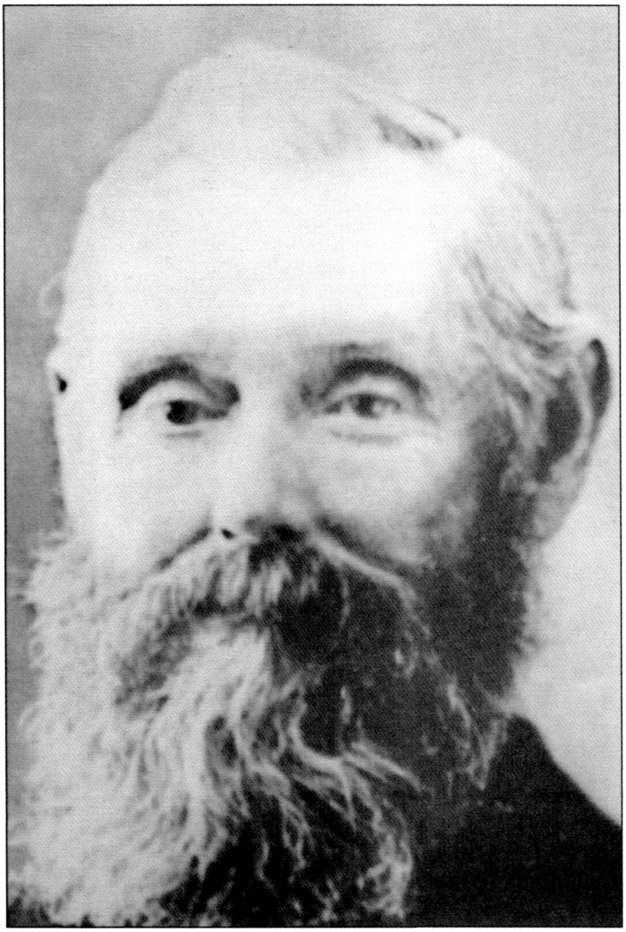

Dr. David Baldwin was a practicing physician in Oakland, California, when he purchased 160 acres of land on Hay Creek from Williamson Allen in 1873. He brought registered Merino sheep from Vermont to raise on his new ranch. He established the Baldwin Sheep and Land Company and his holdings later became known as the Hay Creek Ranch. He built a large sheep empire but failing health led him to sell the ranch in 1884 to C.A. Cartwright, J.P. Van Houten, and H. Lonery.

Mary Brown Webber was among the earliest settlers in the Basin, with a land claim adjoining John Palmehn's, part of which was included in the original plat of Madras. She married Alonzo Boyce, who had come to settle in central Oregon in the late 1870s and became a large sheep operator, often using the Basin for grazing. This early photograph shows their homestead in the Basin.

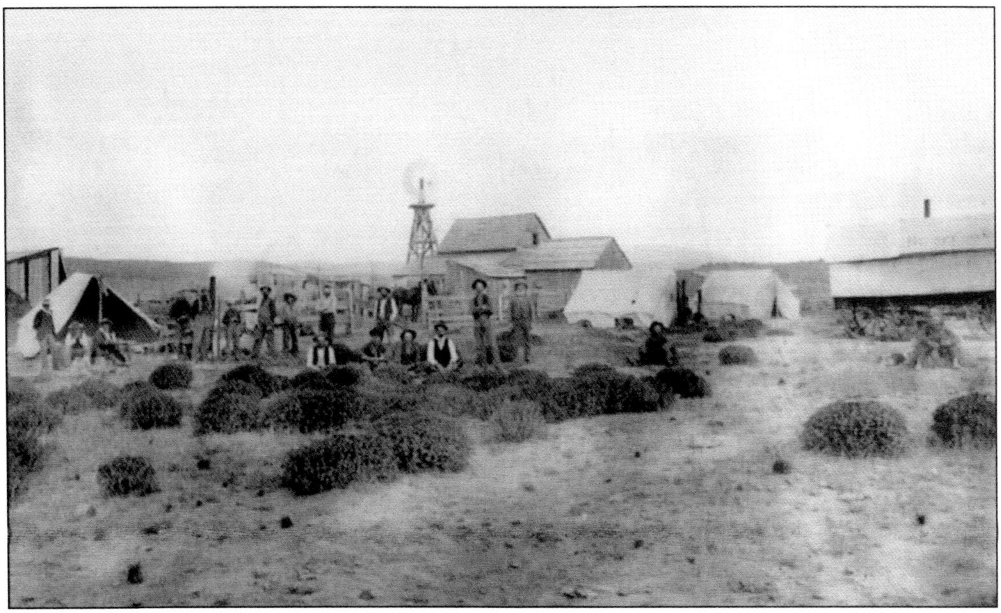

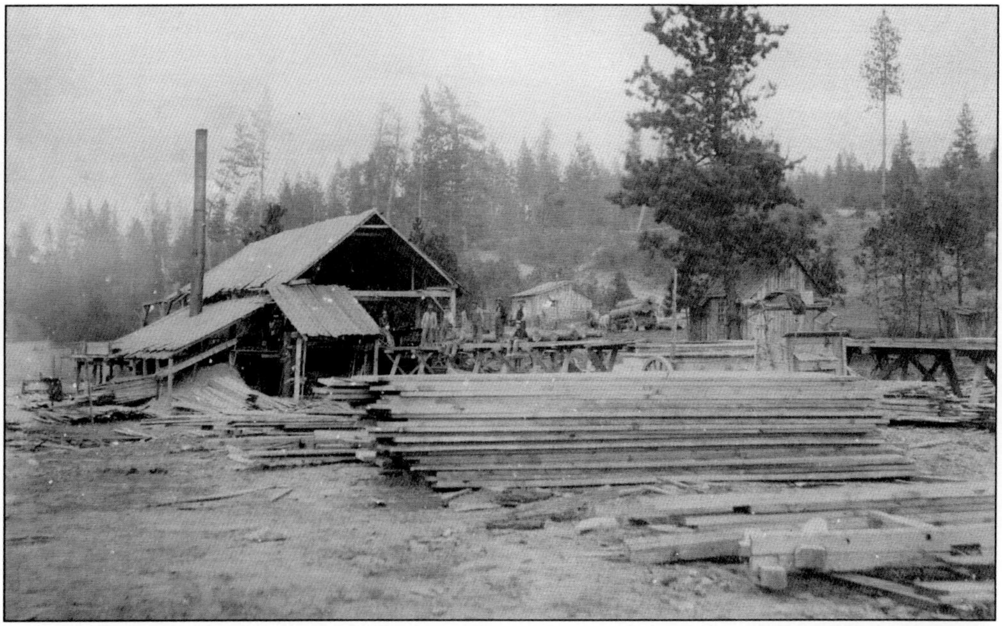

A growing number of homesteaders arrived in the Madras vicinity after 1900 and the developing community needed lumber to construct houses and businesses. The Mailing mill was established in 1877, one of the earliest established mills in central Oregon. It was operated by Charles C. Mailing near the base of Grizzly Mountain on Willow Creek, southeast of Madras. The Mailing mill was the source of lumber, most of which was green and rough cut, for most of the early buildings in and around Madras. The freshly cut lumber was hauled by horse teams from the mill.

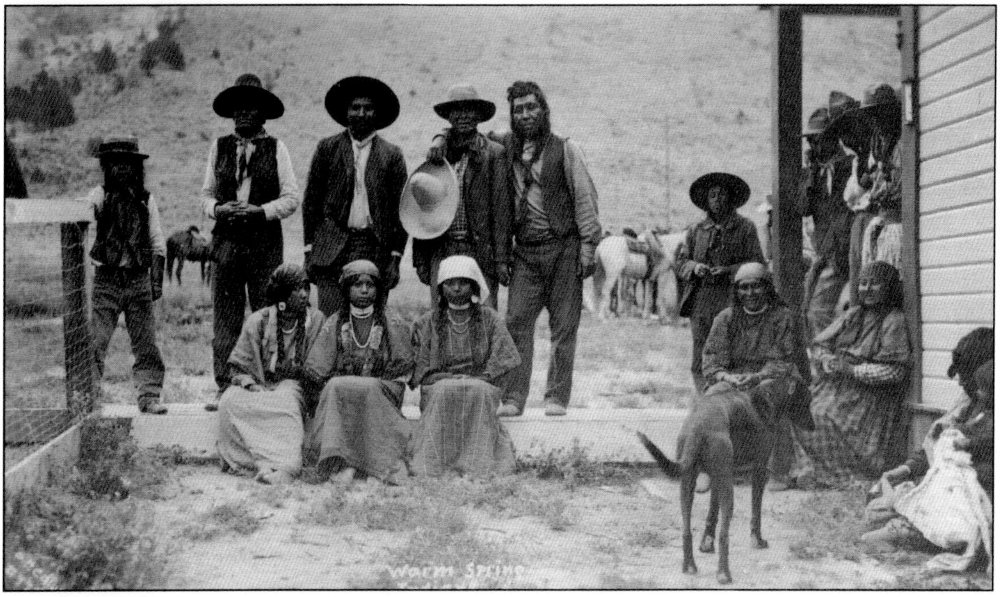

The Warm Springs Indian Reservation is northwest of Madras and has long been tied to the community. On June 25, 1855, the tribes of middle Oregon signed a treaty with the United States, among the first treaties signed in the Oregon Territory. Three tribes are now located at the reservation: the Warms Springs, the Wasco, and the Paiute. This photograph of a group of Warm Springs Indians was taken by local photographer Ole Hedlund around 1911.

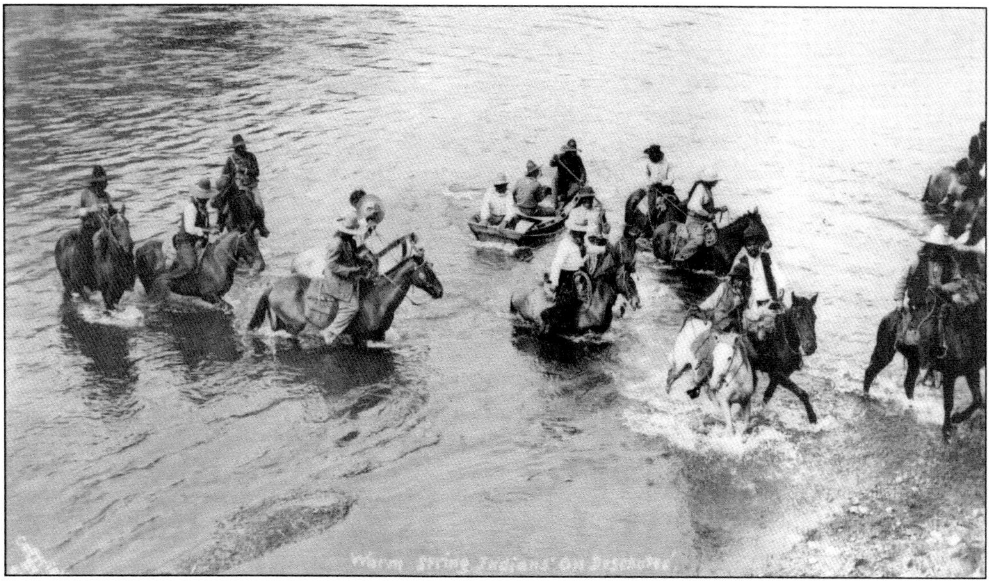

After 1900, the Warm Springs Indians frequently made trips to Madras to conduct business and trade. This group crosses the Deschutes River near the community of Warm Springs to the non-reservation side of the river on their way to Madras. Some of the earliest transportation routes to Madras passed through the reservation, with ferries and bridges constructed to cross the Deschutes River.

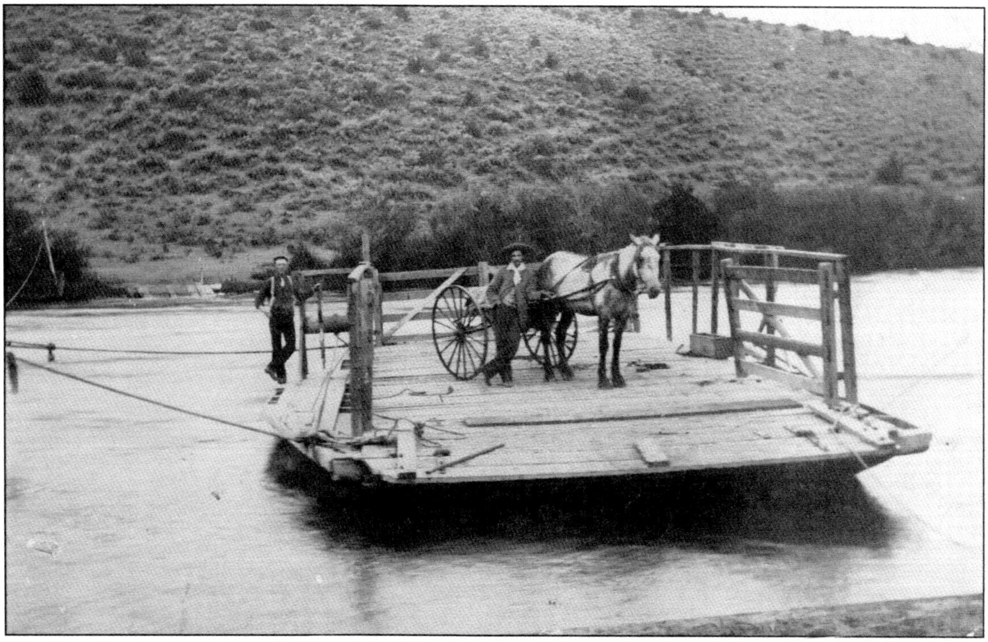

The first ferry site across the Deschutes River near Warm Springs, established in the 1870s, was operated by Chester McCorkle, John L. Luckey, and Isom Cleek. It was about two miles east of the community of Warm Springs. Ed Campbell purchased the ferry in 1895, and his family helped him operate the ferry while he delivered mail and operated a stage line. It became known as Campbell's Ferry. Charges were 25¢ for a man on horseback, 50¢ for a two-horse outfit, and 10¢ for each loose head of livestock. Indians were charged 10¢ for a horse and 10¢ for a man without stock.

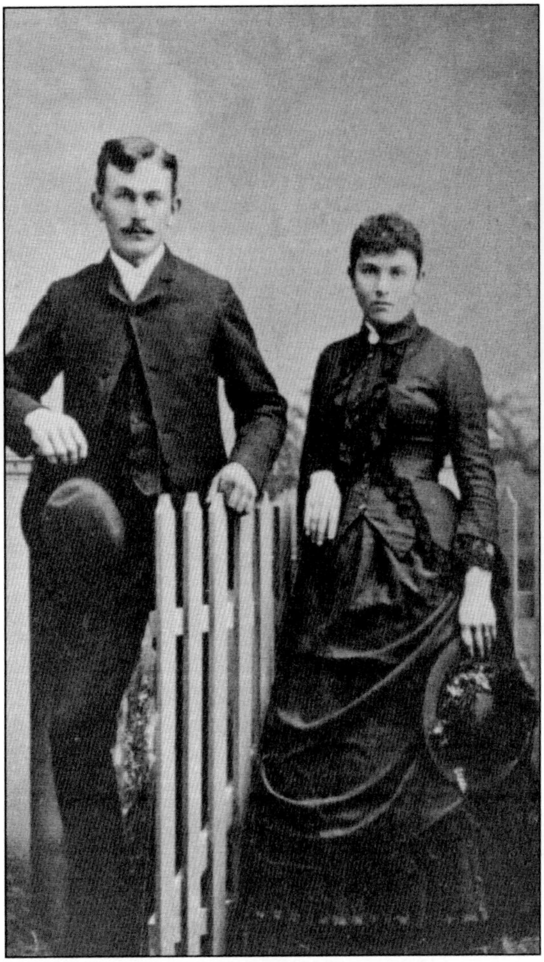

John Edward "Ed" and Sarah Rodman Campbell purchased the Cleek homestead in a canyon northwest of Madras and operated the Campbell Ferry from 1895 to 1905. Ed delivered mail from The Dalles to Prineville from 1896 to 1902. He also operated a stage line from Wapinitia to Madras. The family lived near the Deschutes River for many years. Ed passed away in 1917, and Sarah moved to Madras, staying until her death in 1946. (Courtesy of the Campbell family.)

It was important for the developing community of Madras to have a transportation system to connect to other communities on the frontier of central Oregon. Wagon roads were important, providing the connectivity for growth. One of the first major roads that connected Madras to its neighbors to the south was Trail Crossing. The site was originally a stock trail that forded the Crooked River near the eastern edge of the Crooked River Gorge 15 miles south of Madras. A bridge was constructed in about 1890, and a steep and narrow road allowed wagon travel. It was the main route south of Madras until The Dalles-California Highway was constructed in 1926.

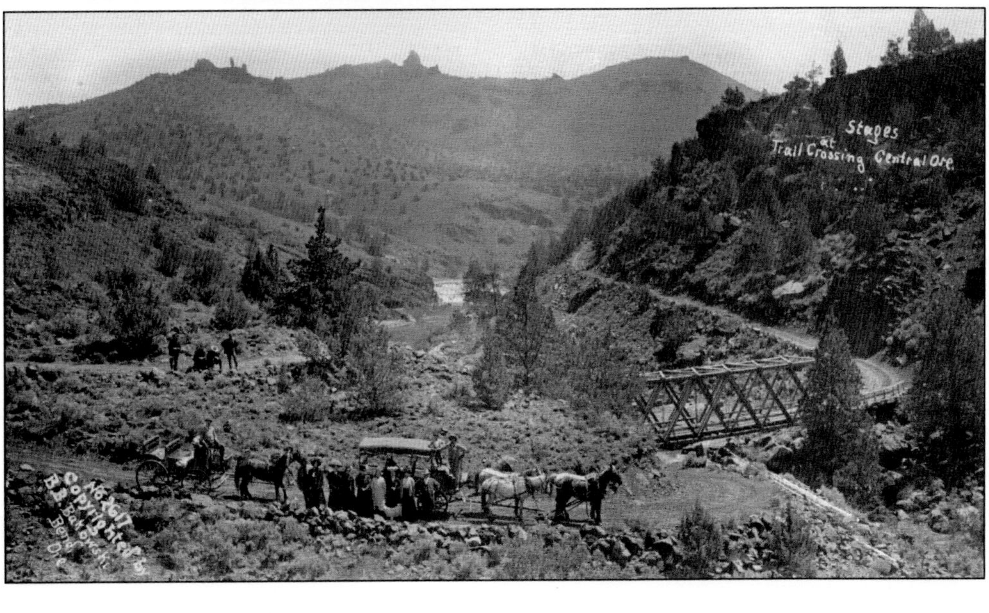

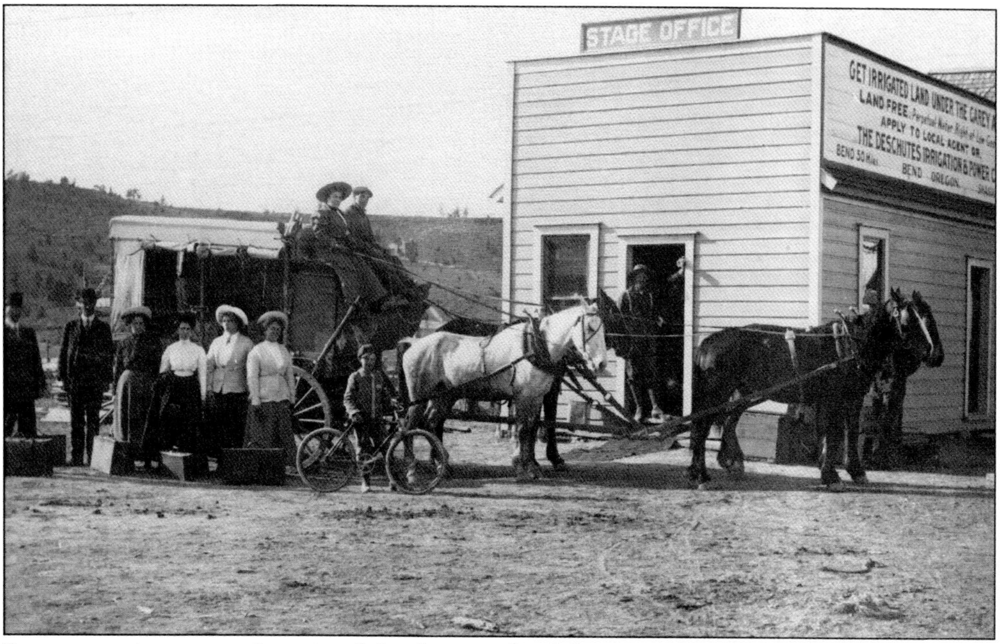

Stage operations were also critical for the growth of the new community. Stages first traveled routes from The Dalles to Prineville via Hay Creek Ranch and later from Shaniko to Prineville. Once Madras was platted, it was necessary to attract stage routes through the community. Here, passengers pose at the stage office in Madras around 1905 with Jim Sears driving and Marie Dizney next to him. The stage office was located at Fifth and B Streets.

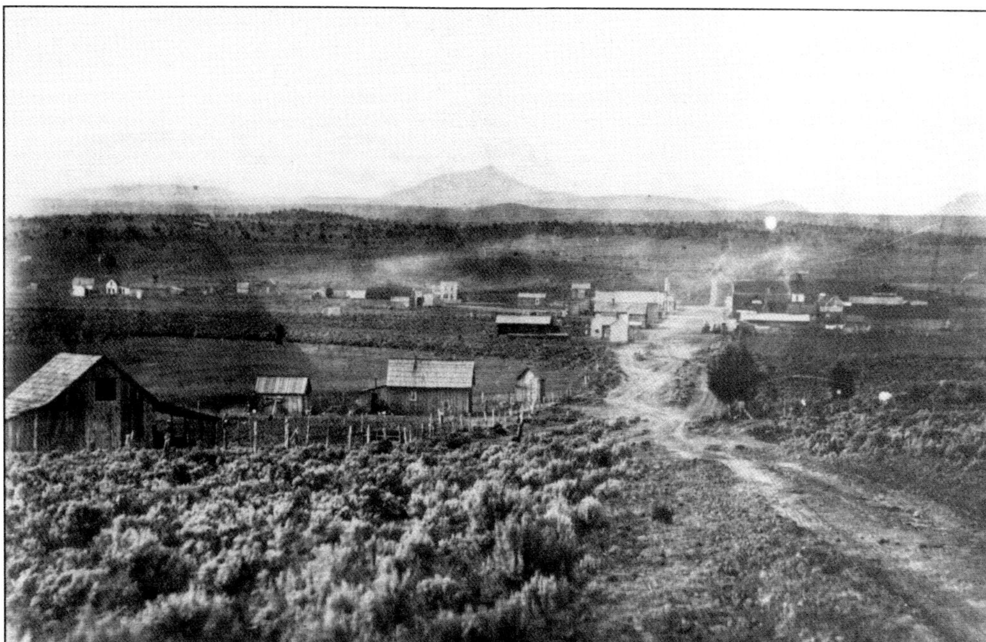

This 1904 view, one of the earliest images of Madras, looks south toward Gray Butte. Notice that buildings are beginning to create a core for the new community. Streets and roads were rutted and had many courses as weather conditions made travel an adventure when it was wet or dusty.

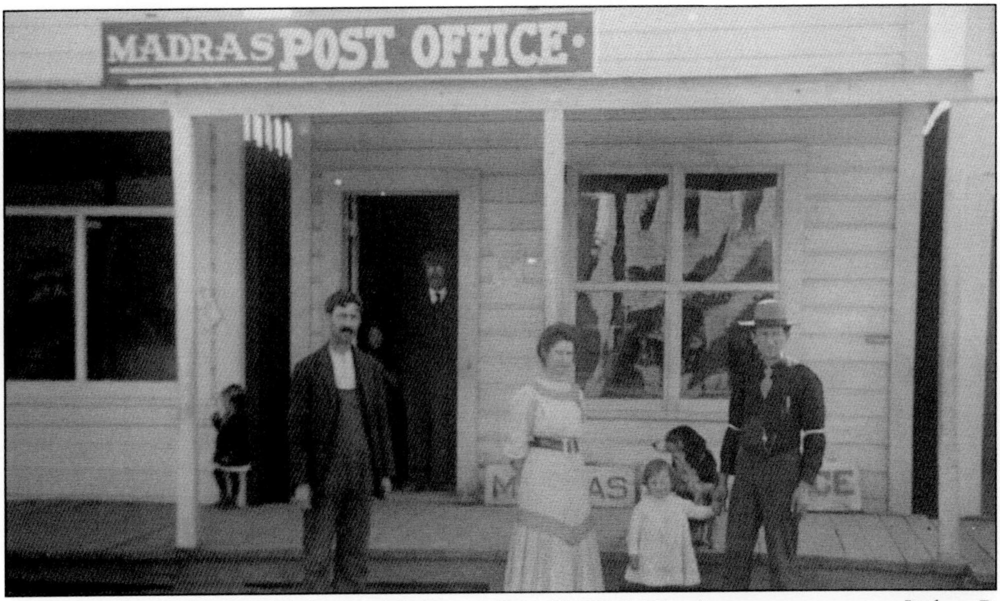

A post office was first established in Madras on July 10, 1902. The first postmaster was Joshua P. Hahn. The name Palmain was first submitted as a name but was rejected by the postal service and a controversy surrounds how the name Madras was chosen. Some stories claim that it was named for a bolt of cloth in a local store while others claim it was named for the city in India. This 1909 photograph includes, from left to right, Charles M. Dizney, clerk; C.R. Randolph; May Davis, assistant postmaster; and Fred Davis, postmaster.

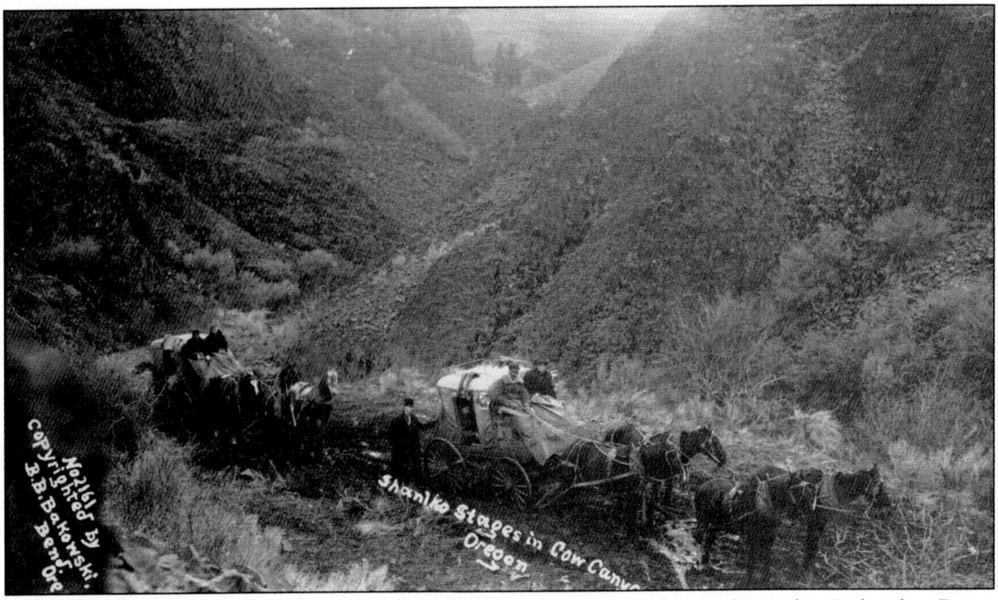

In 1900, the arrival of the Columbia Southern Railroad, which ran from the Columbia River to Shaniko, opened up easier access to central Oregon. Stage and freight traffic began to route south through Antelope and then to Prineville, and another route was developed as a private toll road down Cow Canyon to Trout Creek and on to Hay Creek and later to Madras. Note the muddy road and rugged terrain in this photograph of the Shaniko to Prineville stage at the bottom of Cow Canyon.

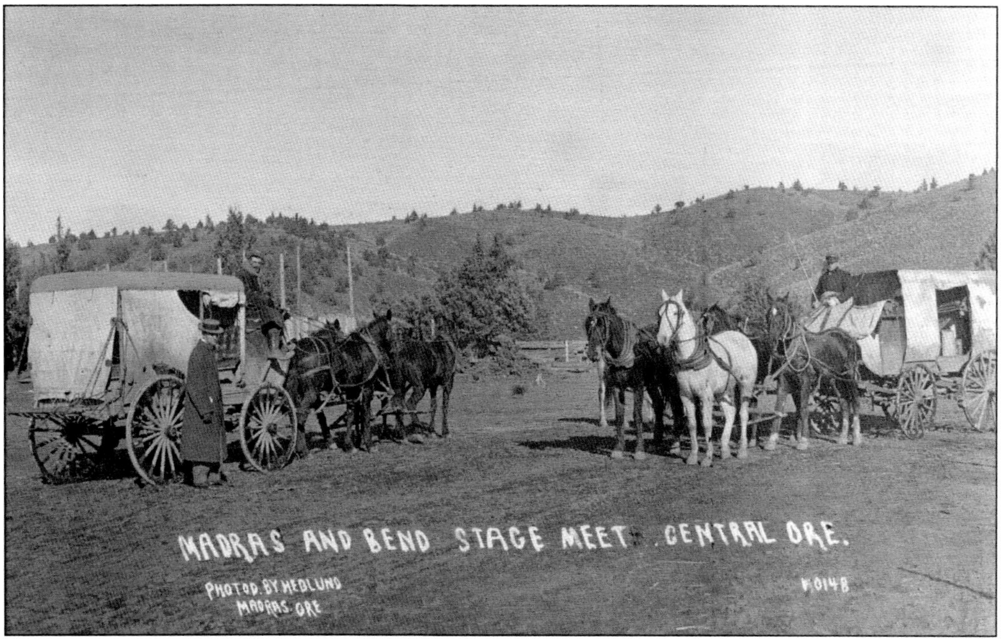

Regular stage routes provided transportation stability for the developing community of Madras. In this photograph, the Madras and Bend stages meet on a section of the stage road south of Madras. Stages carried mail as well as passengers and the travel was often rugged and tiring with frequent stops for passengers and horses to rest.

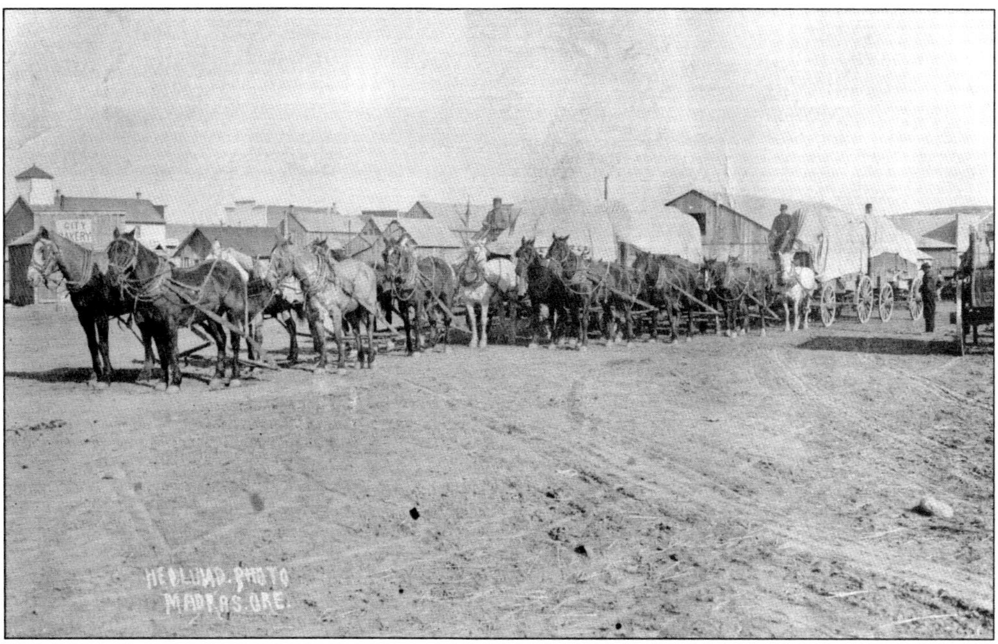

A freight wagon arrives in Madras from the rail terminus in Shaniko in 1909. Freight wagons were important for distributing needed supplies on the frontier. Many local homesteaders supplemented their income by driving freight wagons. Most incoming freight to Madras came from Shaniko or Prineville.

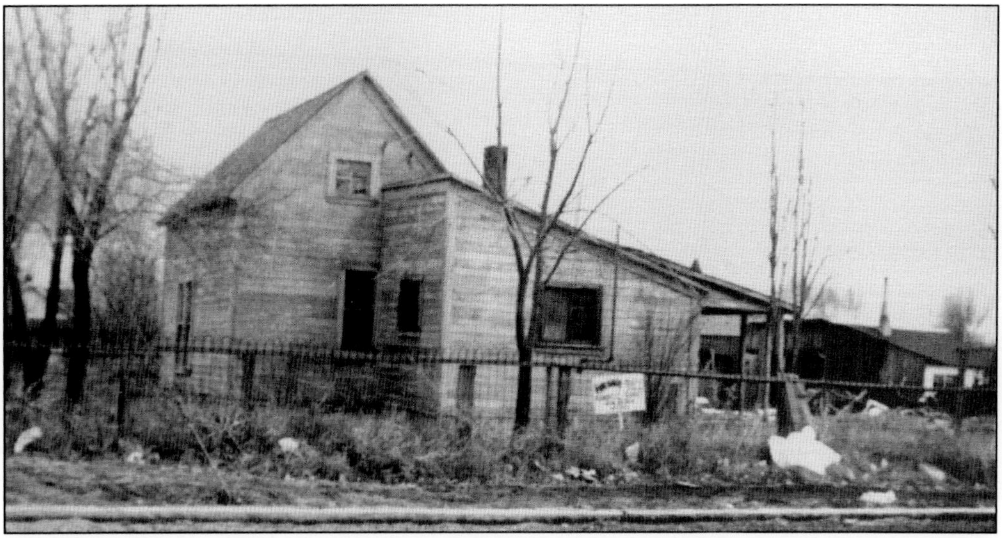

The John Palmehn house, seen here in the 1930s, was the first built in the Basin, on Seventh and E Streets in Madras. A well was located on the property and a water storage tower behind the house allowed for running water in the kitchen. A windmill provided the power to pump the water to a large water trough. Many neighbors would come to fill barrels with water and haul them to their homes because water was scarce in the early settlement era.

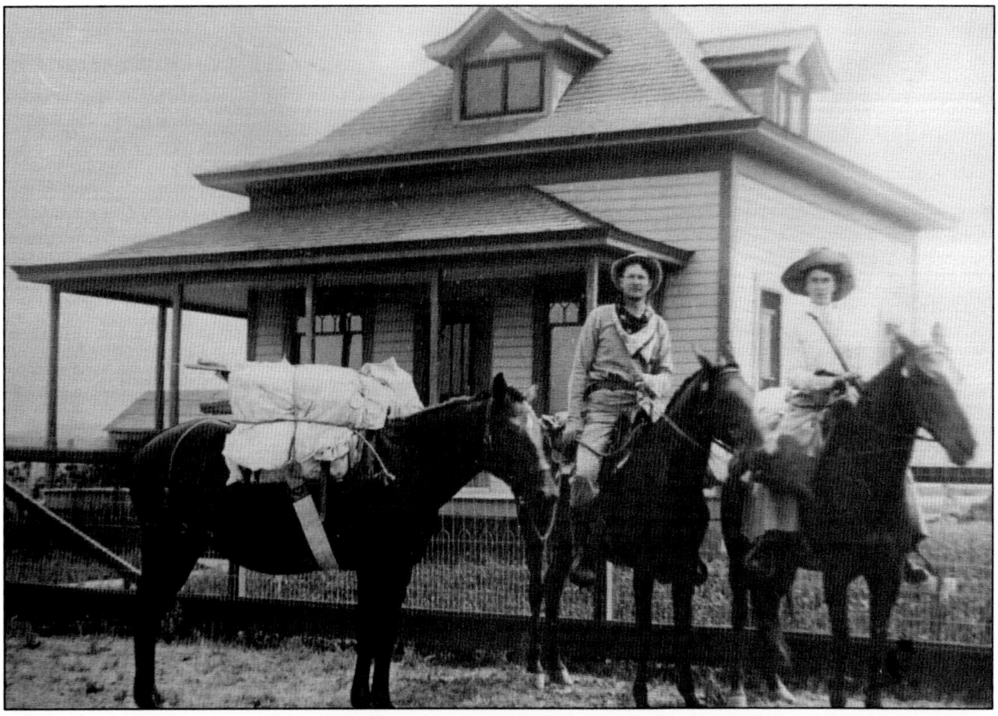

Chester and Katherine Hering Roush prepare to depart on a trek over the Cascade Mountains to the Willamette Valley in front of their home on Sixth Street. Chester came to Madras in 1904 and worked in a meat market, which he later purchased and operated until 1907 when he bought the stock of a mercantile business in Madras and operated the Madras Trading Company. The Roushs operated the mercantile store until 1926.

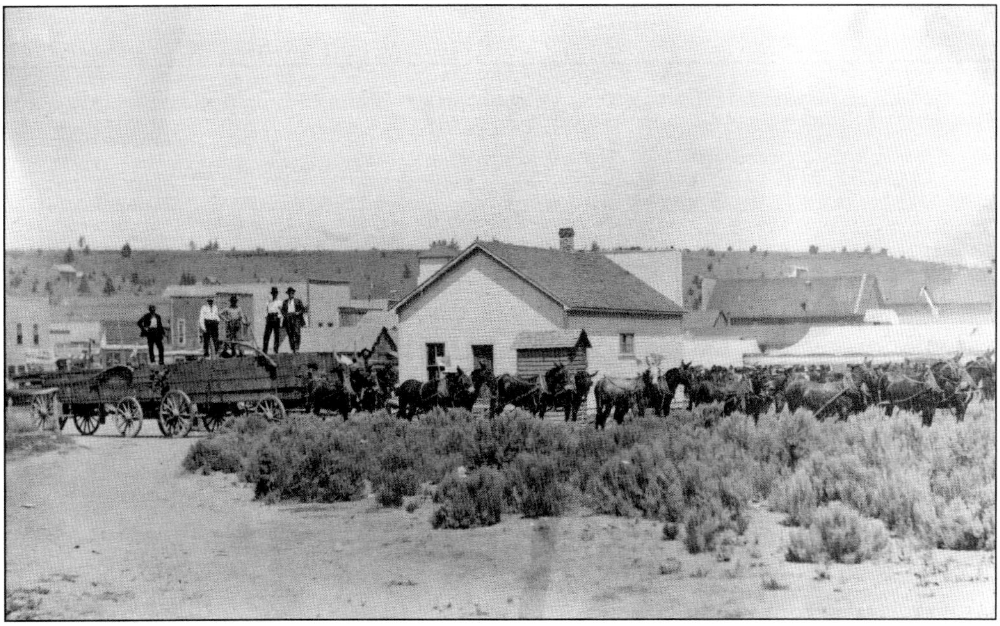

A 14-horse freight wagon has just unloaded freight shipped in from Shaniko in 1909. The horses pull two freight wagons, which appear to be loaded with timbers for railroad construction. Mercantile businesses in Madras frequently shipped merchandise from the rail terminus at Shaniko to keep their shelves stocked with the goods demanded by the growing population of the community.

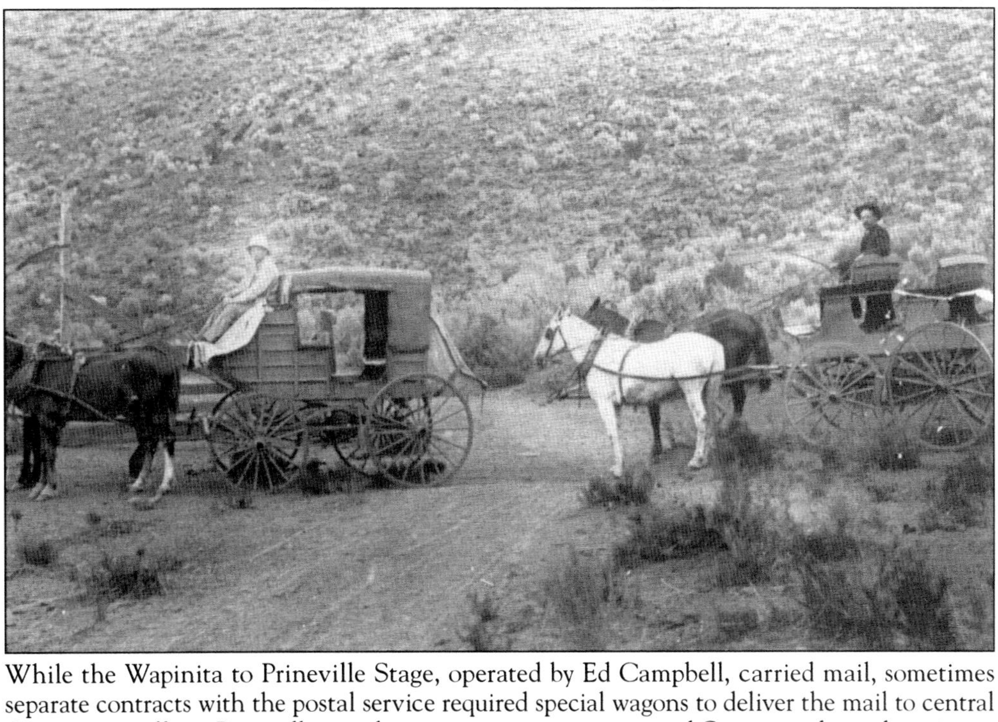

While the Wapinita to Prineville Stage, operated by Ed Campbell, carried mail, sometimes separate contracts with the postal service required special wagons to deliver the mail to central Oregon post offices. Prineville was the main community in central Oregon and was the primary destination of most stages, but mail and stage stops were frequent in Madras. (Courtesy of the Campbell family.)

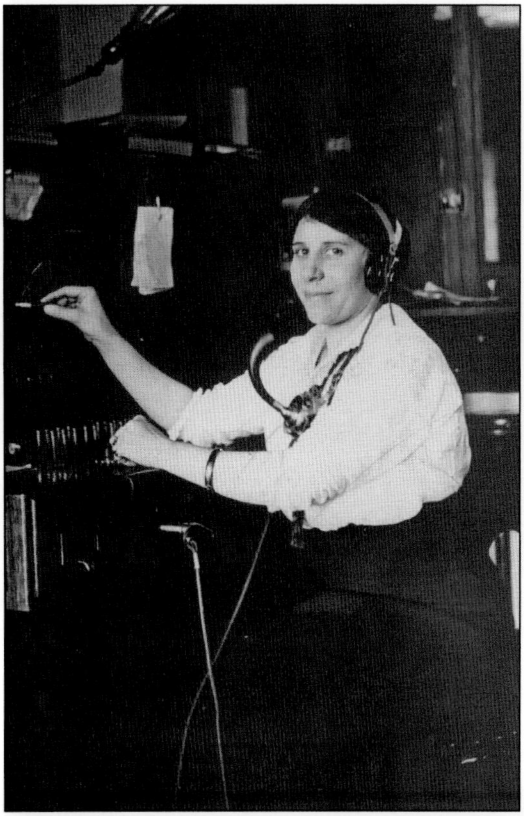

Julia Long Hobson became a night telephone operator for the Pacific Telephone Company in Madras in 1917. She soon became the chief operator for the phone company, serving in that capacity until 1958. The telephone company was among the first to operate in Madras. In 1923, she married Henry Dussault, who later became sheriff and a Jefferson County judge.

Howard Turner, here in front of the First National Bank of Madras at Fifth and D Streets, arrived in Madras when it was an emerging community. He was involved in the banking business for several years and was also an owner of the *Madras Pioneer*. He was selected as the first mayor when the town was incorporated in 1910 and was influential in many of the community's major historical events.

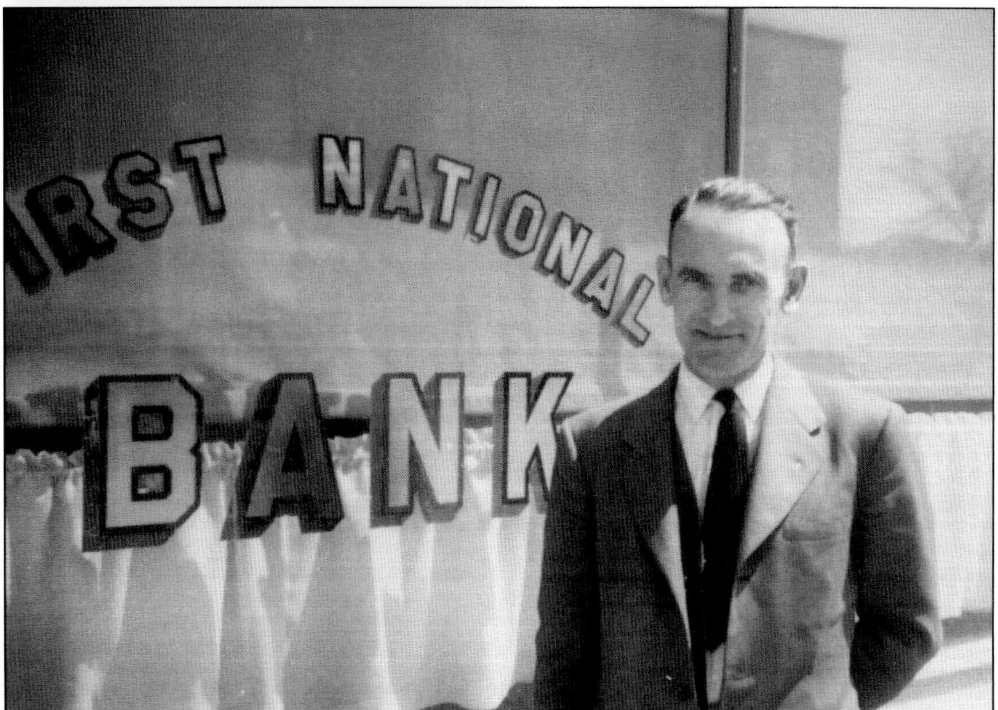

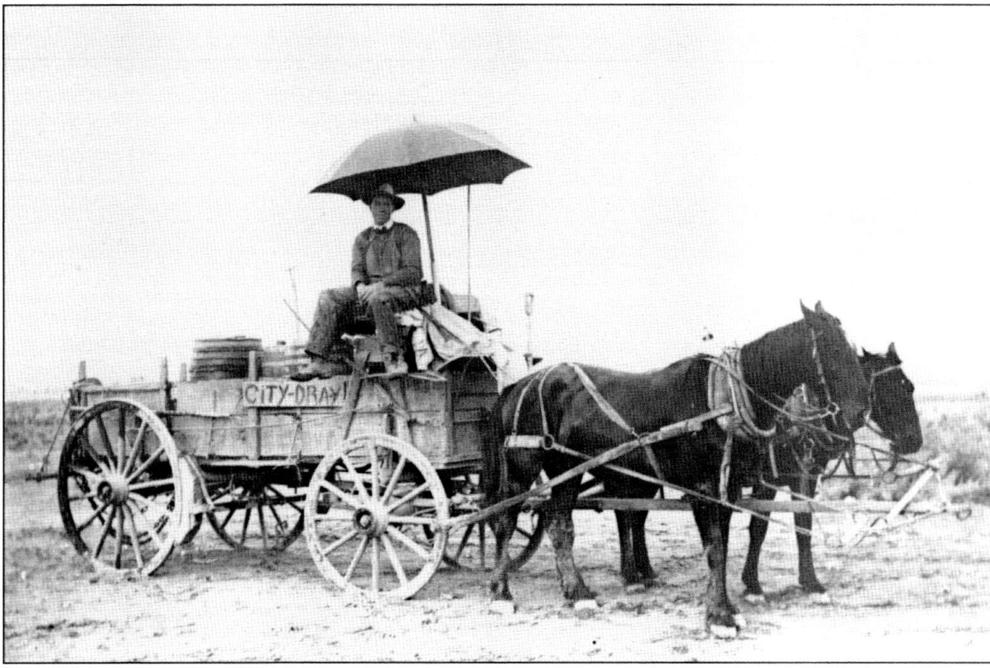

As the population began to grow, the young community created opportunities for entrepreneurship on the frontier. Here, Abe Zell delivers items for local residents on the city dray. Water barrels, like the ones in the back of the wagon, were one of the chief delivery items, hauled from the nearest water source to homes before the community water system was established.

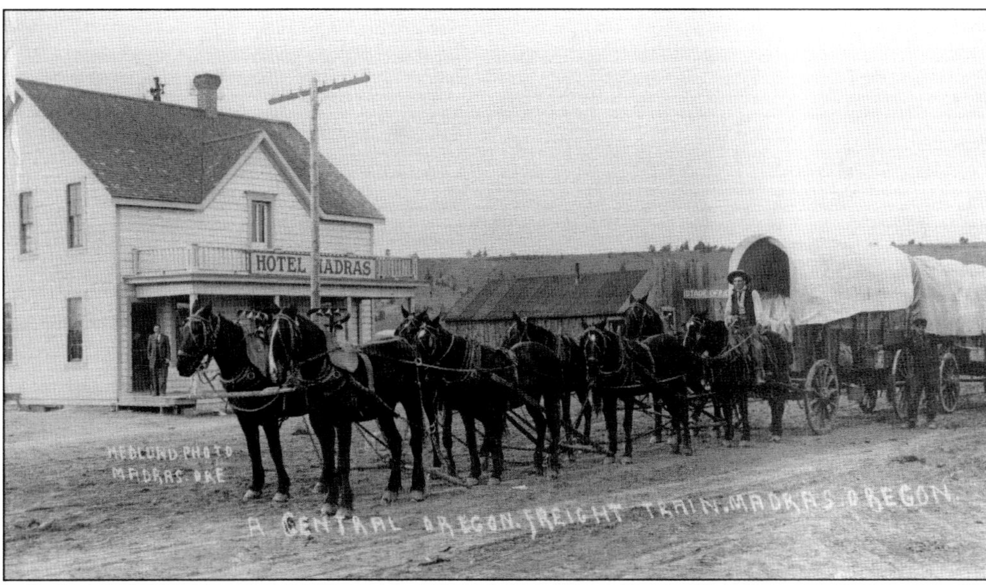

The Hotel Madras was one of the first boardinghouses and was originally known as the Green Hotel because of the green lumber used in construction. It was located next to the stage office and provided rooms and meals for patrons. A team of horses and two freight wagons are stopped in front of the hotel, which was widely known for its hospitality and good meals.

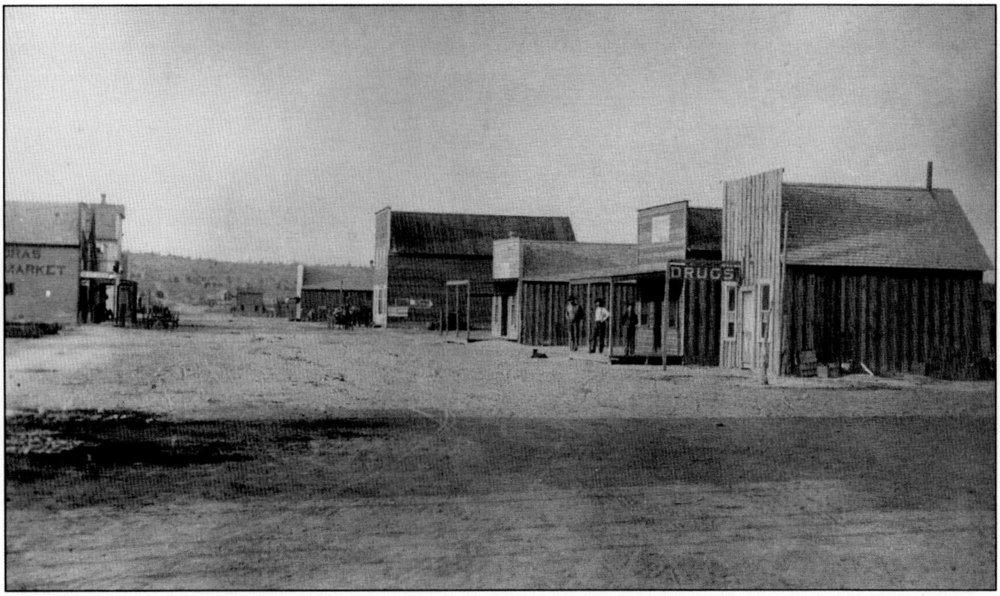

This early Madras street scene looking north on Main Street (Fifth Street) from about 1907 shows several false-front buildings. Madras Market is located on the left and Dr. Snook's drugstore is on the right. The large false-front building on the right is the McTaggert Building. No boardwalks had been constructed yet and dust was a major problem when wagons and horses passed through town.

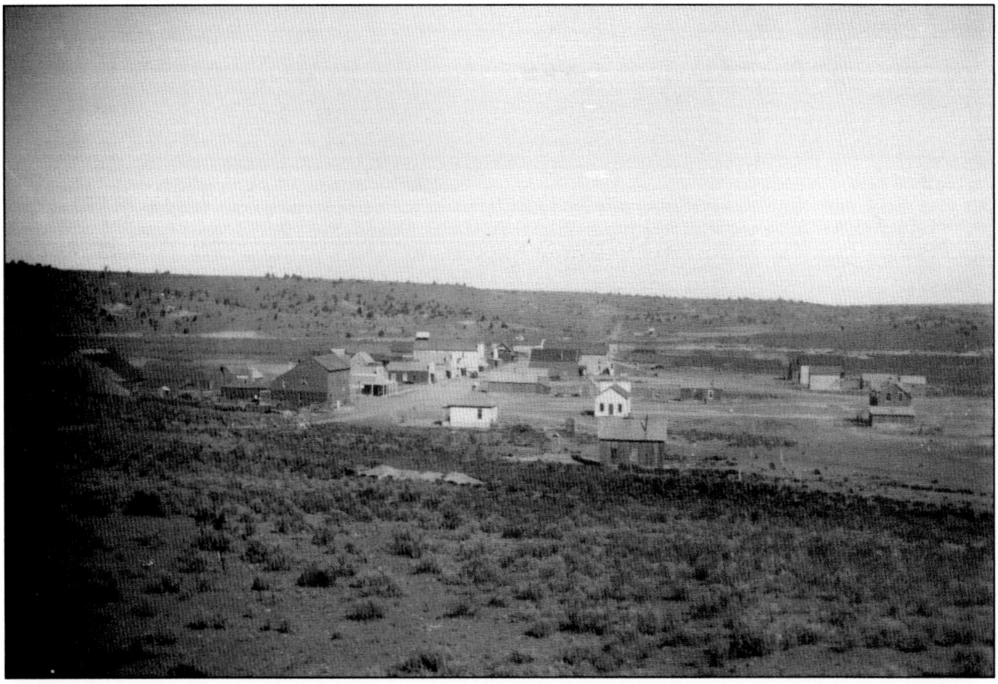

This scene of Madras looks from the south end of town to the north. Most of the buildings are along the main street through town, but some buildings and houses are beginning to spread to the peripheral areas. A feed stable barn has a painted sign on the left and the Hahn Hotel is the dark-colored building on the left side of the street. A pharmacy is also on the left, and the large white building in the middle left is the Central Oregon Mercantile Company.

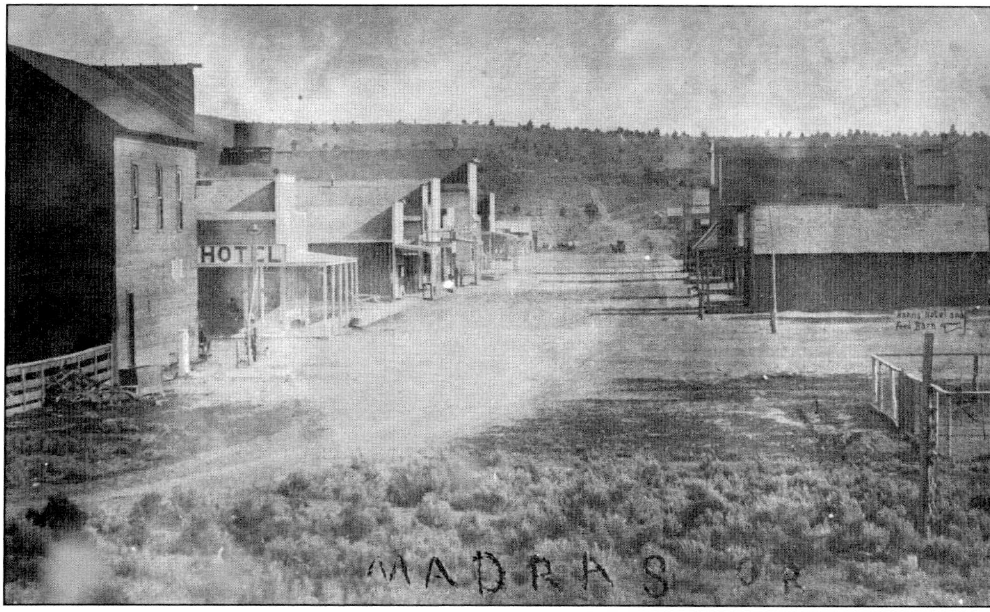

This view looks north of Fifth Street about 1905. The Hahn Hotel is on the left and farther down the street on the left are E.D. Wilson's harness shop and the Madras feed yard. On the right is a sign with a crude hand pointing to the Hahn Hotel and Feed Barn. Some boardwalks are present, and sagebrush is still near the entrance to the community.

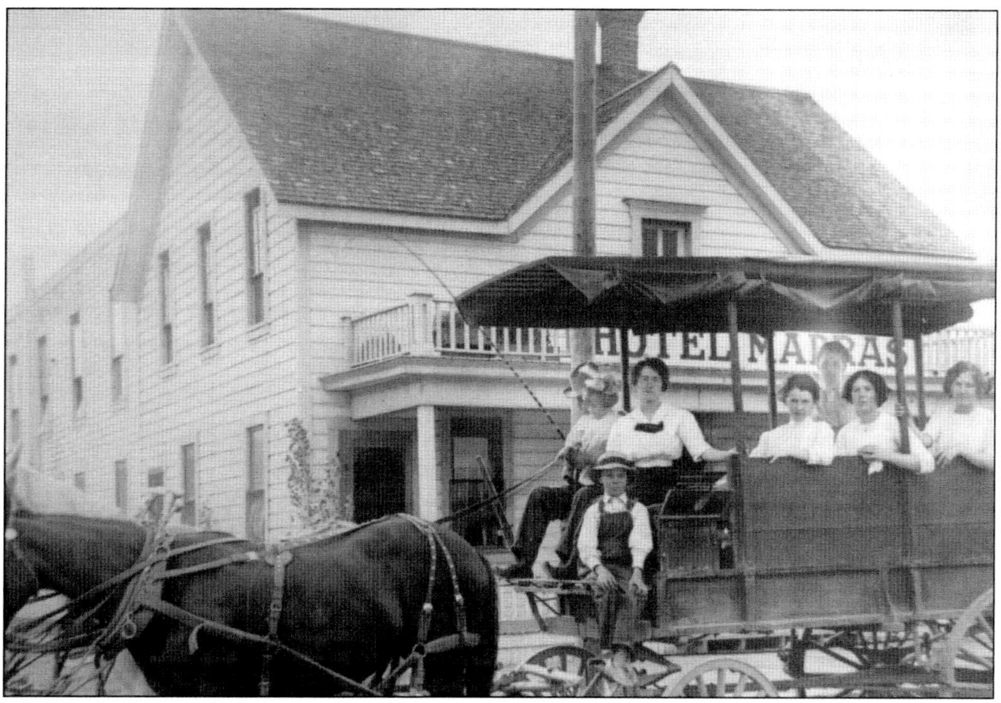

The Hotel Madras is behind this horse-drawn bus at the southeast corner of Fifth Street between A and B Streets about 1913. Mr. Keithly is driving and holding Dorothy Moore. Clara Bliss is on the front seat and Cecil Moore is on the wagon step. In the back are, from left to right, Agnes Moore, Aurel Moore, and Emma White Marshall. The man behind them is the cook, "Lindy."

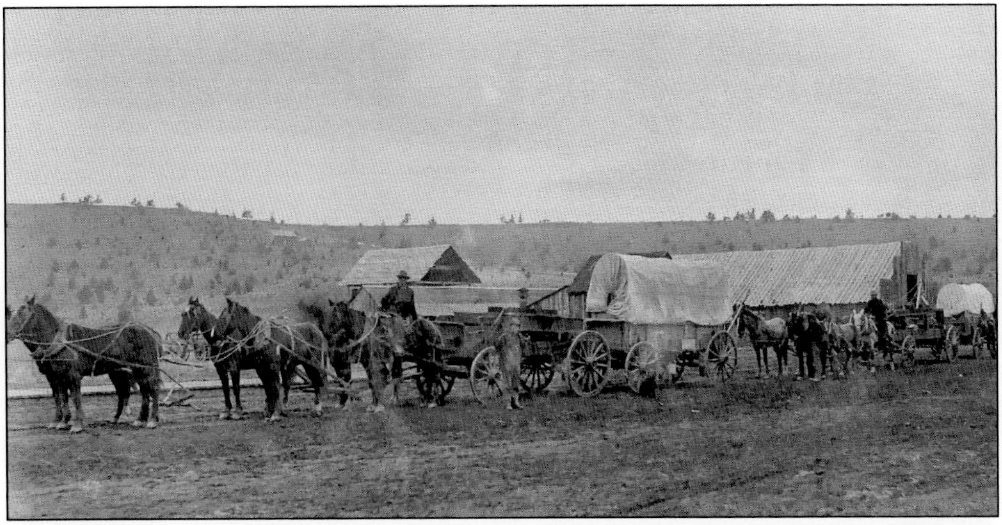

Freight wagons and teams line up in Madras in 1904. Local homesteaders frequently supplemented their income by hauling freight from Shaniko to Madras and Prineville. The Shutt homestead is on the slope in the background.

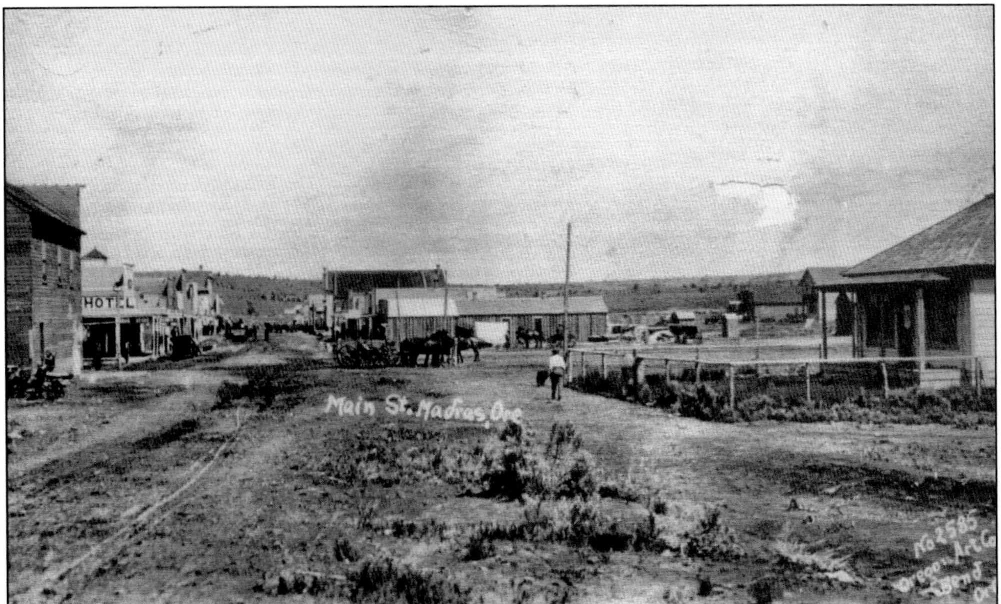

This view looks north on the still-primitive Main Street (Fifth Street) around 1908. The photograph was taken by early central Oregon photographer B.B. Bakowski, who operated a photograph shop in Bend.

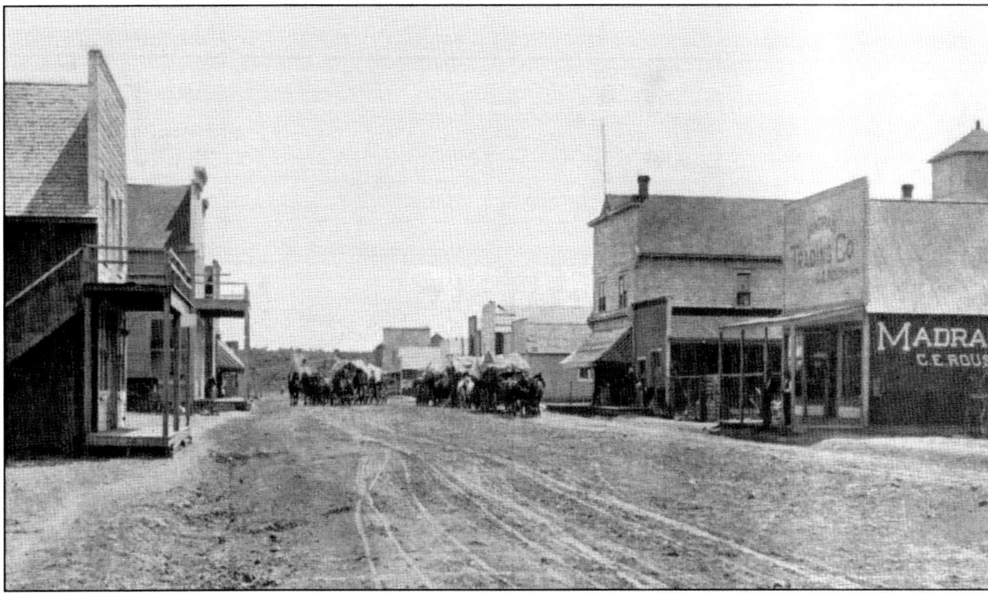

The Madras Trading Company store is on the right as freight teams arrive into town in the background of this 1908 image. Central Oregon Mercantile store is located in the center right.

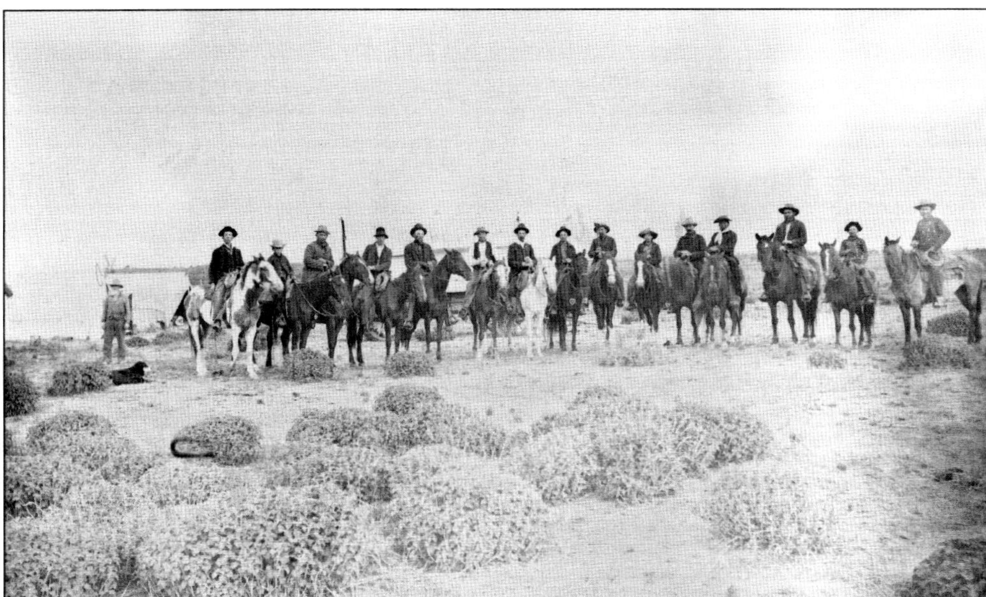

A group of prominent local ranchers in the Basin are gathered for a roundup about 1905. The livestock industry was the major early business in the region. Many local farmers and ranchers grazed sheep and cattle on the lush grass and neighbors frequently assisted each other in roundups for branding and calving.

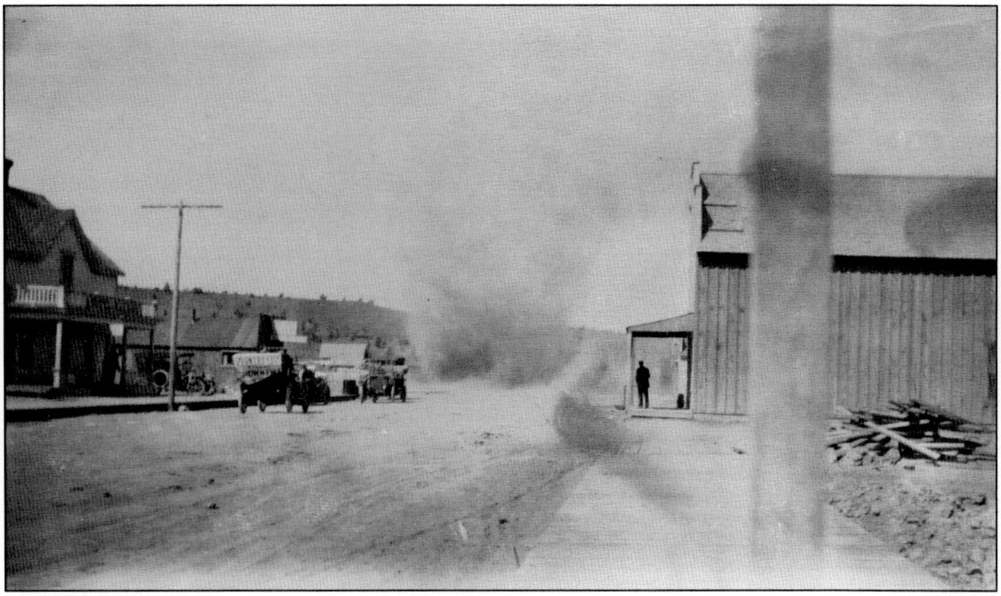

A dust devil winds its way up Main Street in 1912. The Hotel Madras is on the left, and automobiles have arrived in town. Local photographer Ole Hedlund had his shop on the left side of the street and took his camera outside his shop to photograph the whirlwind.

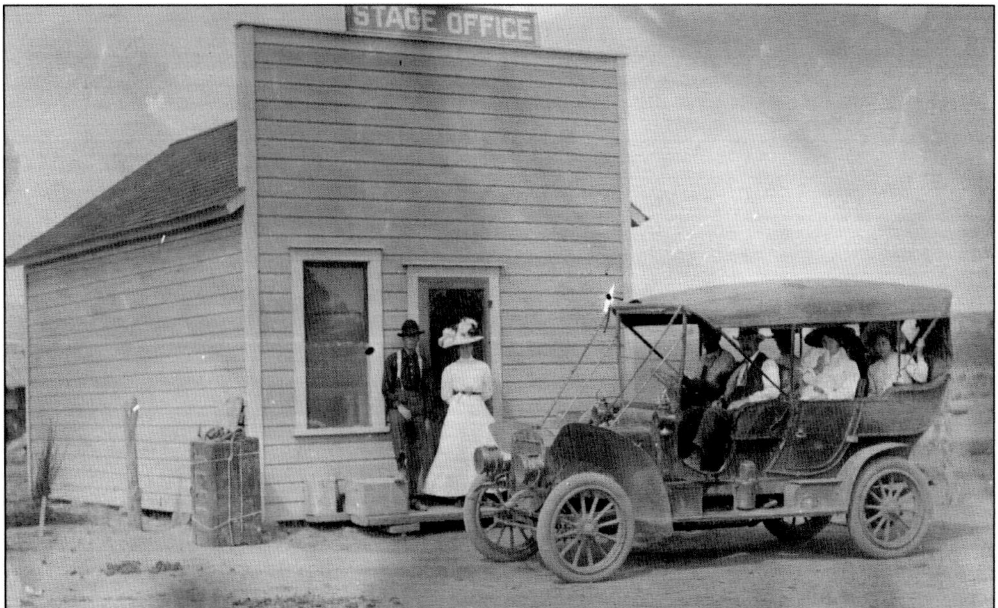

This is the first auto stage to arrive in Madras, in front of the stage station about 1909. Gillis and Marie Dizney stand on the steps of the stage office. While the driver is unidentified, the A.P. Stanford family members are the passengers.

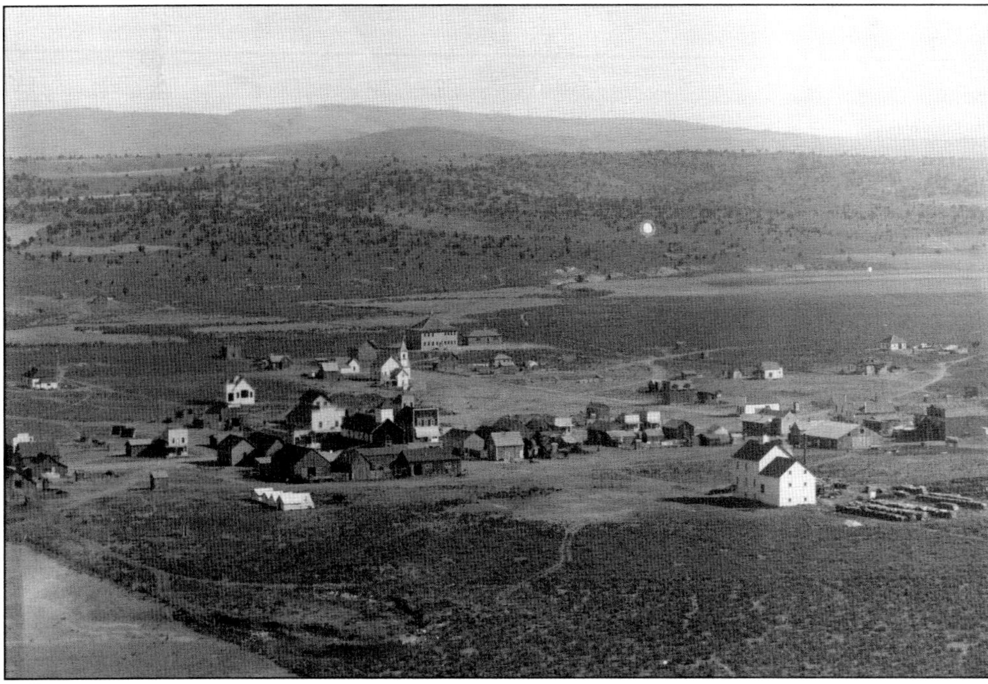

In this 1909 birds-eye view of Madras, Willow Creek flows at the base of the hills in the background and the Madras School is the prominent building in the middle back. Tents in the left foreground were used by surveyors for the railroad being constructed up the Deschutes River to Madras. The large white building in the lower left is the Madras Flour Mill.

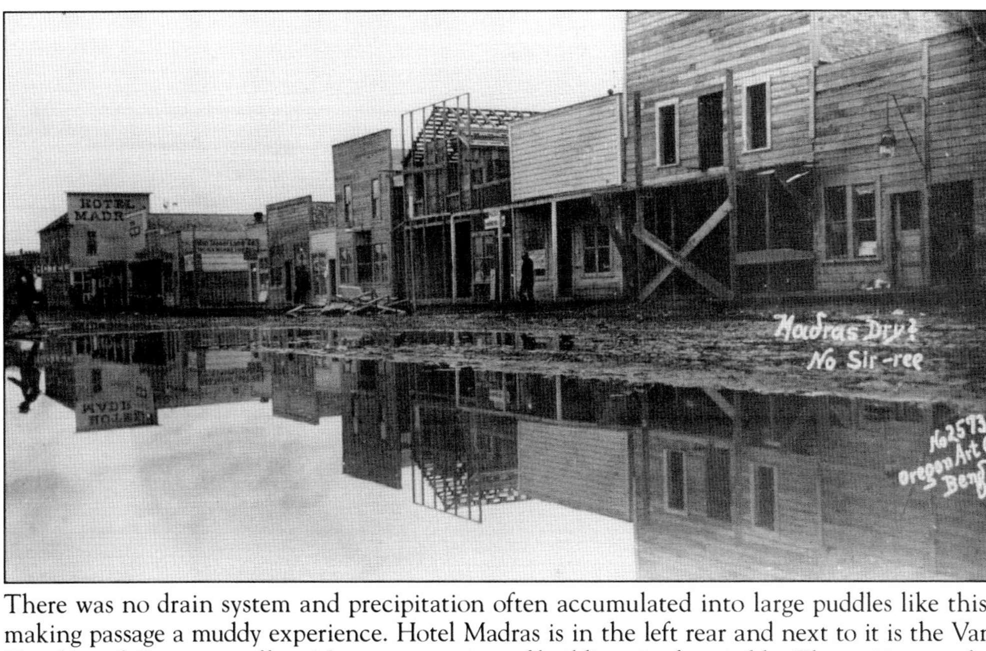

There was no drain system and precipitation often accumulated into large puddles like this, making passage a muddy experience. Hotel Madras is in the left rear and next to it is the Van Tassel Land Company office. New construction of buildings is also visible. The writing on the photograph says, "Madras dry? No sir-ree." A similar photograph was captioned, "Madras, the Venice of Central Oregon."

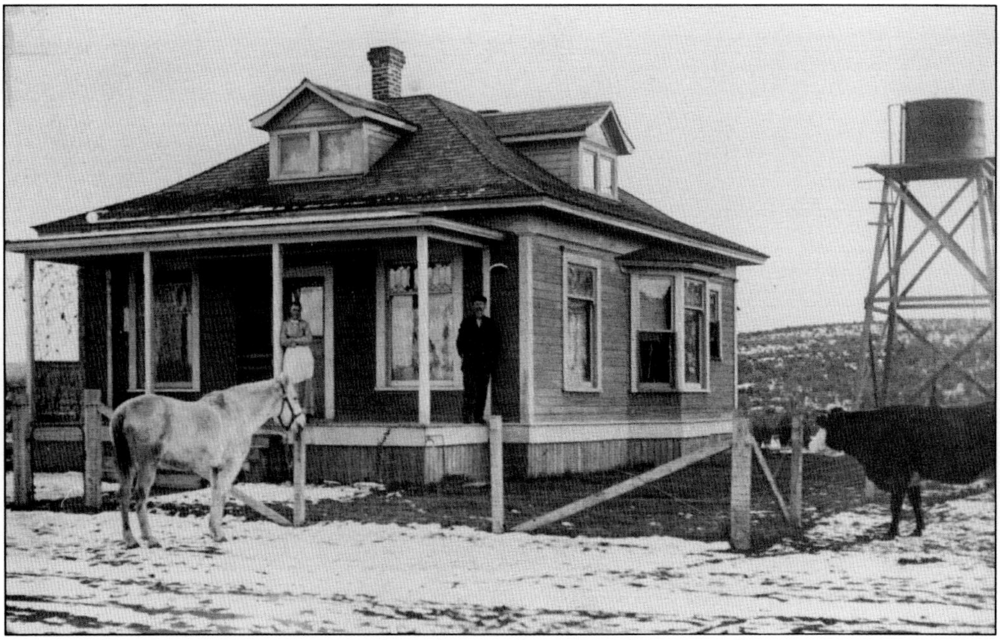

Lillie and William Branstetter stand on the porch of their home at what is now the southeast corner of Seventh and E Streets. The Branstetter's had come to homestead on Agency Plains just north of Madras in about 1905. They later moved into Madras and built this home, seen in 1912. Note the ever-present water tank on the right.

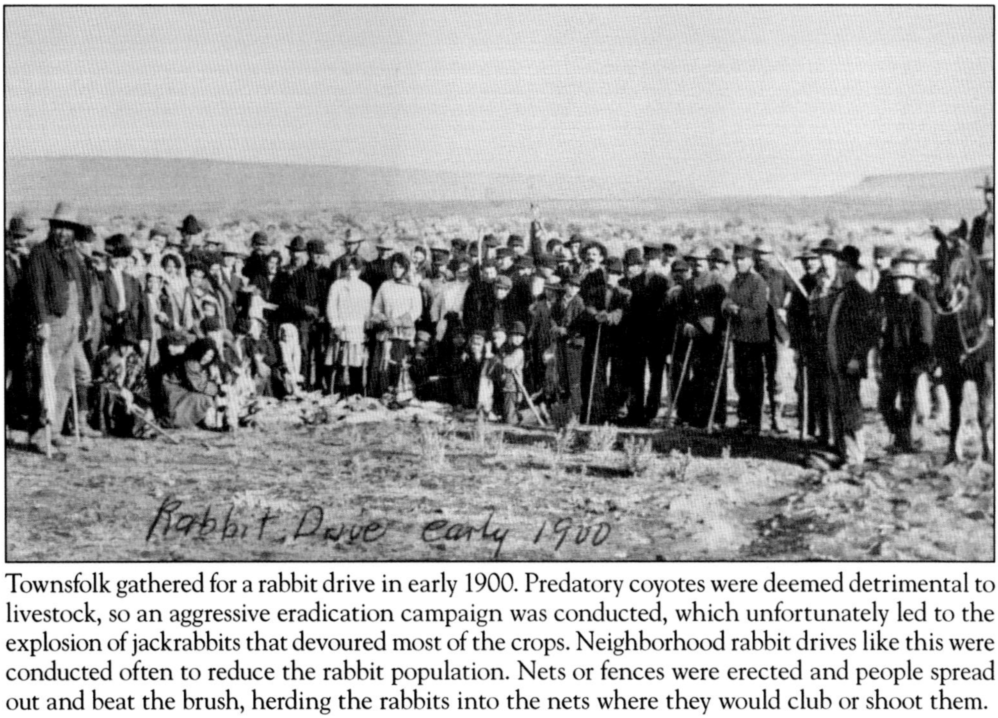

Townsfolk gathered for a rabbit drive in early 1900. Predatory coyotes were deemed detrimental to livestock, so an aggressive eradication campaign was conducted, which unfortunately led to the explosion of jackrabbits that devoured most of the crops. Neighborhood rabbit drives like this were conducted often to reduce the rabbit population. Nets or fences were erected and people spread out and beat the brush, herding the rabbits into the nets where they would club or shoot them.

Two

The Gateway to Central Oregon

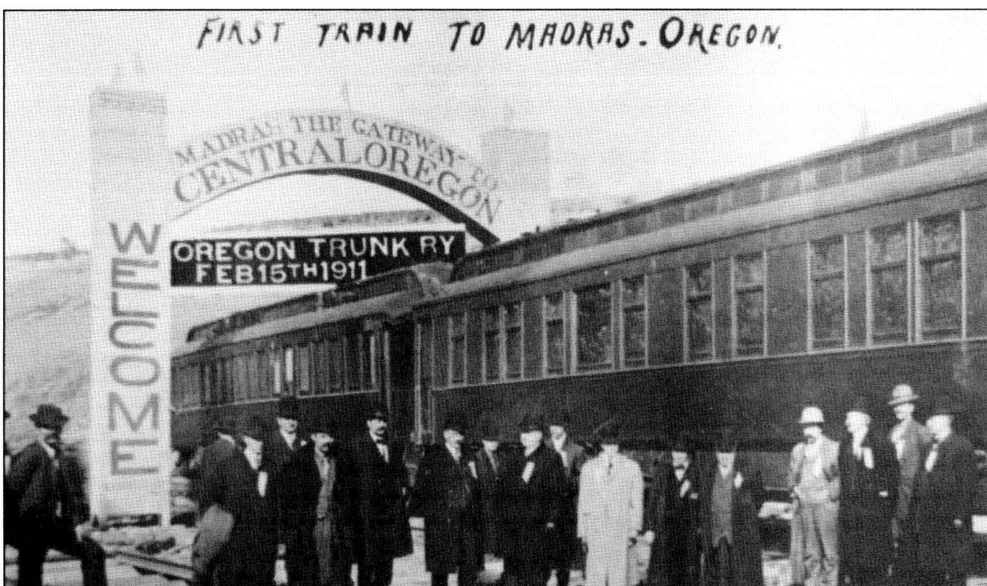

Central Oregon had long tried to lure a railroad to the region, but it did not arrive until 1911, after a battle between two railroad magnates. The Oregon Trunk Railroad arrived in Madras on February 15, 1911, and it was a day of celebration not only for Madras but all of central Oregon. The celebration that followed recognized Madras as the gateway to central Oregon. Several dignitaries arrive on the first train to Madras and the Gateway Arch is on the left. The only identified person in the photograph is Howard Turner, wearing the light-colored coat in the middle of the group.

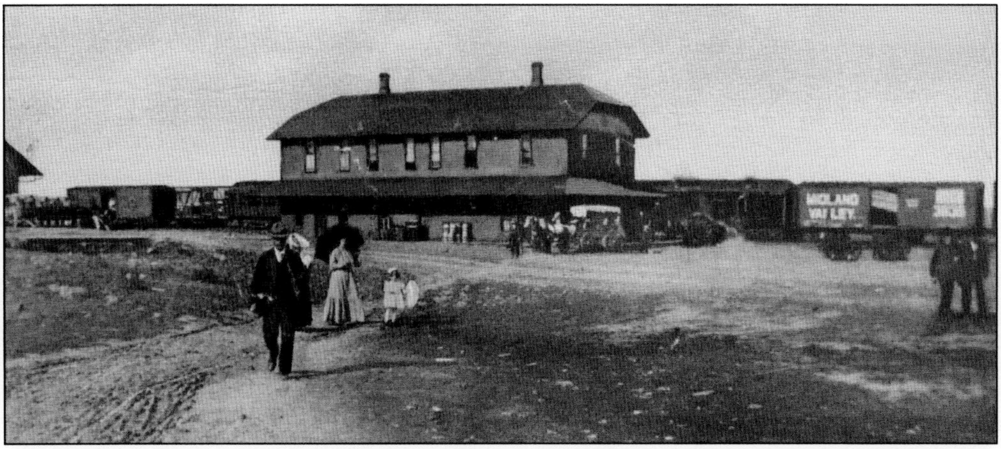

The Columbia Southern Railroad built a trunk line from the Columbia River to Shaniko in 1900. Prior to this time, most freight and stage activities coming to central Oregon came from The Dalles. The rail line, which ended at Shaniko, soon became one of the leading wool-shipping centers in the United States. The transportation pattern changed for central Oregon as the rail terminus at Shaniko now made transportation much nearer although local residents still longed for a direct rail link to the main lines.

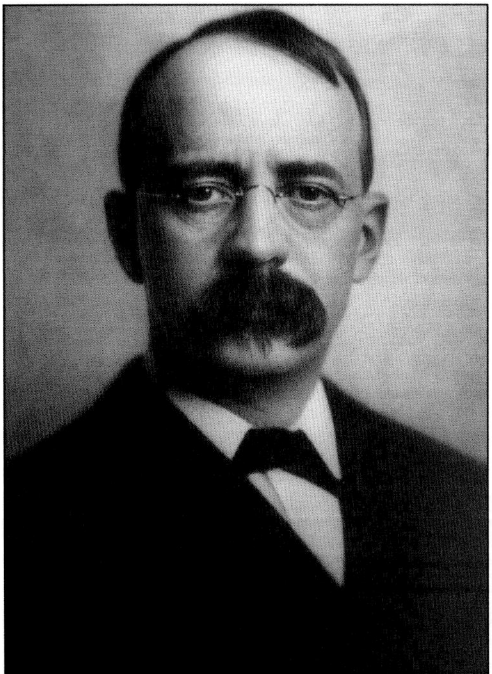

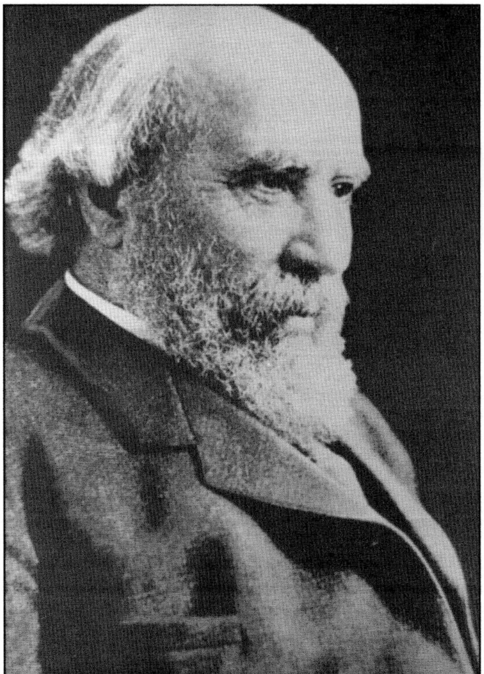

Edward H. Harriman (left) controlled the Union Pacific and Northern Pacific Railroads as well as the Columbia Southern Railroad line to Shaniko. Central Oregonians had long lobbied to continue a rail line into central Oregon, but he monopolized the rails in Oregon and did not see an urgency. It was not until James J. Hill (right) took an interest in extending a railroad into central Oregon that he took action, as he and Hill were bitter rivals. A railroad war began in 1909 between Harriman and Hill. Once Harriman learned of Hill's intentions, he rapidly began operations to construct a railroad on the east side of the Deschutes River known as the Deschutes Railroad.

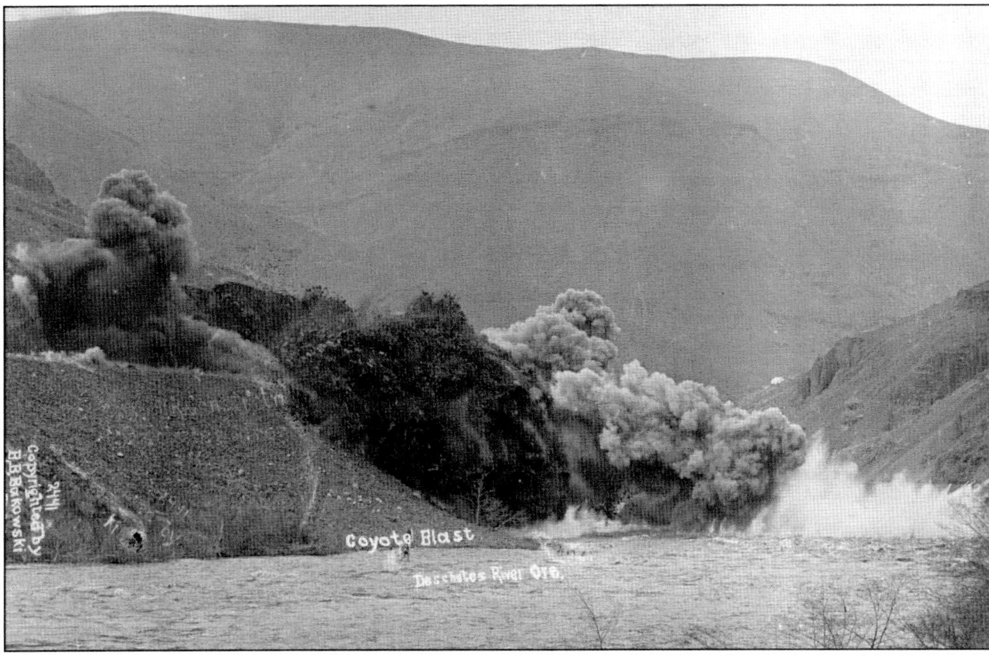

The rival railroads began blasting their way up the Deschutes River from the Columbia River. This is a "coyote" blast on the Oregon Trunk Railroad line, about five miles up the Deschutes River canyon. Tons of rock were blasted into the channel of the Deschutes River as the railroads raced against each other to arrive in central Oregon first.

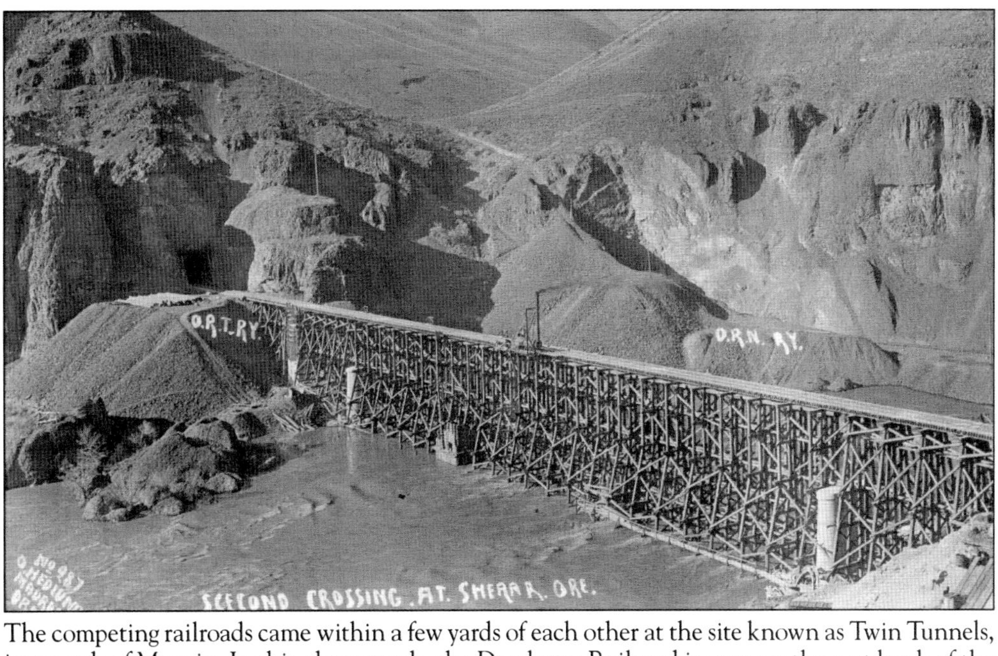

The competing railroads came within a few yards of each other at the site known as Twin Tunnels, just north of Maupin. In this photograph, the Deschutes Railroad is seen on the east bank of the river in the background, and the trestle of the Oregon Trunk Railroad is in the foreground. Note how close the two tunnels are. The construction crews often sabotaged the construction of the other operation in an attempt to gain the advantage.

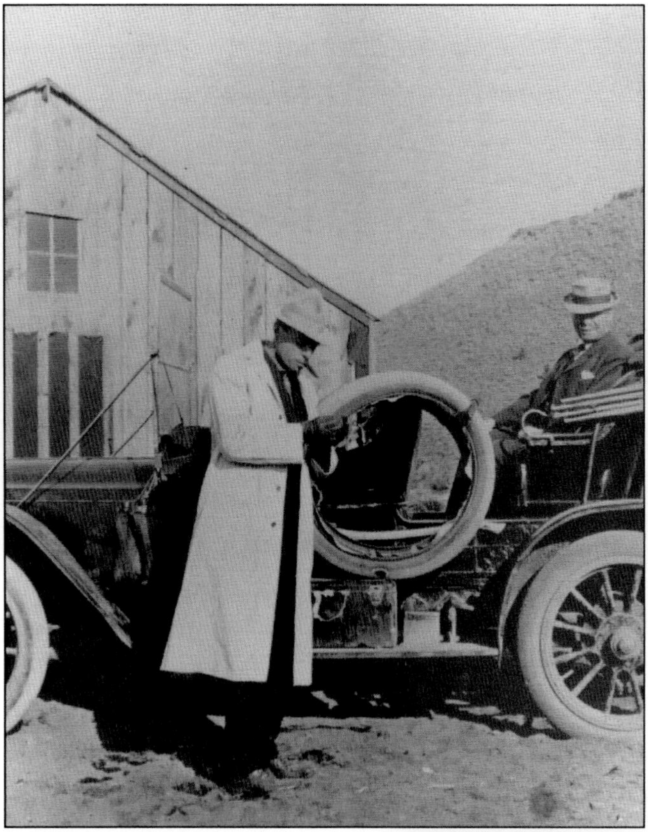

J.D. (left) and Bill Porter, operators of Porter Brothers Construction, were the primary contractors for James J. Hill on the Oregon Trunk Railroad. Here, they oversee their construction operations and prepare supply lines for their construction crews in Madras in 1909.

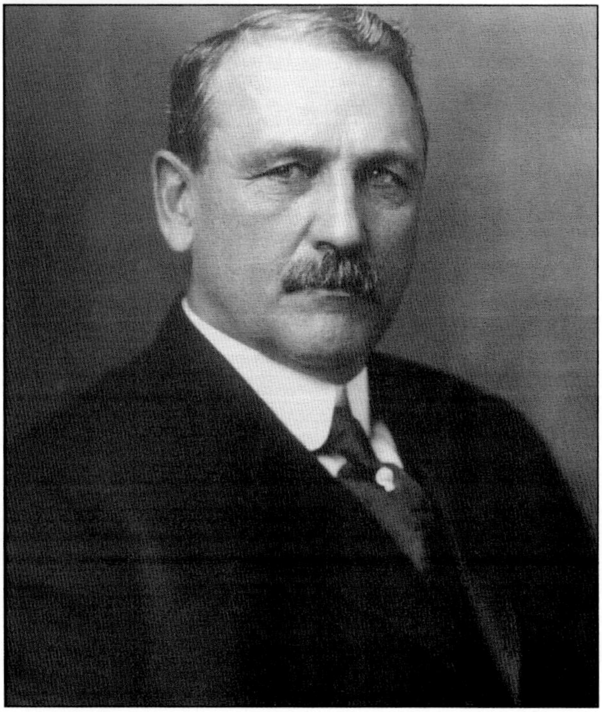

John F. Stevens, who had been the head engineer on the construction of the Panama Canal, was secretly hired by James J. Hill to head his operations for the Oregon Trunk Railroad. He came to central Oregon and, under an alias so as not to arouse the suspicion of the Harriman interests, began acquiring right-of-way property in critical areas along the construction route. (Courtesy of the author.)

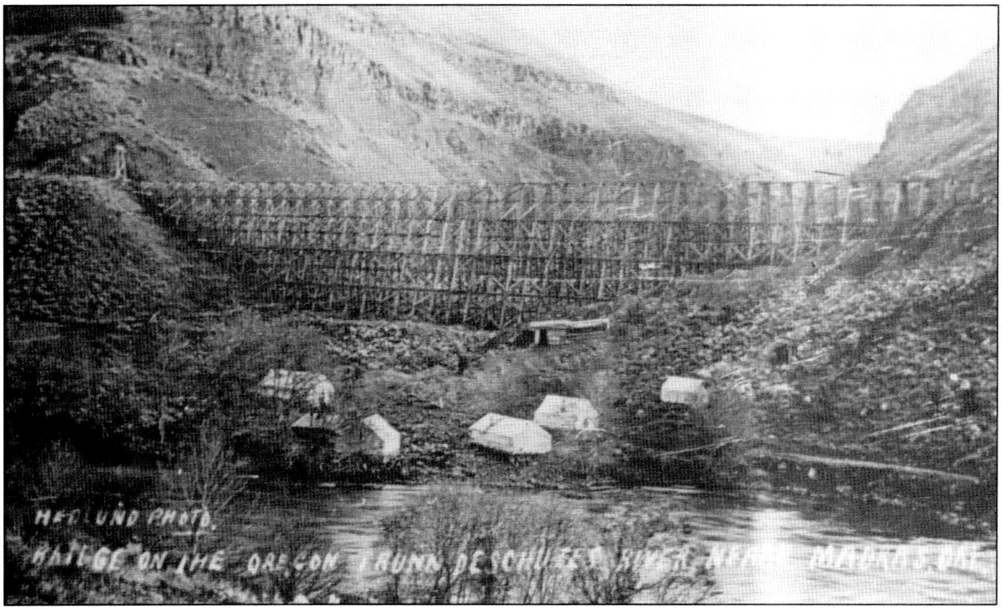

Because of legal issues and difficult terrain, the two railroads were forced to share a single line from North Junction to South Junction, just north of the mouth of Trout Creek. Once the two lines reached Trout Creek, they took separate paths, with the Oregon Trunk Railroad continuing up the Deschutes River to Willow Creek and the Deschutes Railroad going up Trout Creek to Gateway. This photograph shows the Oregon Trunk building a trestle across Rattlesnake Canyon just southeast of Warm Springs. Highway 20 now follows below the old rail line.

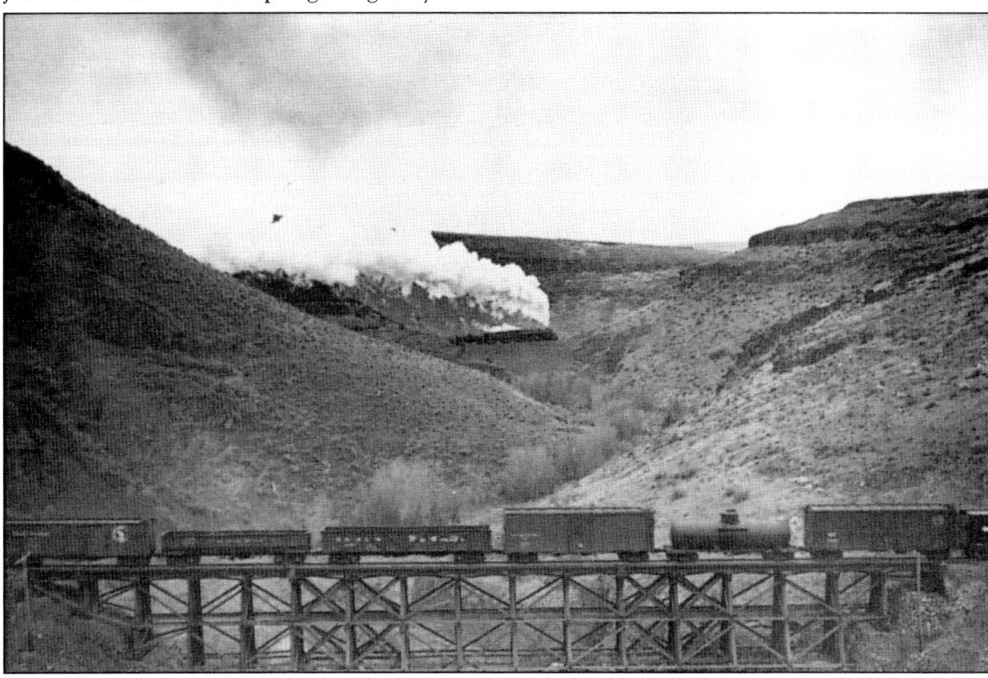

The Deschutes Railroad worked its way up the canyon from Trout Creek to Gateway, with its engine far up the hill and the end in the foreground on a trestle bridge. The climb out of the Trout Creek drainage was relatively steep for a railroad.

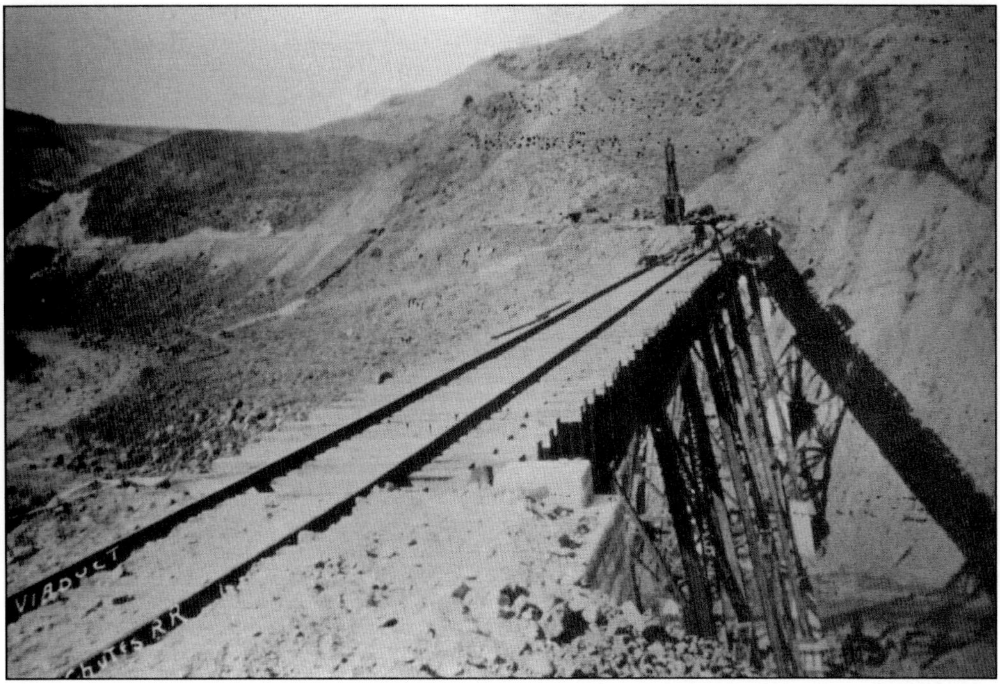

This viaduct bridge was built on the Deschutes Railroad over Trout Creek where it begins its ascent out of the canyon toward Gateway. Most of the Deschutes Railroad bridges were made of steel with similar designs.

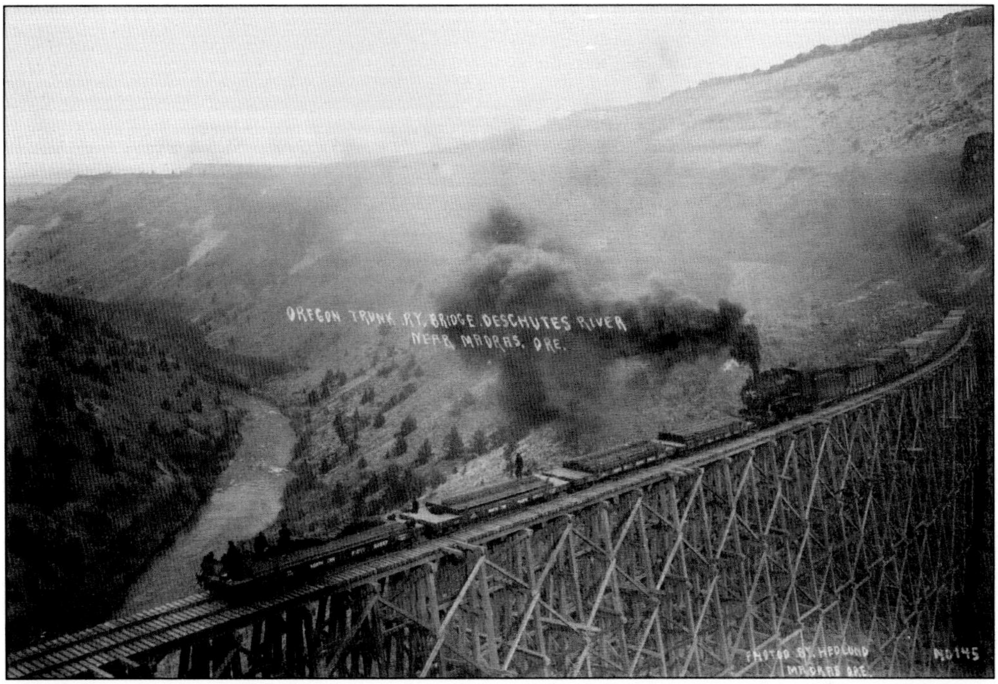

The Oregon Trunk Railroad line constructed a trestle near the rail station at Pelton over a side canyon of the Deschutes Canyon near the mouth of Willow Creek. Most of the Oregon Trunk bridges were constructed of wood.

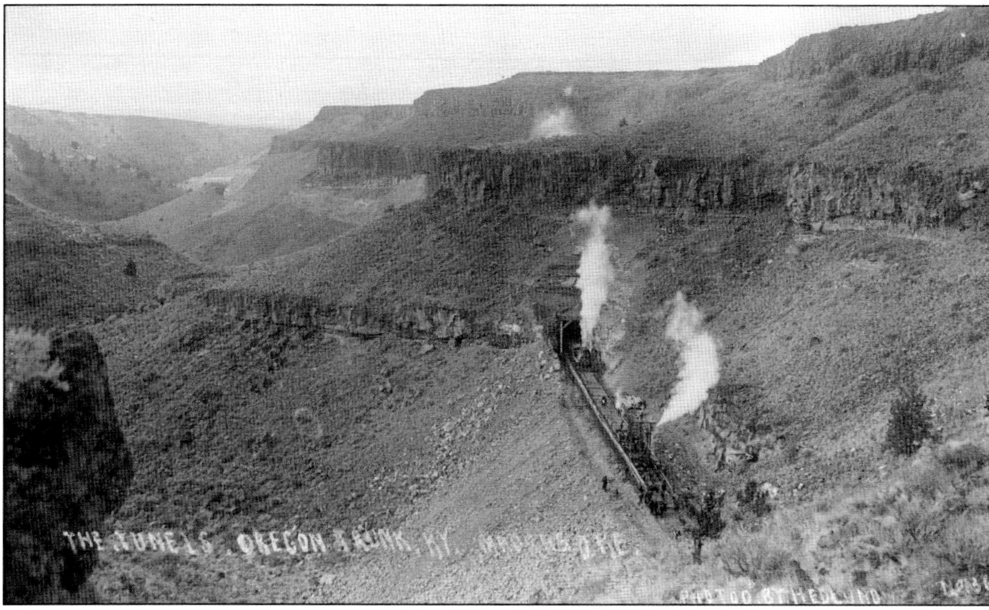

The Oregon Trunk Railroad is being constructed up Willow Creek Canyon toward Madras from the Deschutes River. Tunnels had to be constructed as ridges extended into the canyon. At this point, the Oregon Trunk Railroad is only a few miles from Madras and the rugged canyon country soon gives way to easier construction.

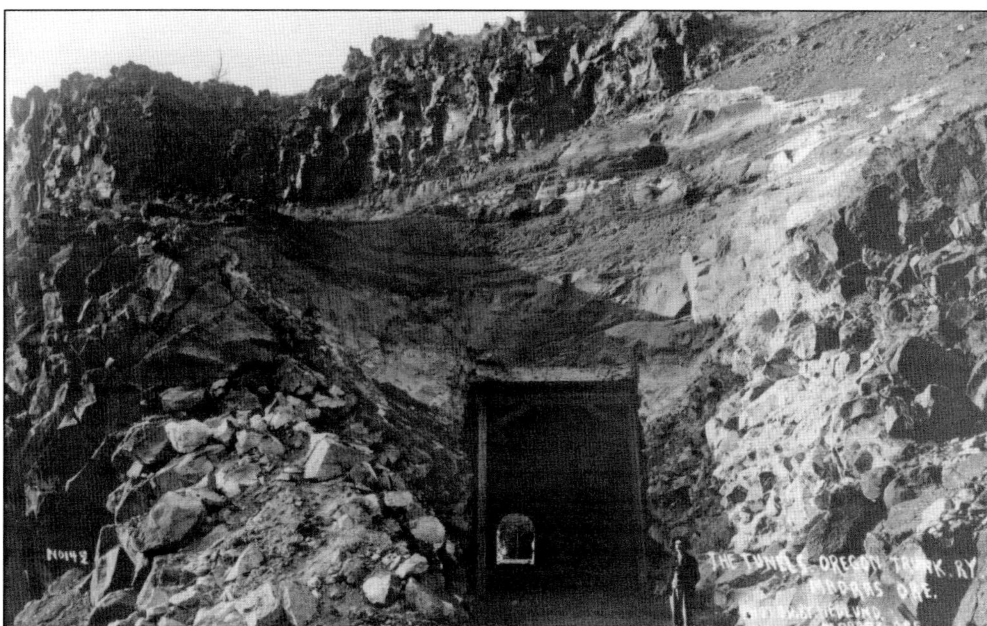

This tunnel, along the slopes of Willow Creek, is one of several tunnels along the Oregon Trunk line.

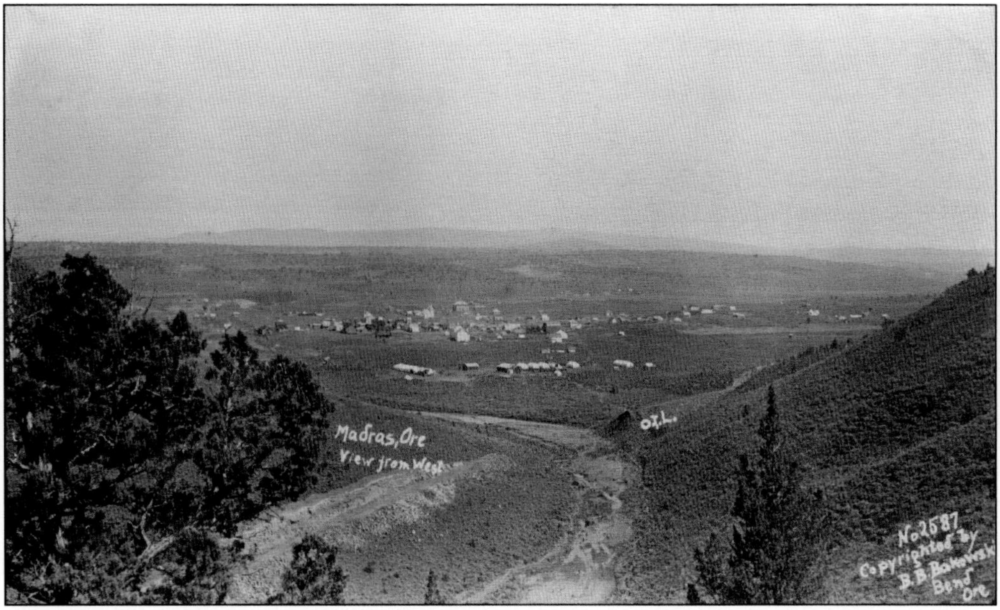

This view looks east toward Madras with Willow Creek in the foreground. The Oregon Trunk Railroad has constructed some preliminary grade up the canyon and will soon arrive as the first of the competing lines to reach Madras. The tents in the foreground were temporary housing for construction and engineering crews.

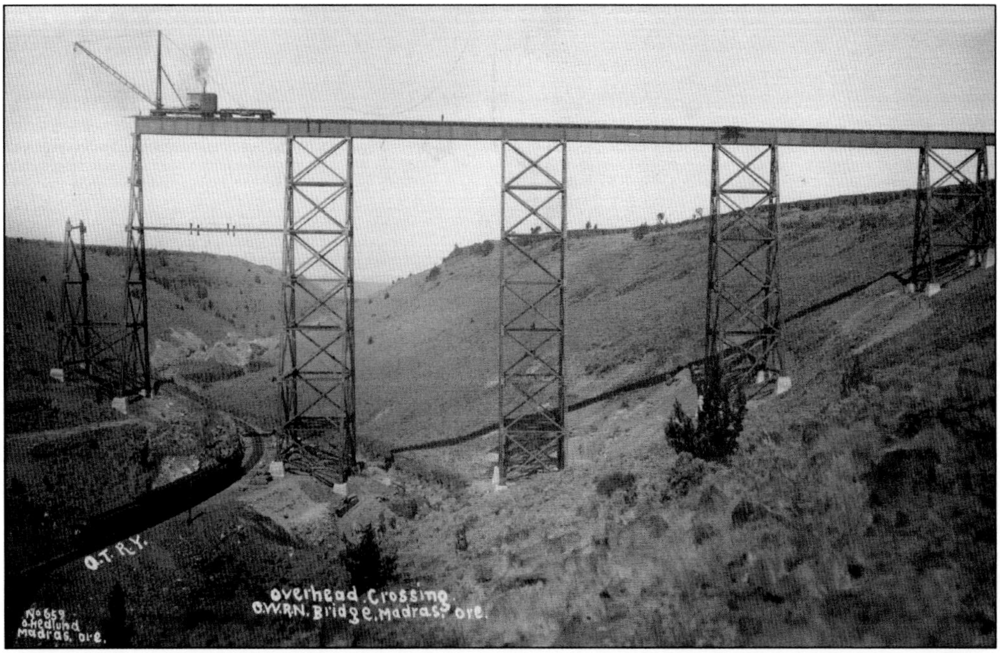

This interesting photograph shows the Deschutes Railroad viaduct bridge being built over Willow Creek Canyon while underneath it, the Oregon Trunk Railroad has already reached Madras. The railroad war was an extravagant expenditure of money between egotistical railroad magnates but was a boom for local residents.

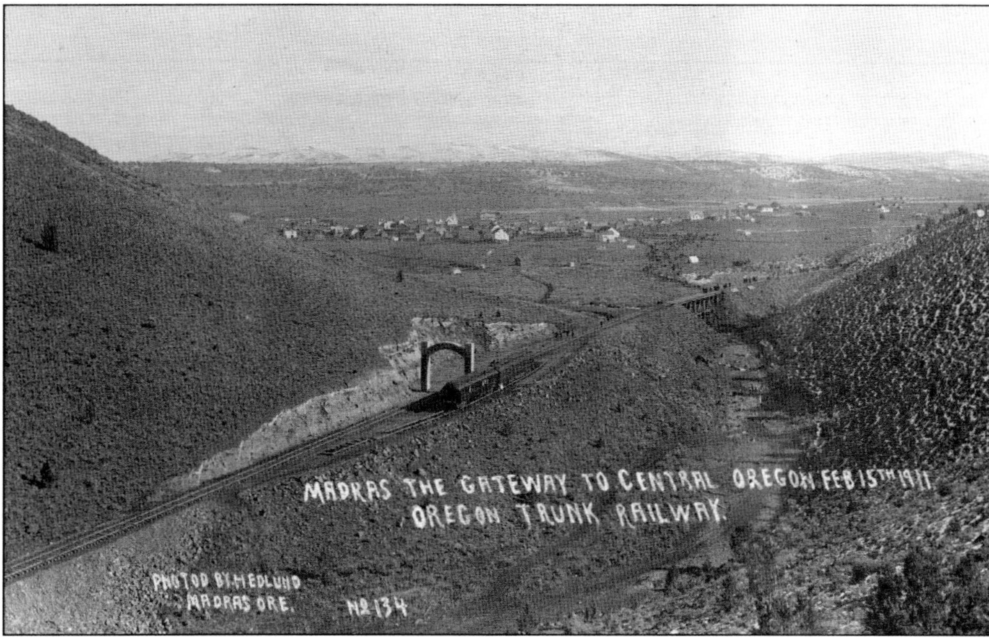

This view looking east from the top of Willow Creek Canyon shows the Oregon Trunk Railroad reaching Madras. The Gateway Arch is visible in the middle of the photograph near the railroad car. The Deschutes Railroad had not yet completed the viaduct bridge over Willow Creek.

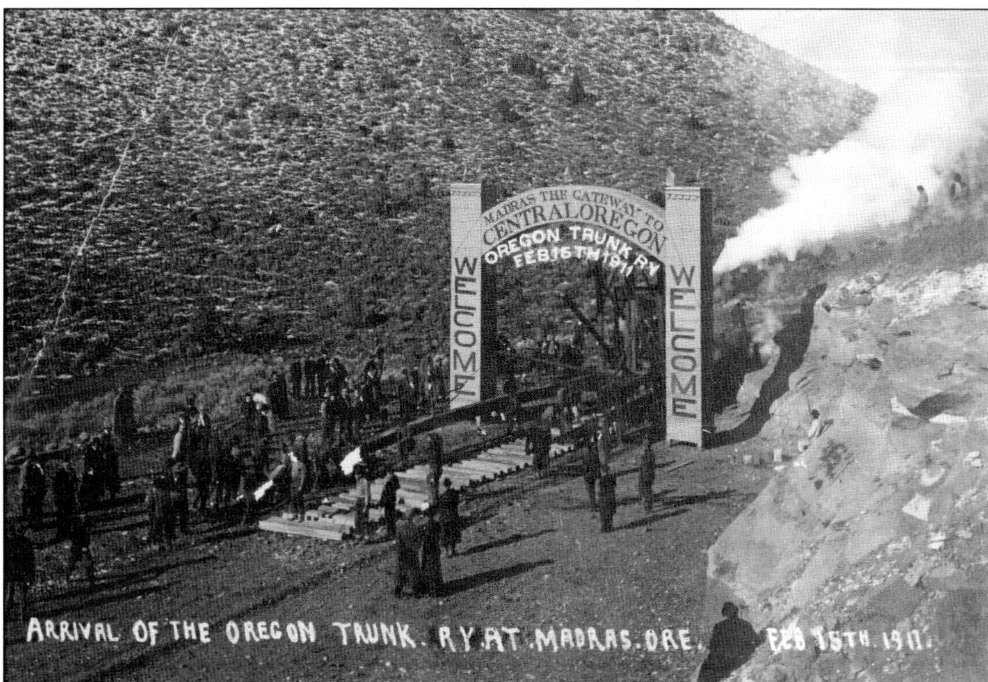

This photograph shows the rail-laying machinery passing under the Gateway Arch and railroad ties being laid in front as the Oregon Trunk Railroad arrives in Madras. The construction crews made it to Madras in early February 1911 and a grand celebration was planned by the Madras community to commemorate the great occasion.

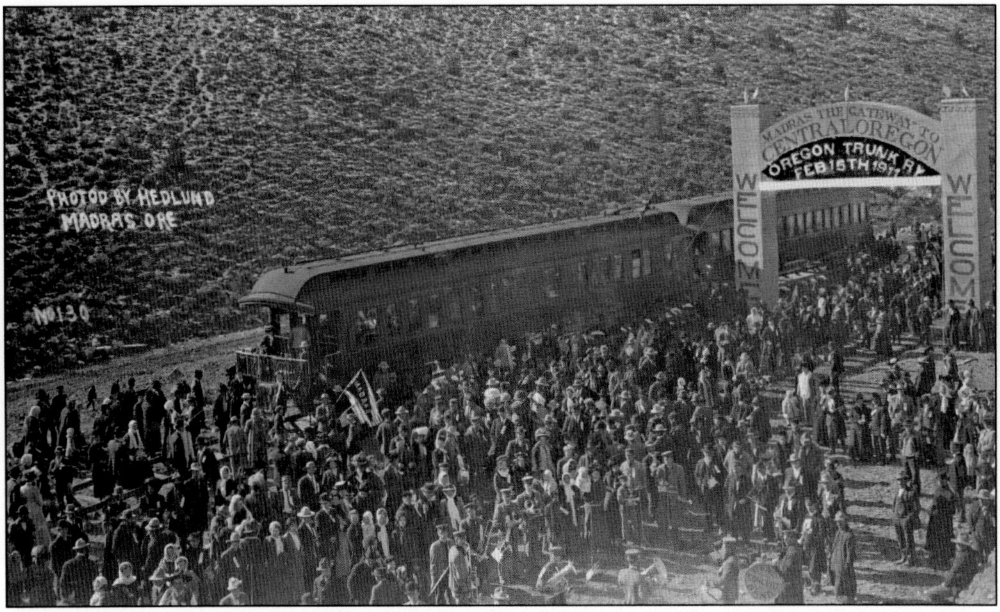

The arrival of the railroad to central Oregon was a long-awaited dream of local residents. Since the Oregon Trunk Railroad was the first to arrive, a major celebration took place on February 15, 1911. Dignitaries from the Oregon Trunk Railroad, including James J. Hill and prominent local and regional officials, gathered to celebrate the beginning of a new era of anticipated prosperity. A large crowd of more than 1,000 people attended the celebration in Madras.

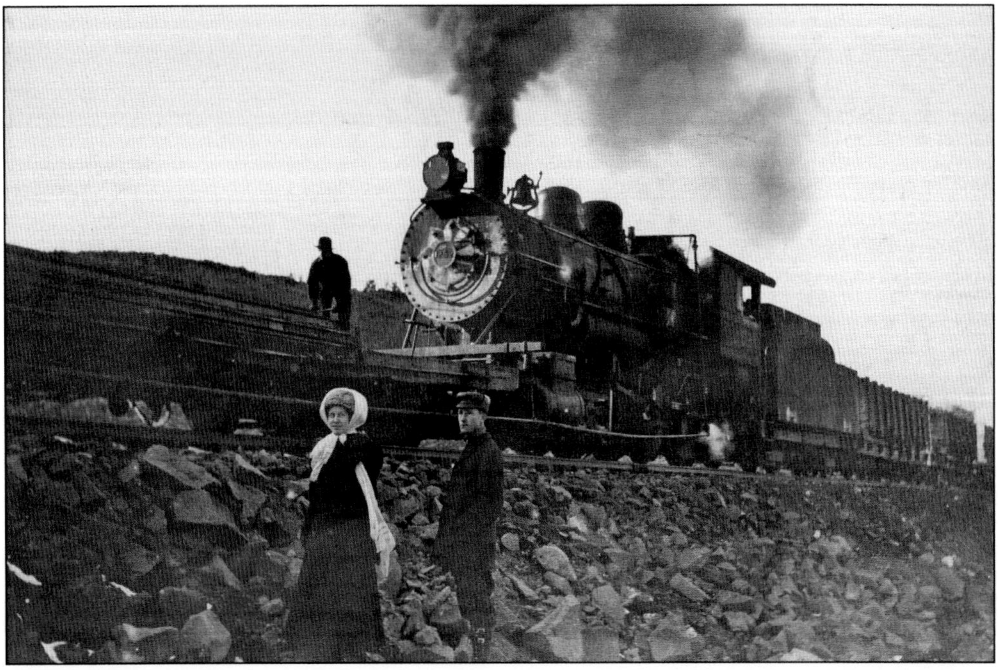

Eva and Warren Crooks of Prineville are spectators along the tracks at the celebration of the arrival of the first train arriving in Madras. People from central and eastern Oregon were extremely joyous at finally having a connection with the main rail lines of the Northwest. (Courtesy of Bowman Museum.)

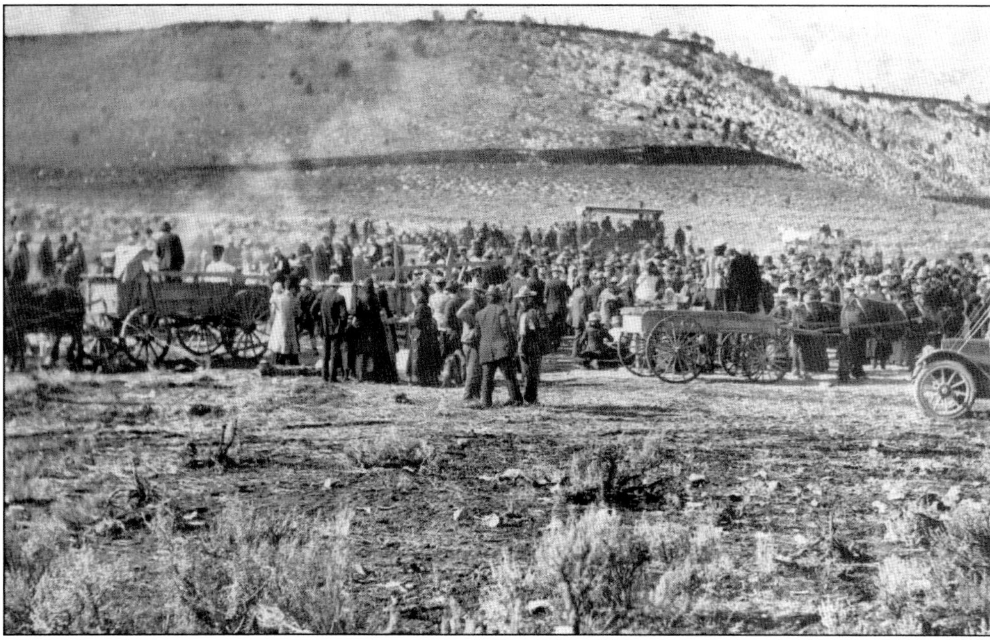

A large crowd gathers early in the day for the big celebration. Wagons are full of passengers eager to glimpse the railroad. Residents had waited a long time for this event after several years of disappointment, with rumors of previous railroads to be built ending in failure. The railroad was massively important to the residents of frontier central Oregon because for the first time they had a way to ship lumber, produce, and livestock to a national market.

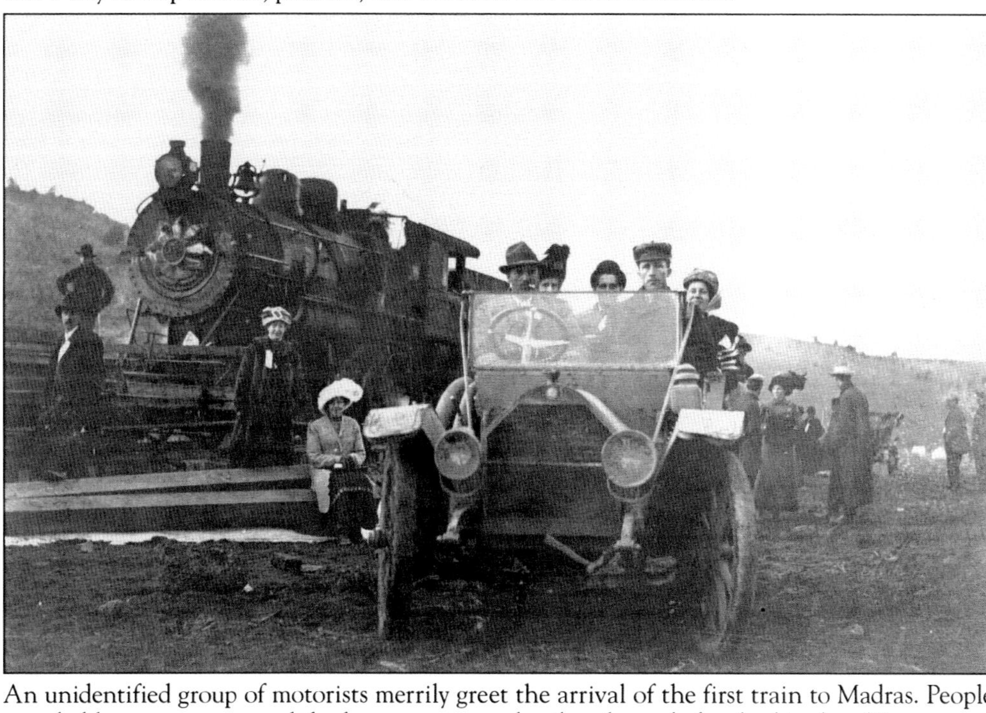

An unidentified group of motorists merrily greet the arrival of the first train to Madras. People traveled by wagon, automobile, horse, stage, and railroad coach for the big day. (Courtesy of the author.)

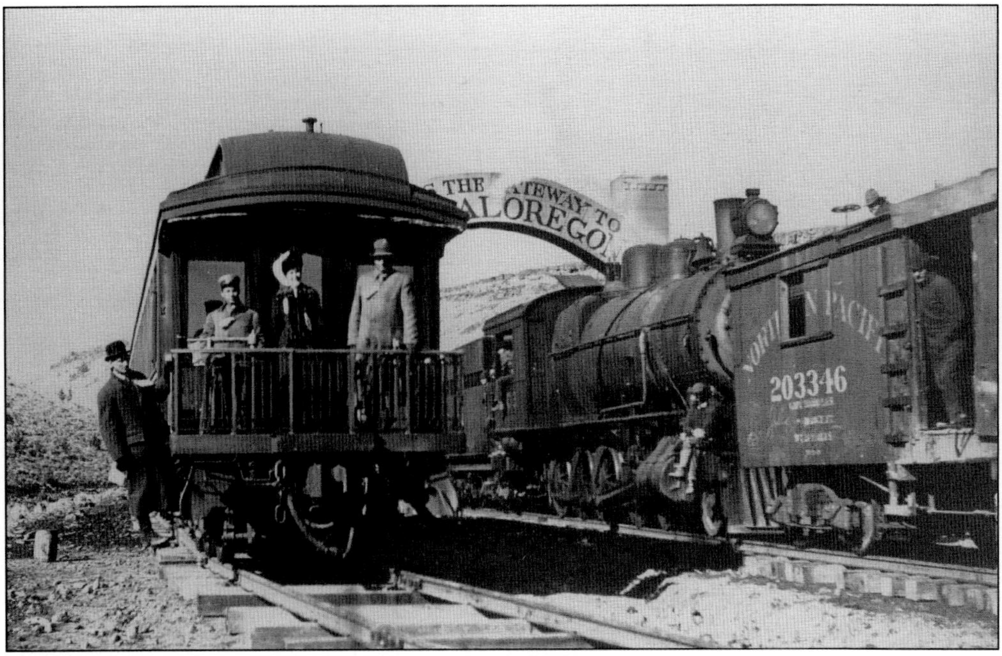

Dignitaries stand on the back of a passenger car alongside the first train at the Gateway Arch. The passenger car was one of James J. Hill's private cars, which brought politicians and dignitaries from Portland and other points to the Railroad Day Celebration.

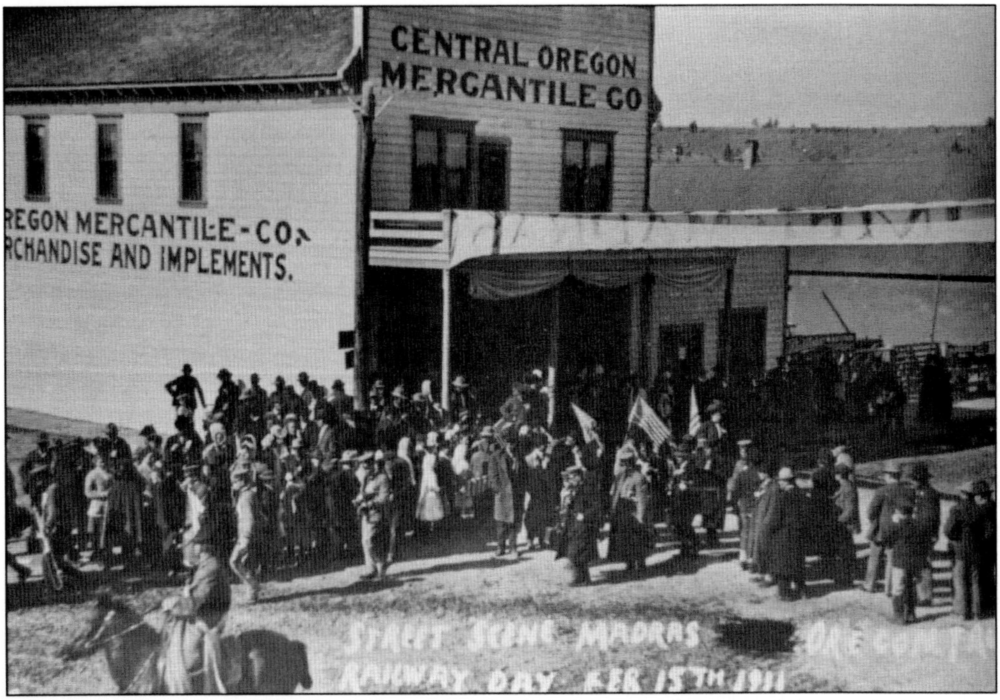

The main street was lined with spectators in front of the Central Oregon Mercantile Company to celebrate the new railroad.

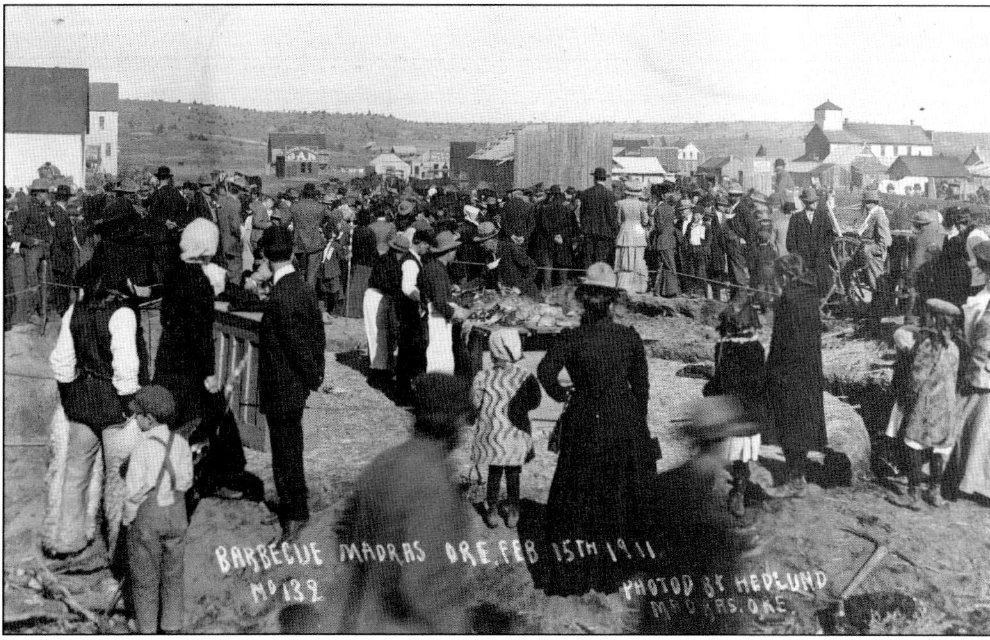

A large barbecue was planned for the celebration in Madras. People gathered on the outskirts of Madras, wearing some of their best finery and in a joyous mood. The community skyline can be seen in the background. The Atwell & Milak Bar can be seen in the middle background and the Near Beer Garden is to the right of it.

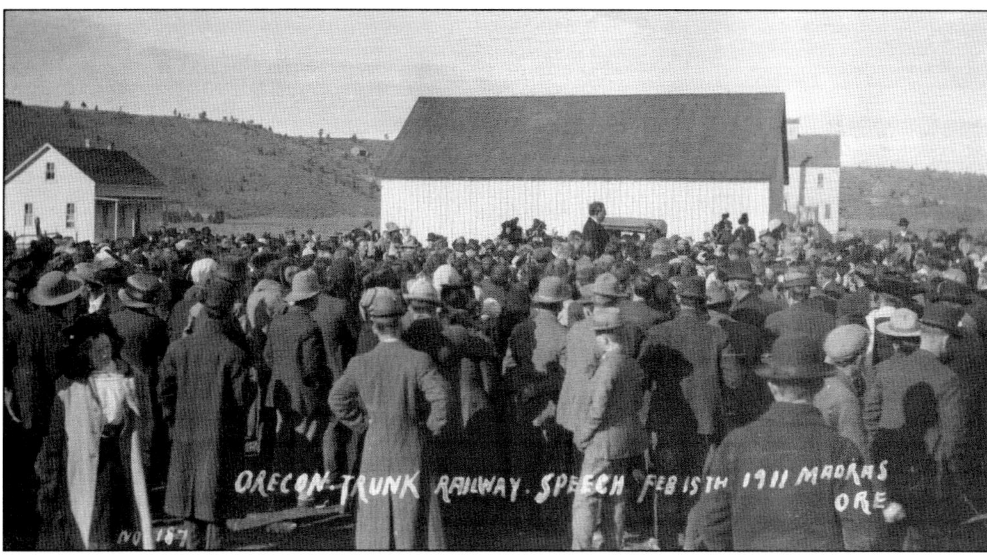

The crowd cheered during and after many of the speeches given on the momentous day of the arrival of the railroad. Among the speakers were legislators, railroad officials, and prominent local citizens. It was such a joyous occasion that every speech was applauded, even if the crowd did not know who the speaker was.

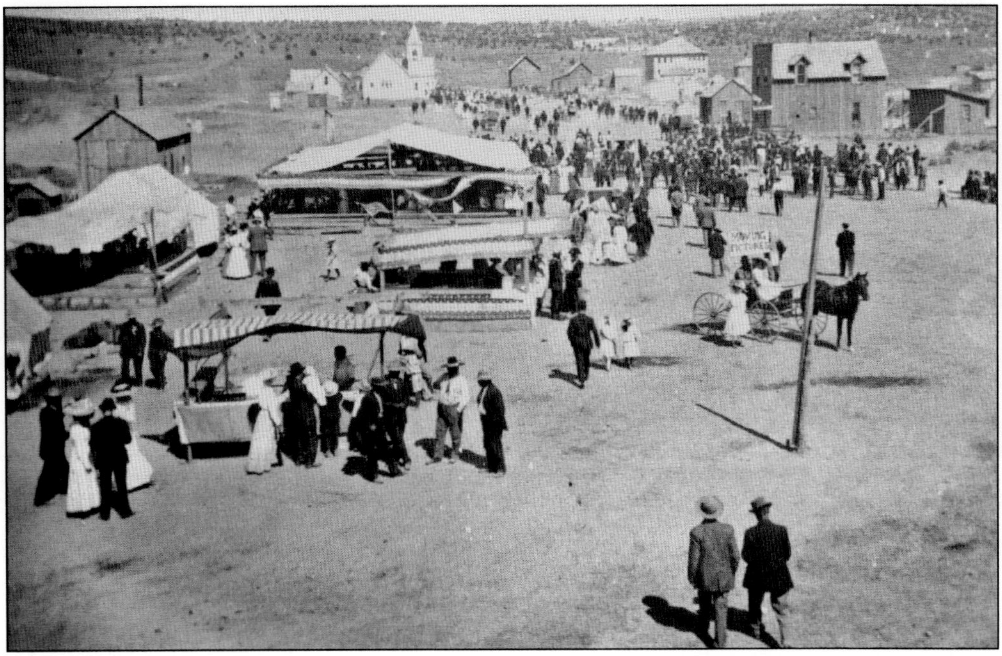

This elevated view looks east on D Street months after the arrival of the railroad. Notice the large crowd walking the main section of town. Side tents and booths had been erected for promotional purposes and for the sale of souvenirs.

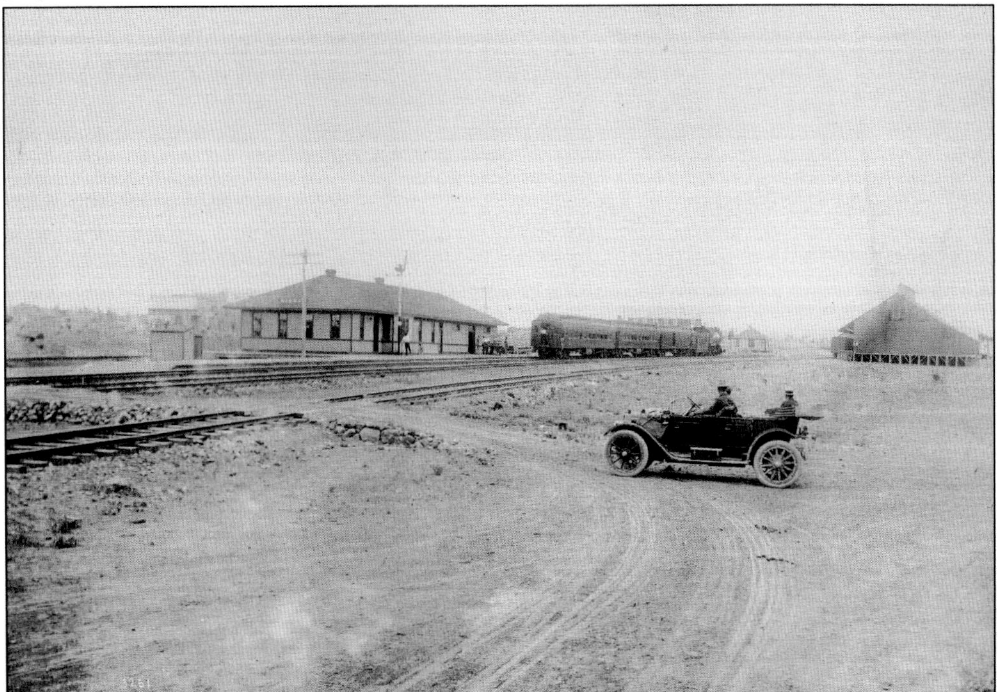

The Oregon Trunk Railroad depot, on the west end of Madison Street, was constructed in the typical Great Northern design and completed a few months after the first train. The Farmers Union Warehouse can be seen to the right of the tracks.

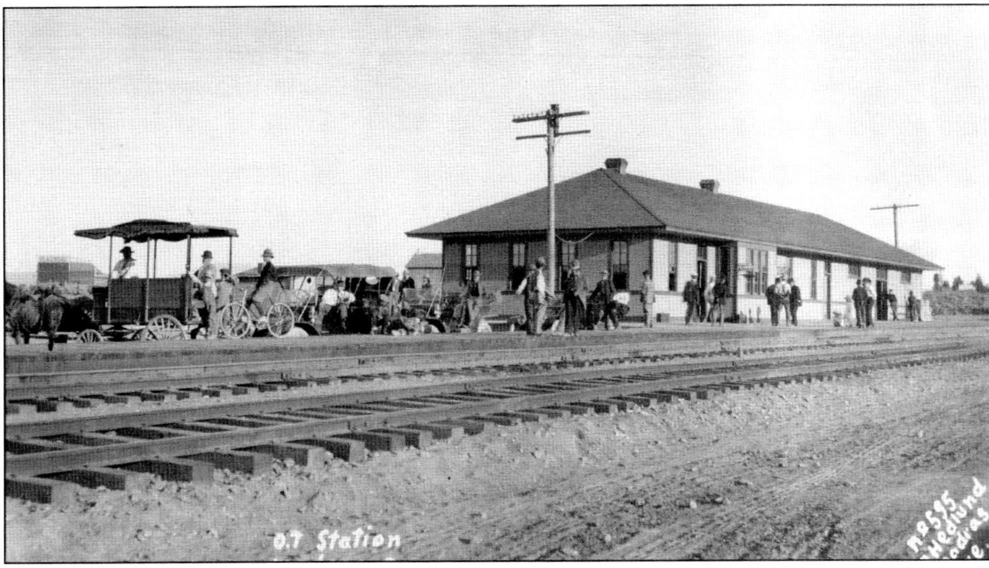

Residents often planned visits to the depot on train arrivals to see who was arriving and to enjoy the excitement of the moment. The Oregon Trunk Railroad eventually abandoned its line from Trout Creek to Madras and shared the Deschutes Railroad line from Trout Creek to Madras via Gateway in 1923. The depot was eventually dismantled and moved to Eugene where it was rebuilt as the terminal for the Oregon Electric Railroad.

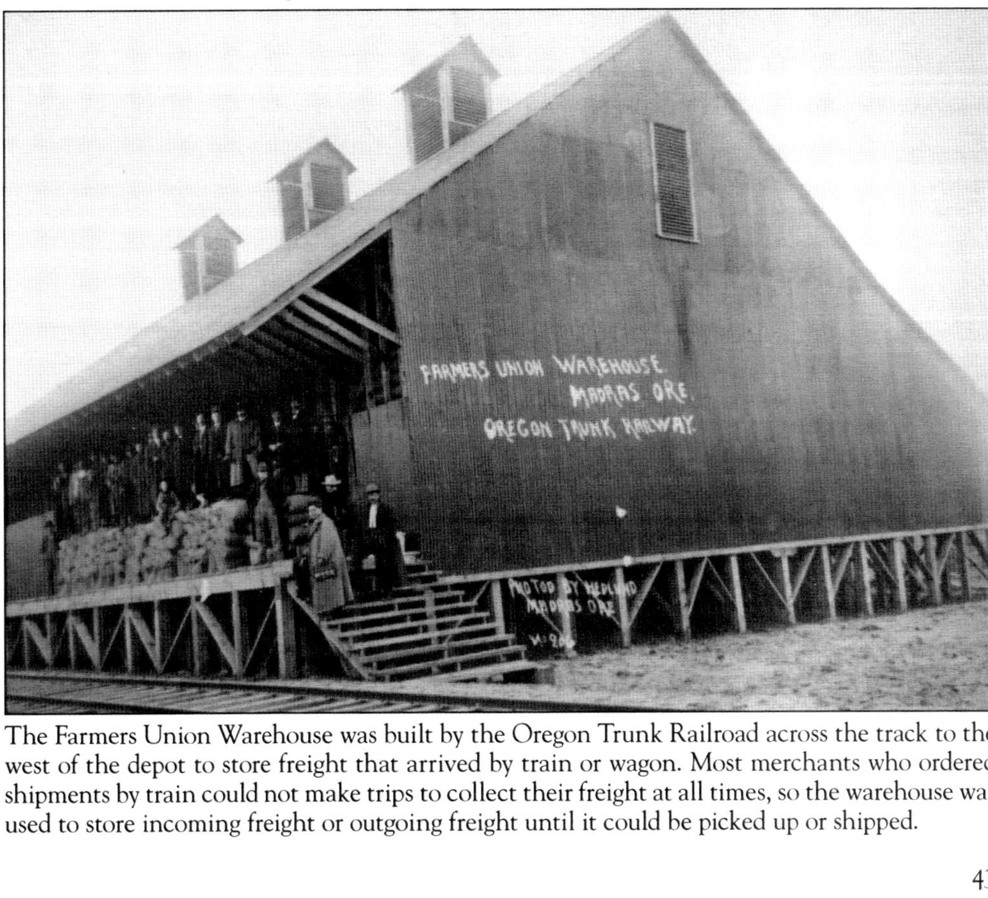

The Farmers Union Warehouse was built by the Oregon Trunk Railroad across the track to the west of the depot to store freight that arrived by train or wagon. Most merchants who ordered shipments by train could not make trips to collect their freight at all times, so the warehouse was used to store incoming freight or outgoing freight until it could be picked up or shipped.

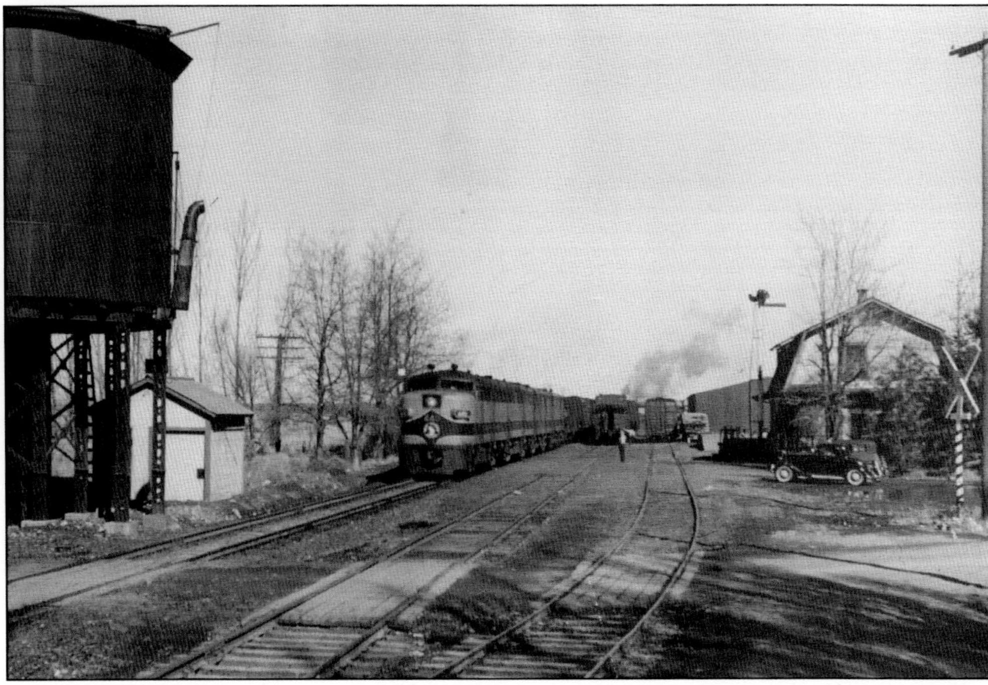

The Deschutes Railroad depot, seen here in 1936, was north of the Willow Creek Viaduct Bridge on Agency Plains, just north of Madras. It became the main station in Madras when the Oregon Trunk Railroad abandoned its line up Willow Creek in 1923. The depot is no longer standing.

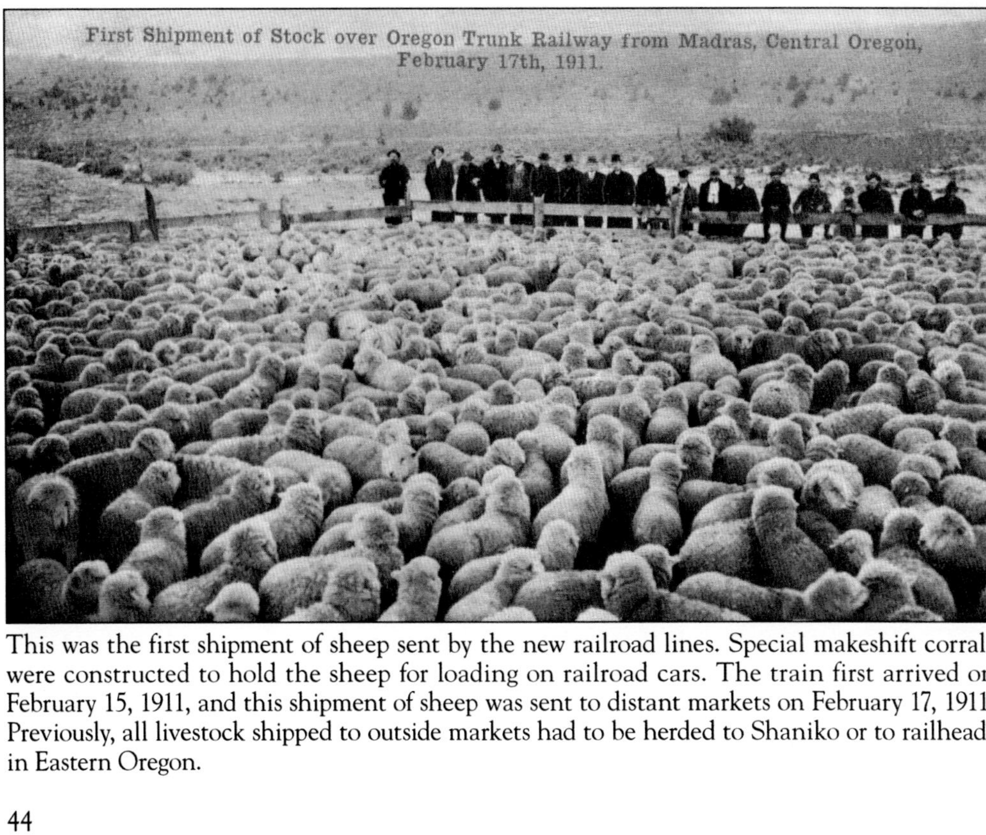

This was the first shipment of sheep sent by the new railroad lines. Special makeshift corrals were constructed to hold the sheep for loading on railroad cars. The train first arrived on February 15, 1911, and this shipment of sheep was sent to distant markets on February 17, 1911. Previously, all livestock shipped to outside markets had to be herded to Shaniko or to railheads in Eastern Oregon.

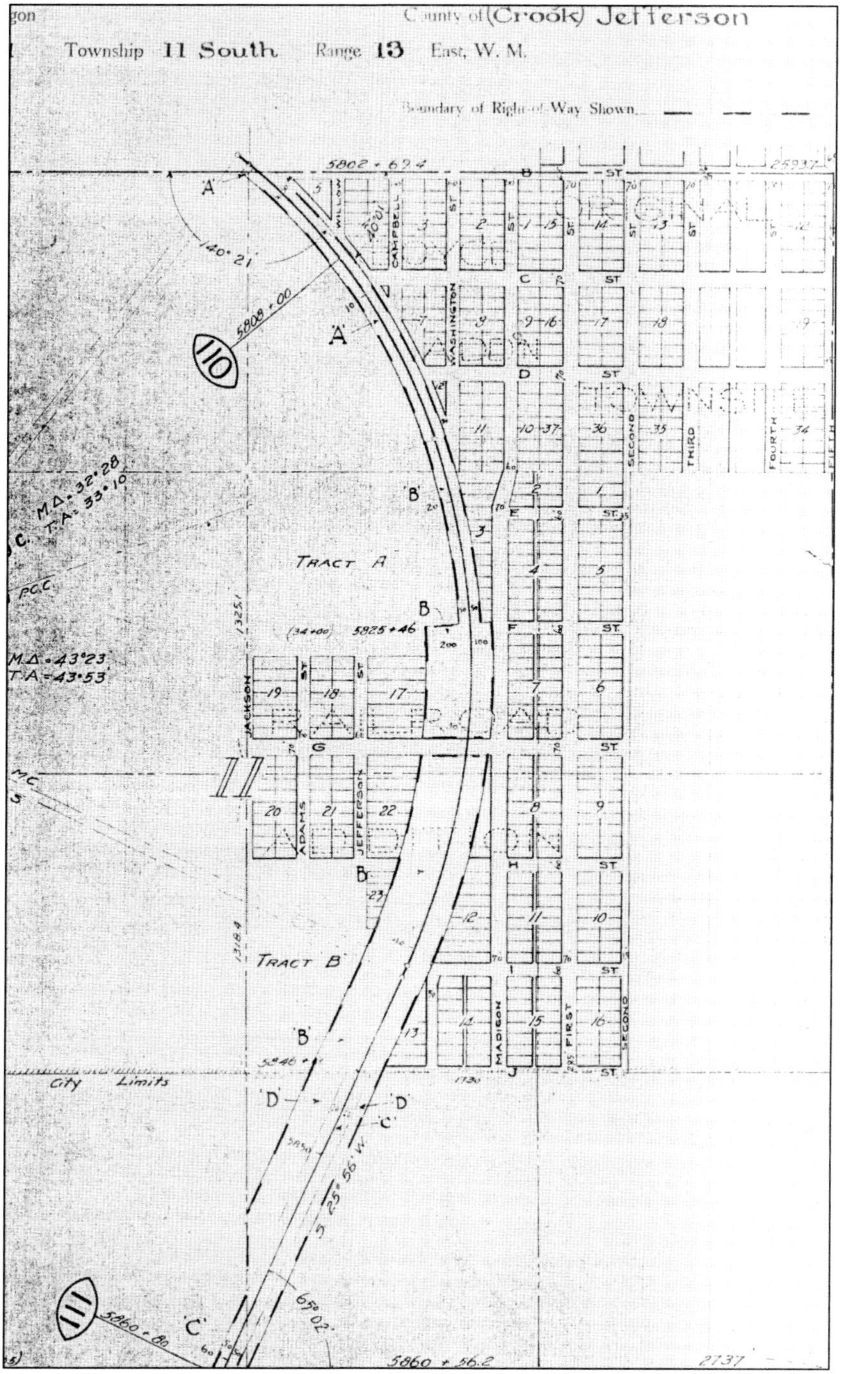

This right-of-way map for the Oregon Trunk Railroad delineates the route of the railroad through Madras. The depot was located near Madison Street between H and I Streets. Madras residents were happy to give the right-of-way to the railroad so near the community. Although the depot was located on the western fringe of the community, homes were soon built near the depot. Today, there is little trace of the once-revered symbol of transportation history. (Courtesy of Beth Crow.)

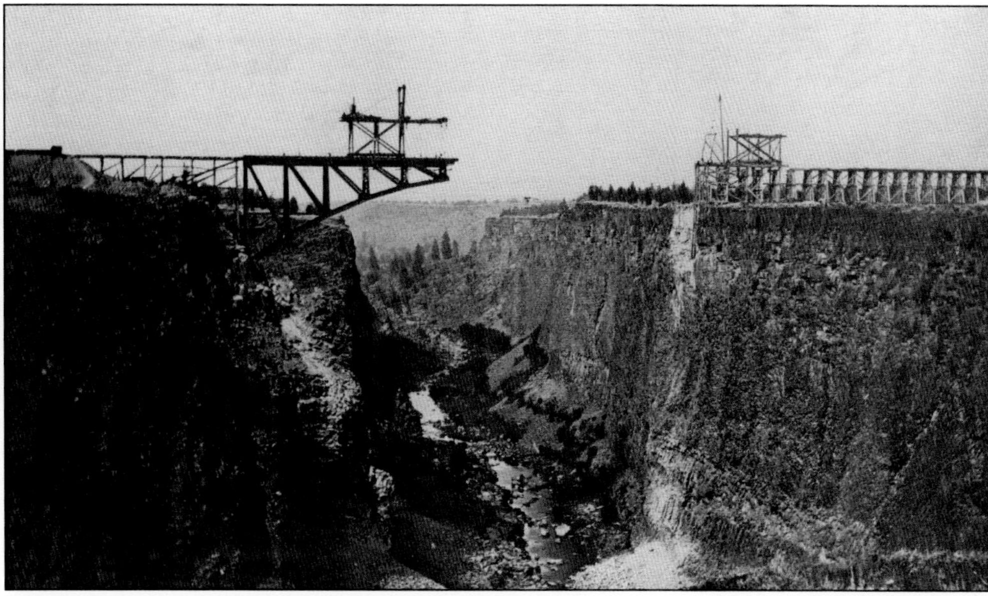

Madras was not the final destination of the railroads; construction continued south across the Crooked River Gorge to Redmond and Bend. The most difficult obstacle along the rail route was the crossing at Crooked River Gorge. Here, crews work on the bridge from both sides of the canyon. Because of the expense and limited construction opportunities, the two railroads shared the same line into Redmond and Bend once the bridge was completed. Madras was a major supply center for the construction crews working on the bridge.

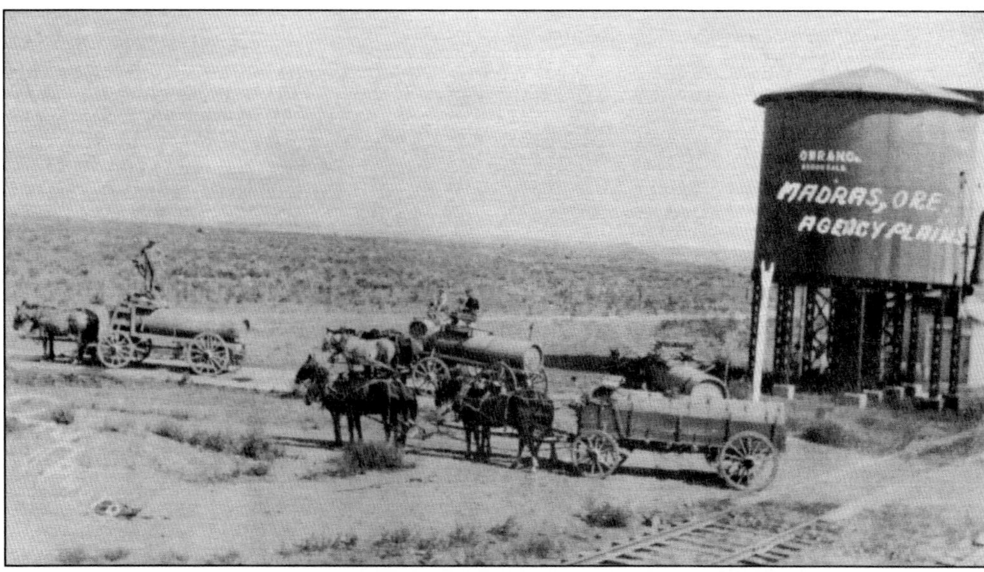

Another benefit the railroads brought were water towers, built to supply engines with water for the steam engines. This tower is located on Agency Plains just northwest of Madras. The railroad allowed homesteaders and residents to fill up wagons and barrels like the ones seen here with water from the towers, which were fed by deep wells. However, the availability of water still remained a problem for most farmers and community residents.

Three

The Growth of a Community

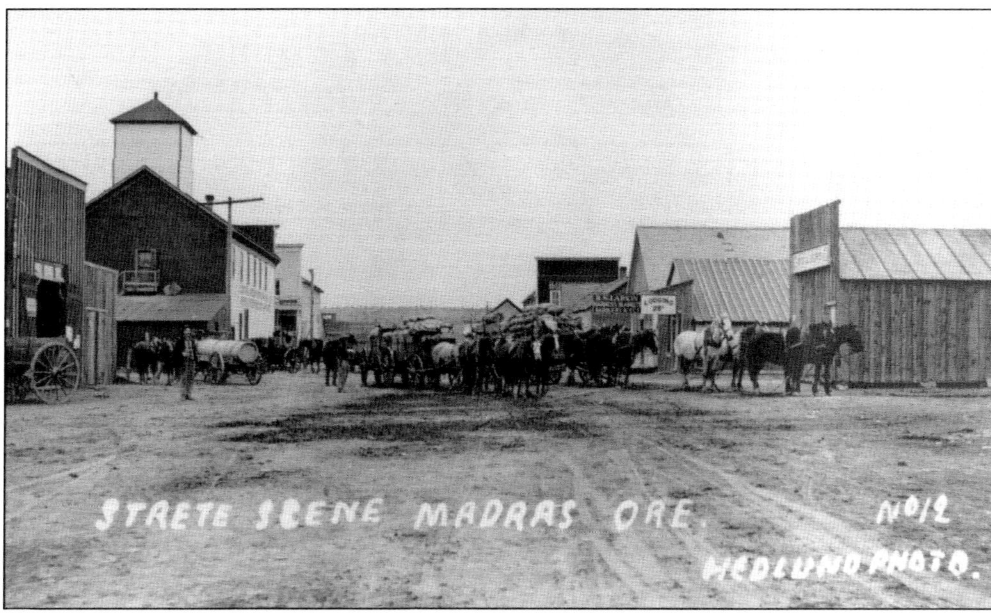

The arrival of the railroad brought an economic boom to Madras. This photograph, looking east on C Street, shows the community at the time of the railroads' arrival in 1911. The town would soon begin a transition from horses and wagons to early automobiles, which meant improved roads and the opening up of new trade markets.

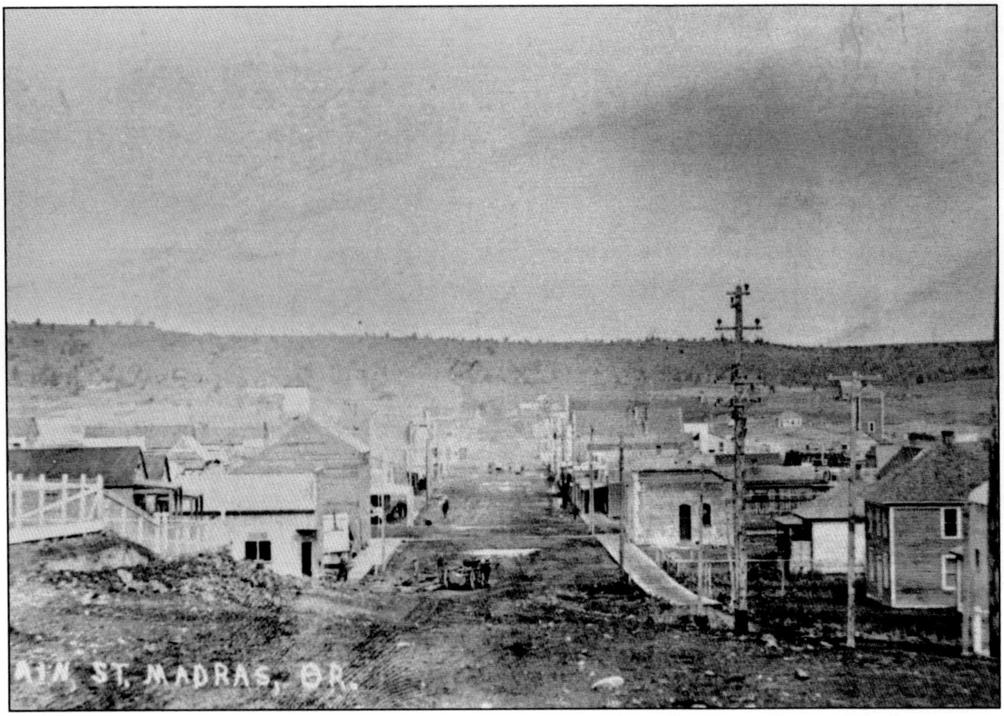

A dusty Fifth (Main) Street is bordered on both sides with boardwalks in front of the businesses in 1909. Combined telephone and electrical lines parallel the street on the eastern side signaling that the frontier town is beginning to modernize.

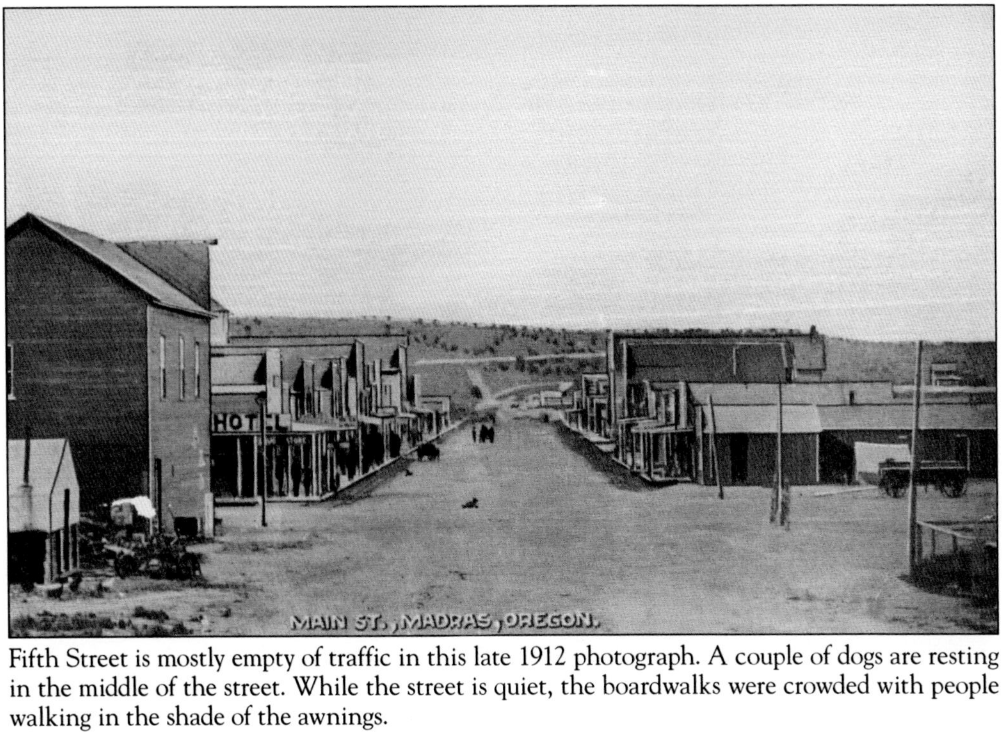

Fifth Street is mostly empty of traffic in this late 1912 photograph. A couple of dogs are resting in the middle of the street. While the street is quiet, the boardwalks were crowded with people walking in the shade of the awnings.

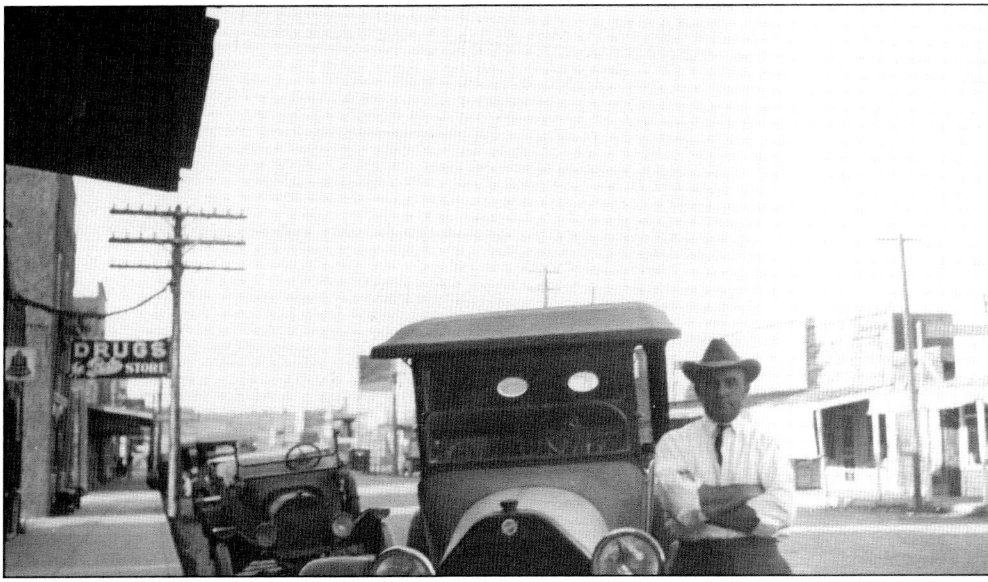

More and more automobiles were seen in the community after 1912. Here, Howard Turner leans against his new vehicle with other automobiles parked along the street behind him. One of the obstacles to motorized vehicle use was the lack of fuel depots. Gas was first delivered in five-gallon cans by horse-drawn freight wagons. The railroad provided a means of transporting more fuel to the community.

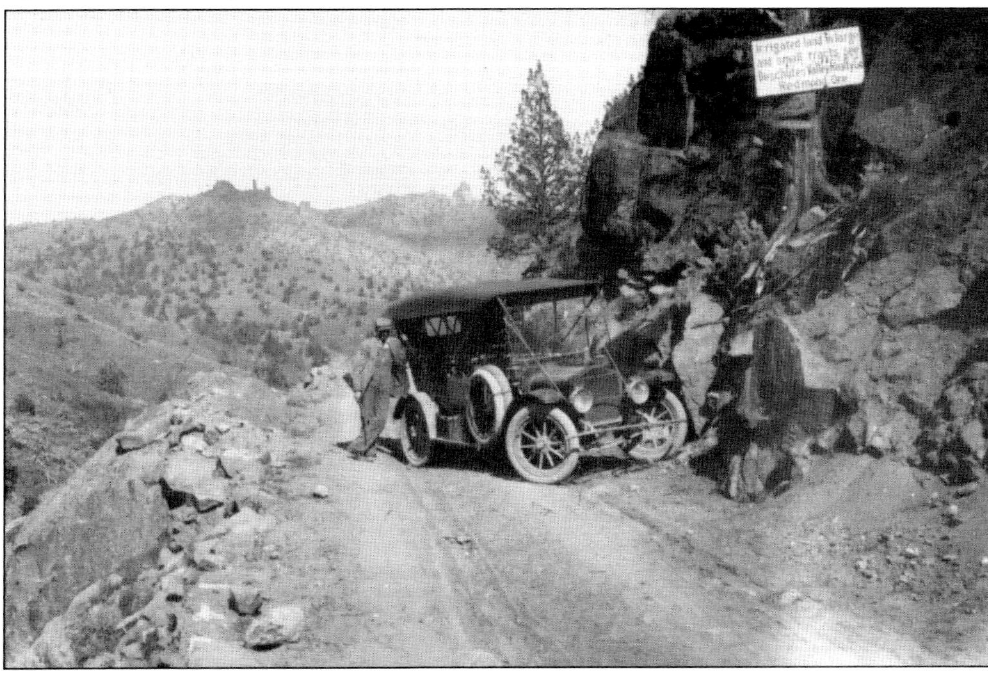

An automobile owned by the Campbell family is stopped along the grade on the south side of Trail Crossing en route from Redmond to Madras in 1912. A sign along the road advertised irrigated lands in the Terrebonne and Redmond vicinities. An innovative artist hired himself out to paint a large advertising sign on the flat surface of a rim rock on the north side of the canyon. The lava rock billboard is still visible today. (Courtesy of the Campbell family.)

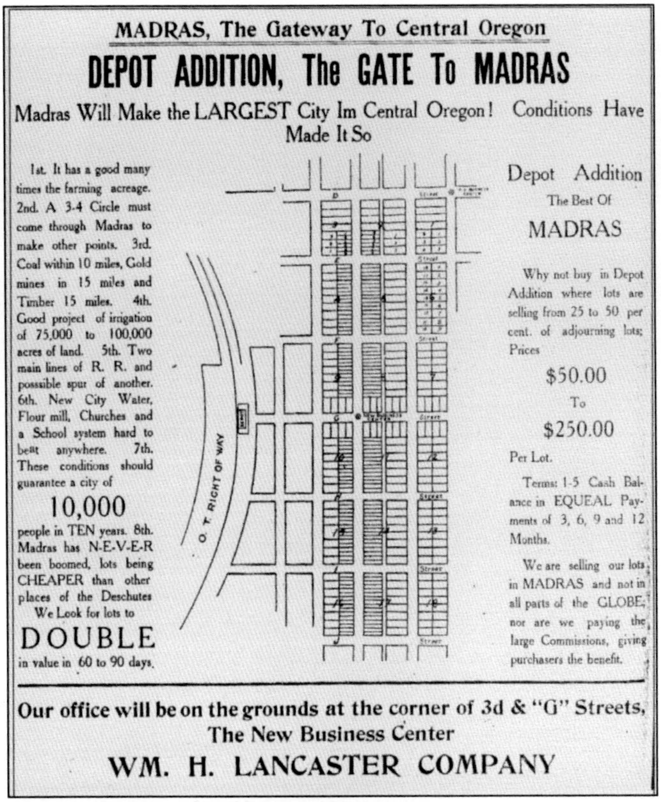

This 1911 advertisement proclaims that Madras is the gateway to Central Oregon and will become the largest city in central Oregon. Lots are advertised for sale, ranging in price from $50 to $250. The advertisement states that it is expected that Madras will reach a population of 10,000 in 10 years.

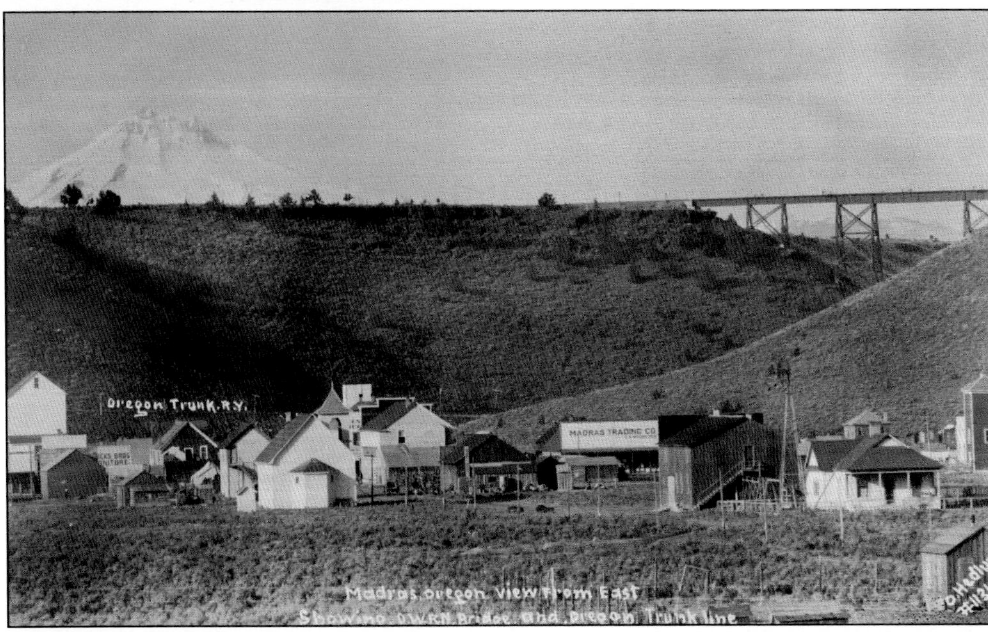

This view of Madras looks west toward Willow Creek Canyon and the Deschutes Railroad Viaduct Bridge. Mount Jefferson appears larger than life in the background on the left. This photograph was taken in 1912, and the Madras Trading Company is plainly visible in the middle section of town with a furniture store and a few buildings to the south.

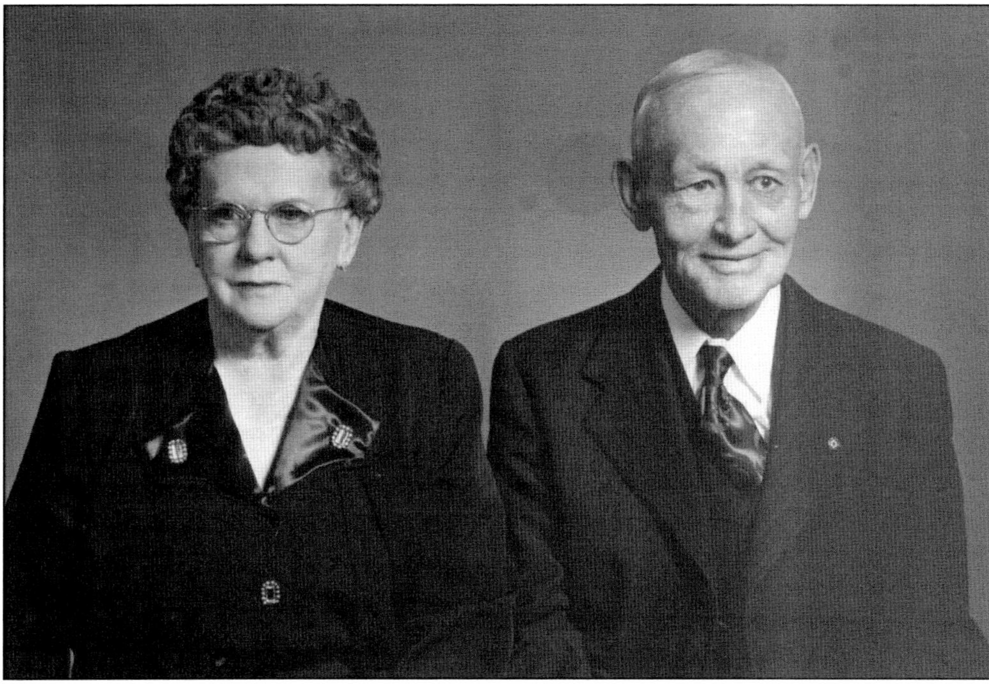

William R. Cook was the first principal of Madras Grade School. He and his wife, Pearl, seen here in their later years, came to the Basin in 1901. He began teaching in the small one-room school nearby and moved to Madras in 1909. He held many prominent positions in the community after serving as principal.

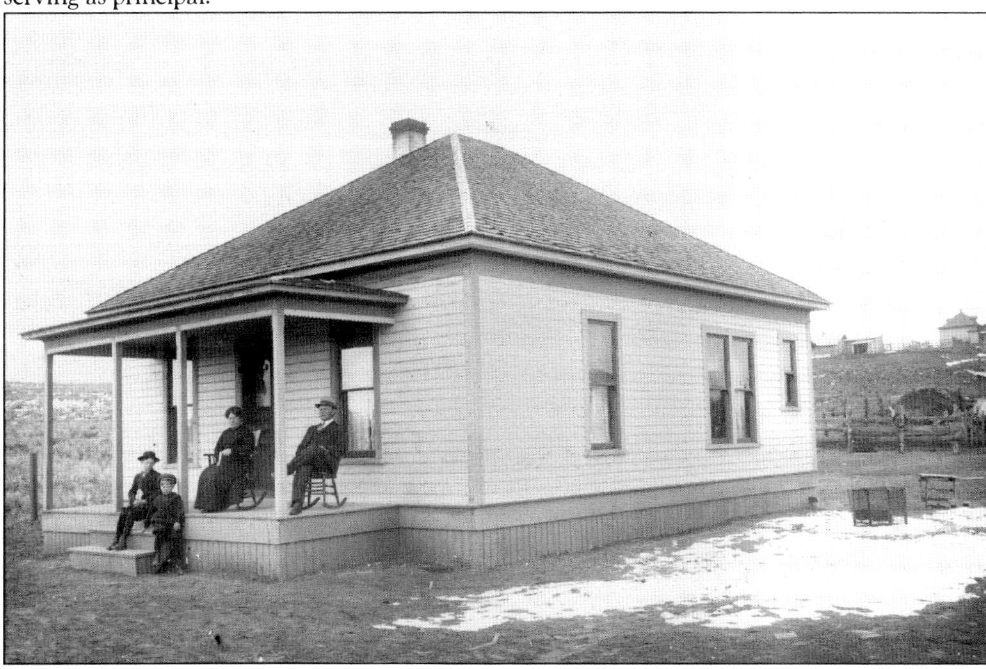

After moving to Madras in 1909 from their homestead south of town, the Cooks built this house—one of the finer homes in the new community—on East Tenth Street. Pearl and William sit on the porch and their two sons, Robert (left) and Eugene, are on the steps.

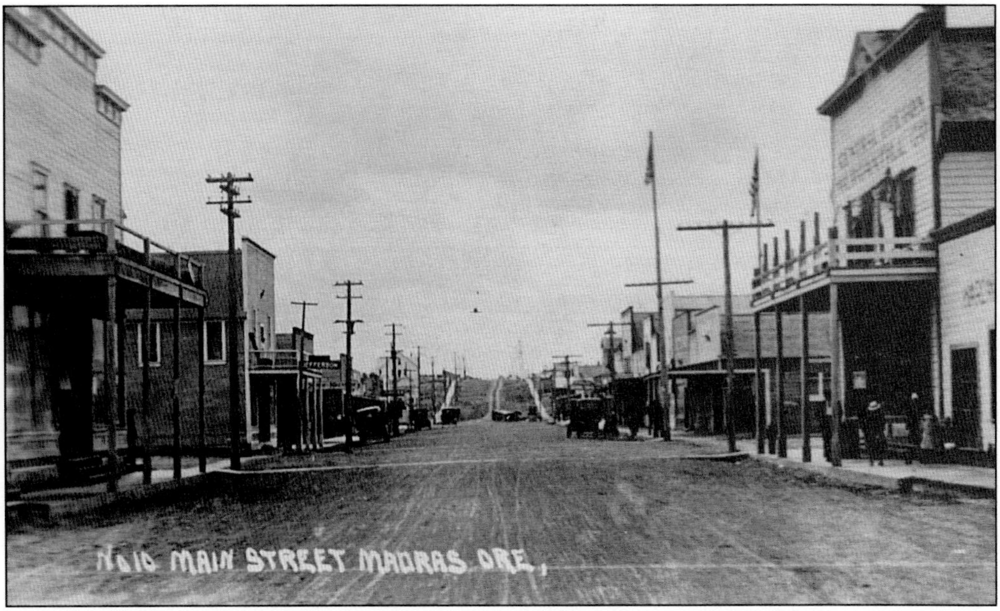

In 1914, Fifth Street was wide and had boardwalks stretching into the distance even though there were few buildings on the outskirts of town. Residents took pride in their prosperous new community. In the background, the street fades to a rutted lane as it approaches a slope.

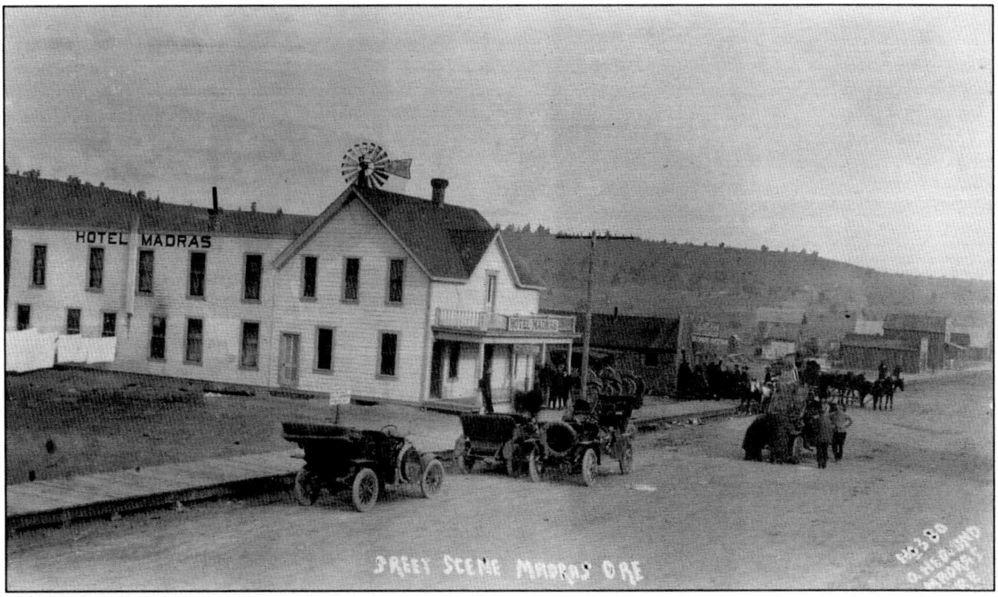

Some automobiles and a horse-drawn wagon stand beside each other in front of the Hotel Madras in 1912 as sheets dry in the wind to the left of the building and a sign advertises a lot for sale. The stage office is now known as the Cornett Stage and Auto Company. Transportation operators quickly made the transition from horses to automobiles.

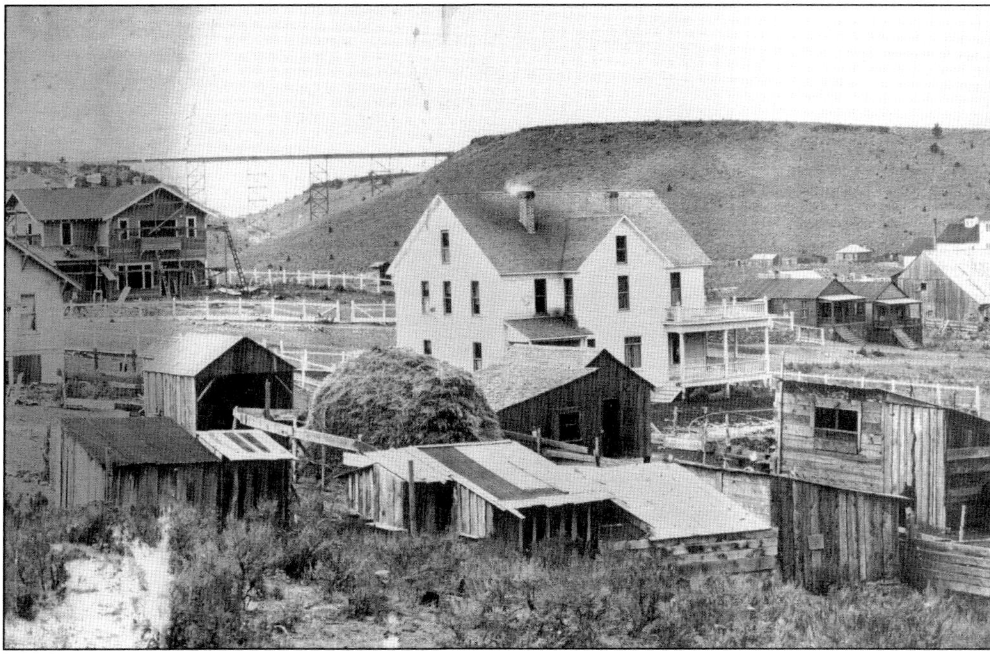

A panoramic photograph of Madras was taken in late 1911 and the next series of photographs shows segments of it. The Mason house is in the center of this image looking west toward Willow Creek Canyon and the viaduct bridge. A small haystack is located in a back lot in the center. Livestock was commonly penned inside the city limits.

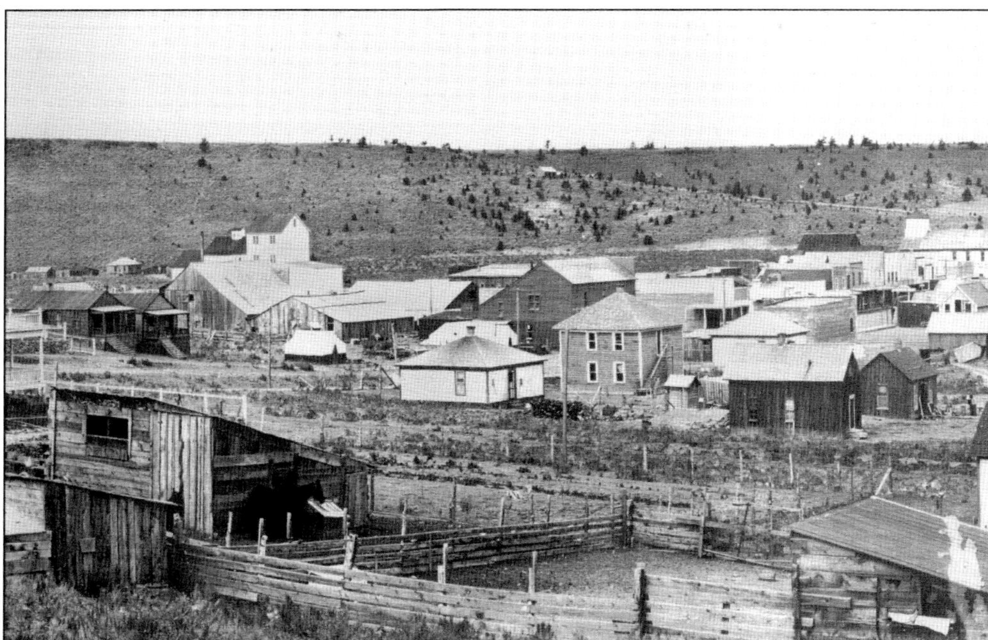

This portion looks northwest toward a ridge and Agency Plains. The main section of town is in the middle of the photograph. A chicken coop and a small stock corral are in the foreground. Although not visible above the ridgeline in the background, the Deschutes Railroad Depot was located just out of sight. The flour mill is the large white building on the left.

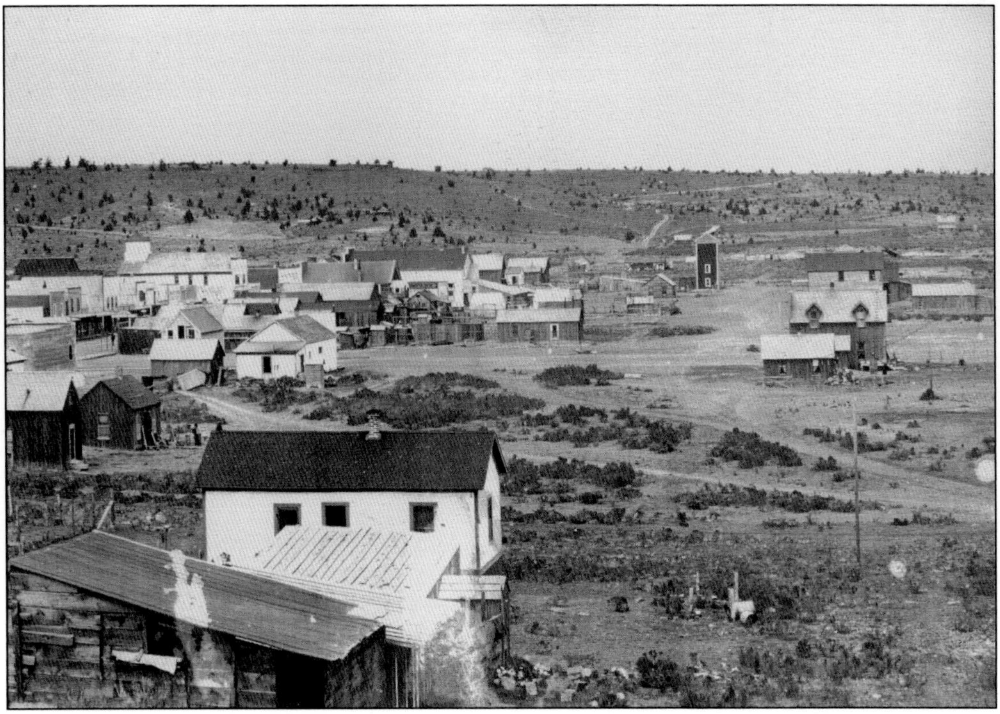

This image looks north with the main section of town to the left. Some structures and plenty of open space are visible to the right. Sagebrush is still growing near buildings in the foreground. D Street is in the middle of the panoramic photograph traversing from left to right.

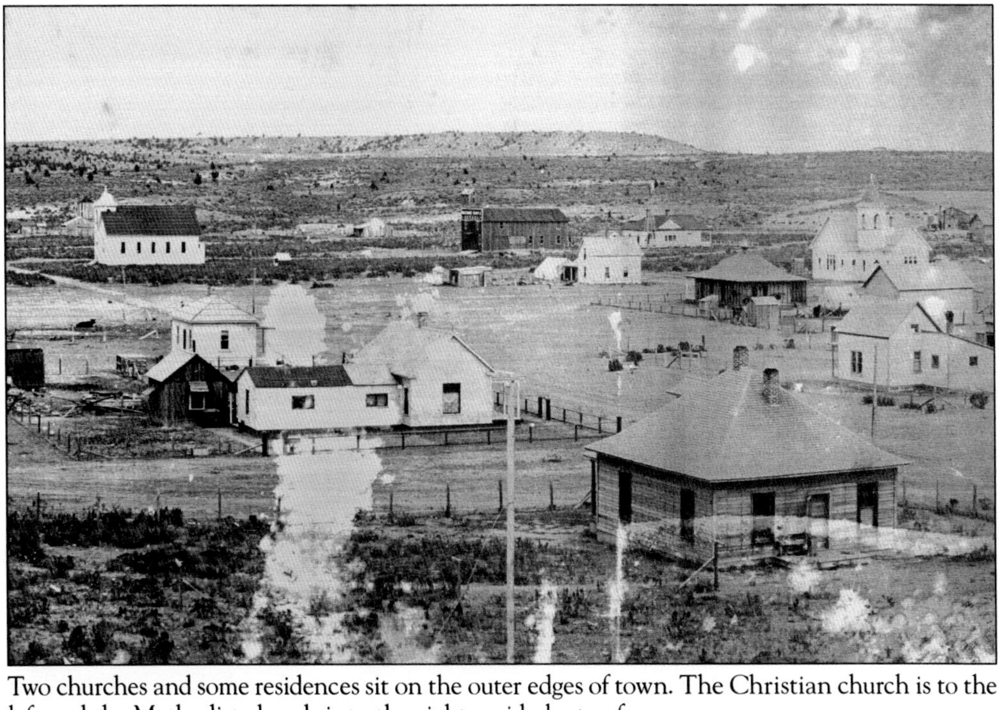

Two churches and some residences sit on the outer edges of town. The Christian church is to the left and the Methodist church is to the right amid plenty of open space.

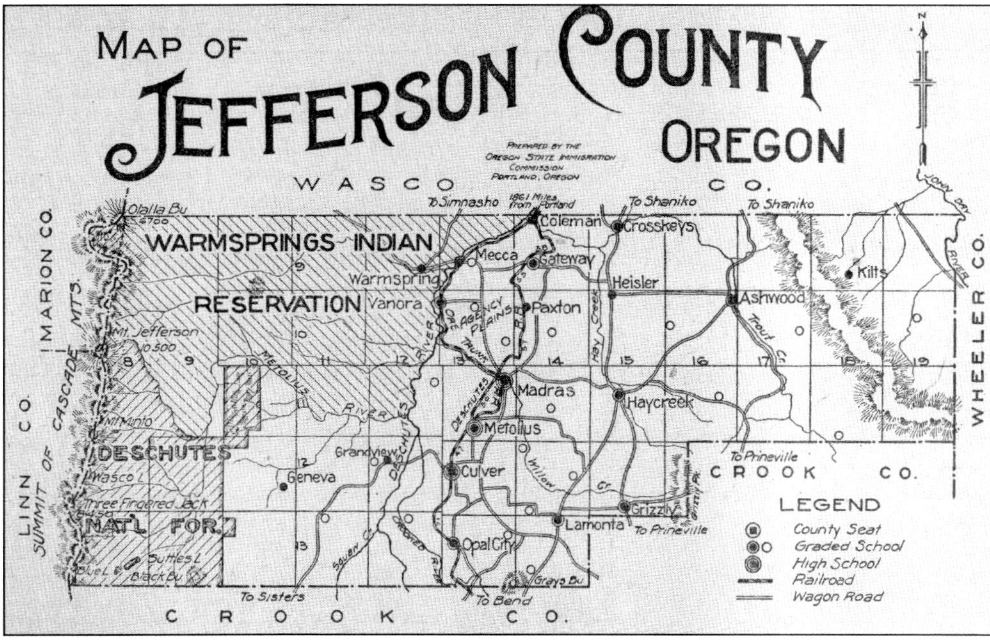

The residents of Madras and its outlying areas wanted to have government closer than Prineville, the Crook County seat. In 1914, residents convinced legislators that a new county should be created out of northern Crook County and named Jefferson County. The county was named for Mount Jefferson, which was along the western border of the new county. It was officially created on December 12, 1914. This is the first map of Jefferson County.

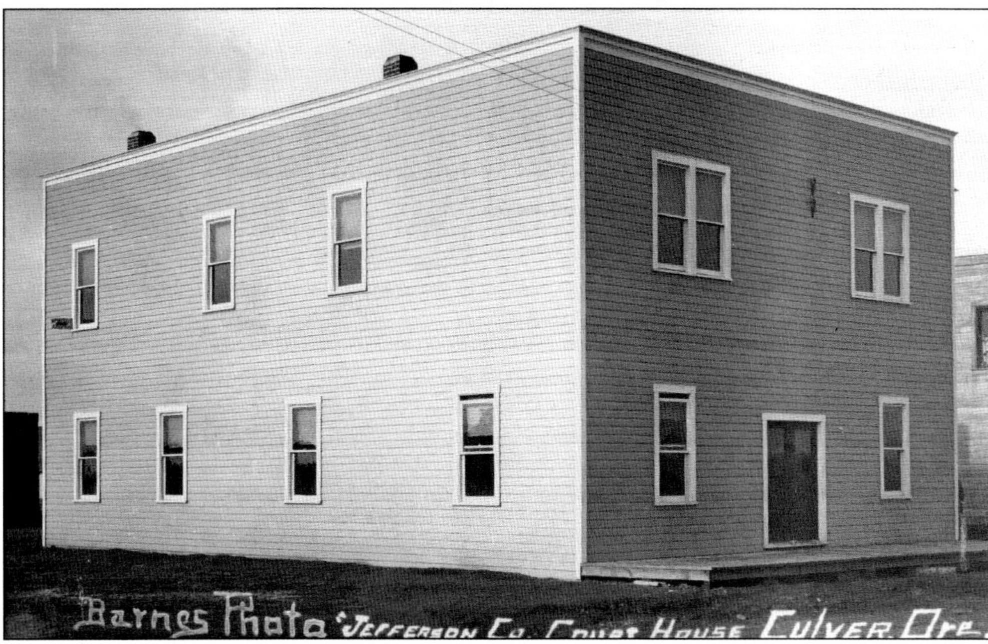

When Jefferson County was created, the governor of Oregon appointed the first county officials, and Culver was selected as the interim county seat until elections could be held to determine the official county seat and this building in Culver served as the interim courthouse. Madras was the larger community, but many influential people lived near Culver.

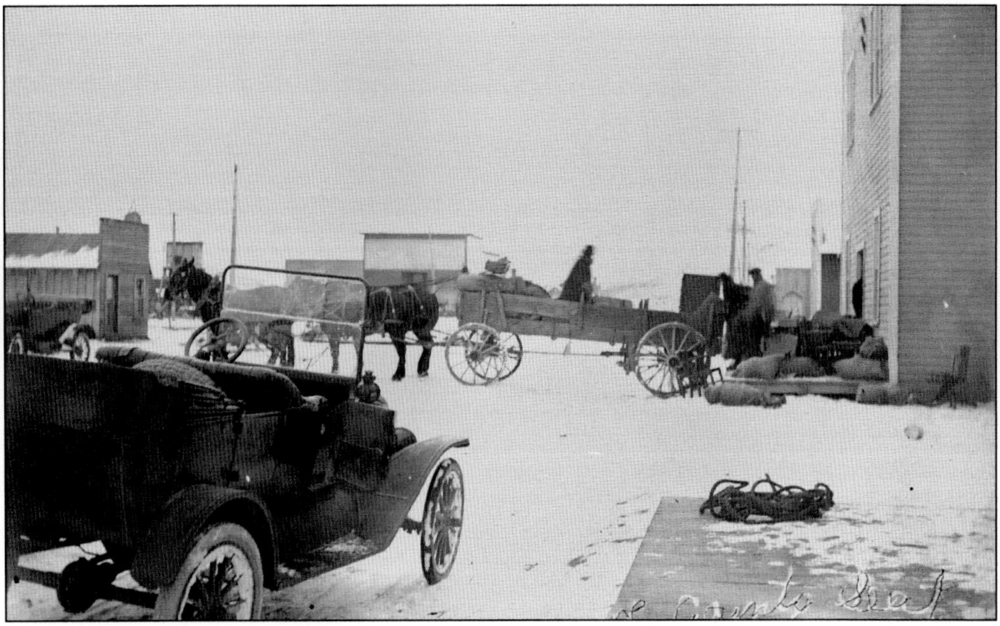

When the first election for Jefferson County was held in November 1916, Madras was voted as the official county seat. Culver residents resented Madras being voted the county seat and refused to give up the county records. Officials from Madras had to drive to Culver and physically remove the records and take them to Madras. In this photograph, a horse-drawn wagon backs up through the snow to the courthouse in Culver to load the county records.

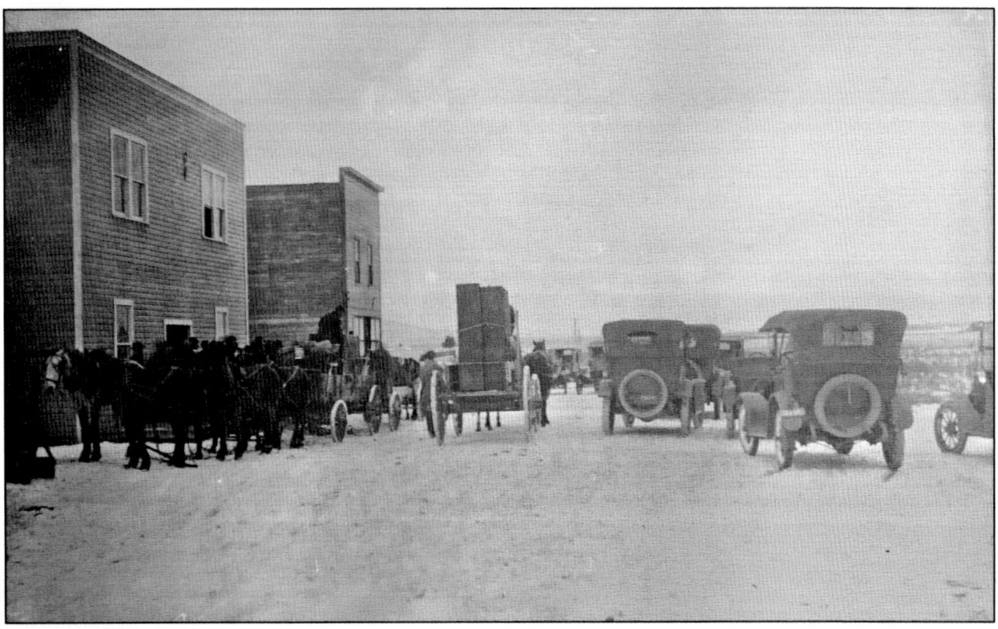

Escorted by automobiles, the record-carrying wagon headed north to Madras. Culver residents were bitter about losing the county seat and threatened counteraction. Efforts were being made to prevent the election from being certified, so Madras officials quickly went to gather the records and office fixtures and took them to Madras. Eventually, the election was certified, making Madras the official county seat.

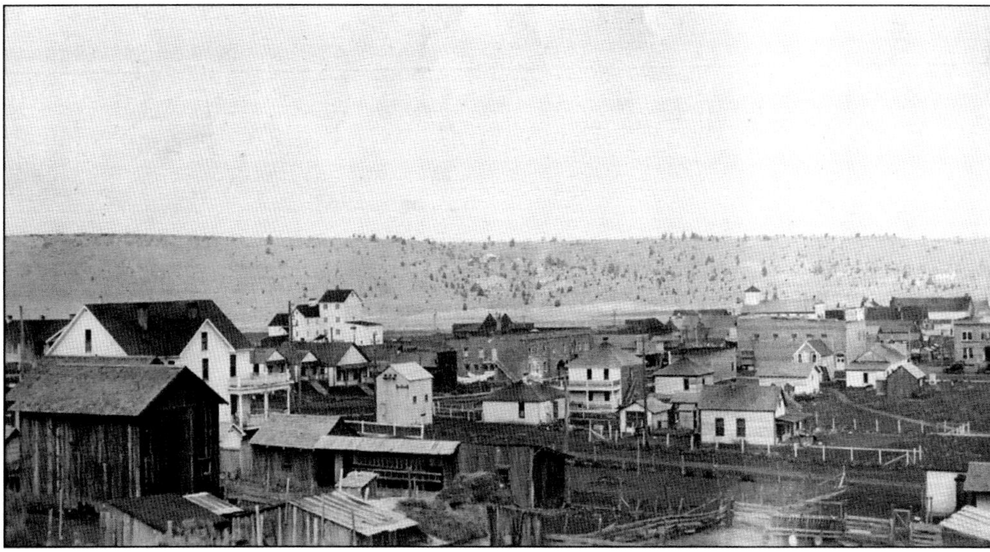

Madras is seen here in 1917, shortly after it became the official county seat of Jefferson County, which began a new era for Madras as an important community in central Oregon. The Mason house is the large white building to the left and the flour mill is in the left middle.

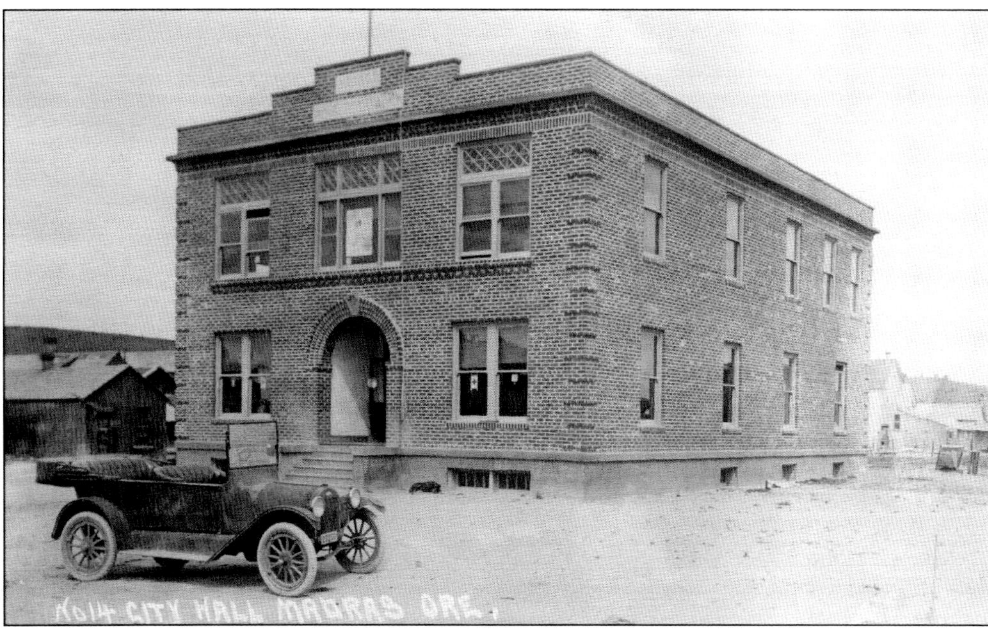

The new county seat needed a building to house government offices and records so an agreement was made and the brick city hall building was leased as the Jefferson County Courthouse. The building, seen here in 1917, still stands today, between Fifth and Sixth Street on the north side of D Street.

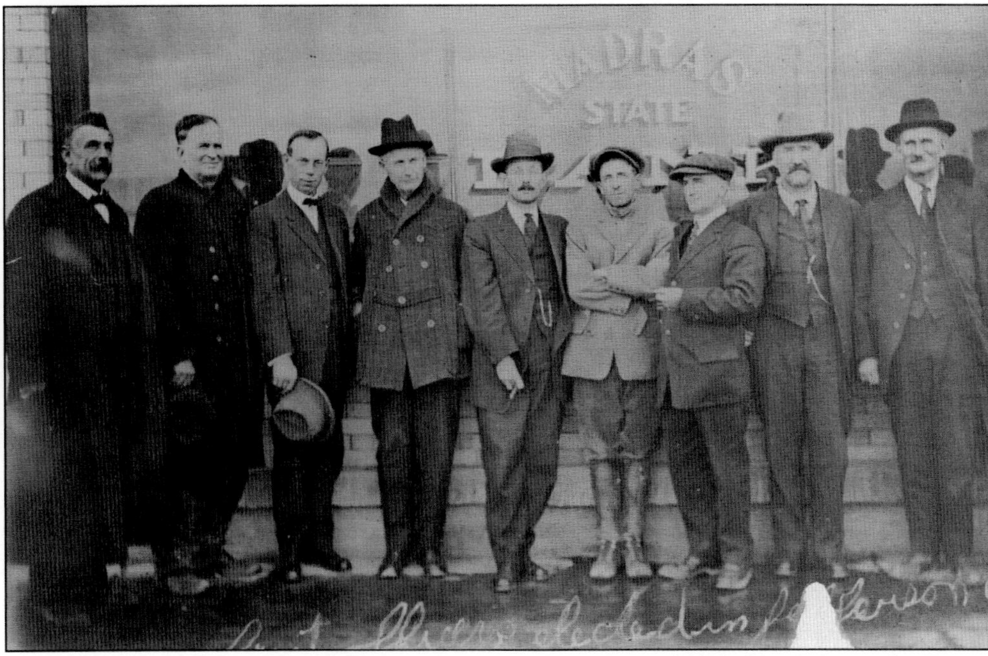

The first elected officials of the Jefferson County government included, from left to right, county director Doctor Snook, Sheriff James Wood, assessor Walter Arney, treasurer Dave Barnett, district attorney Bert Bylar, surveyor W.M. Eaton, clerk Sid Percival, commissioner P. Chitwood, and county judge A.W. Boyce. Not pictured was school superintendent Lillian Watts.

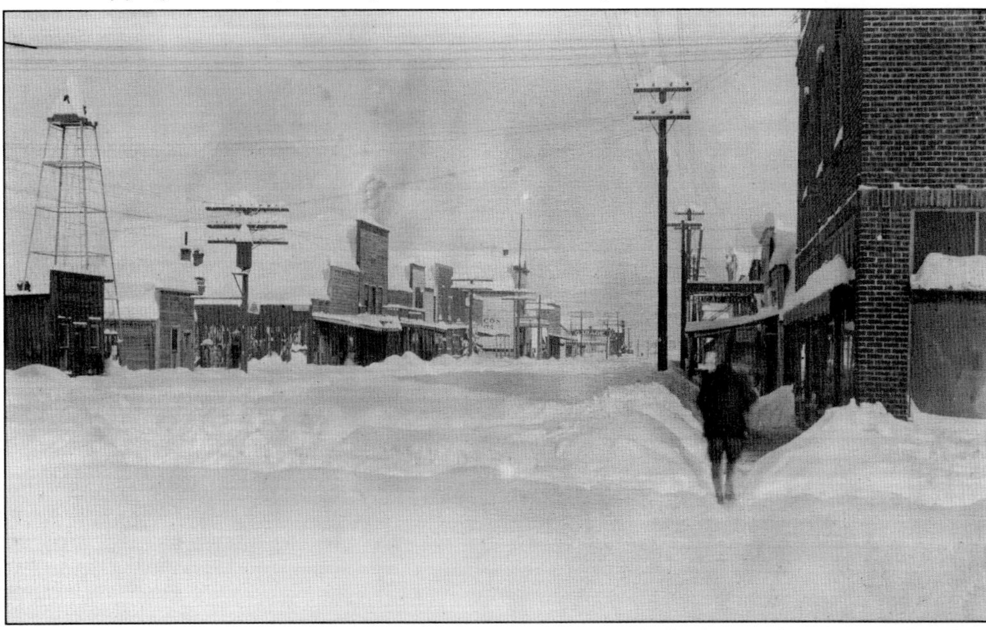

A major snowstorm known as the "great blue snow" blanketed all of central Oregon with a deep snow in 1919. Up to 36 inches of snow fell on Madras and essentially stopped all traffic and business. Many outlying areas became isolated and train traffic was slow; even with a plow engine it took a long time for the train to get to the community. This photograph shows the lack of activity on the streets of Madras while the snow was on the ground.

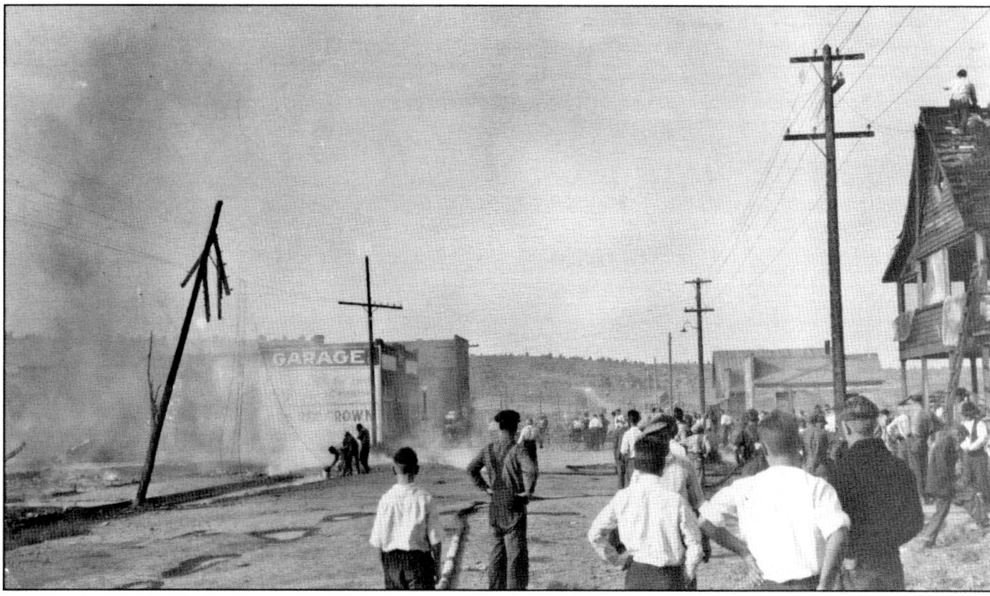

Fires were a constant fear for frontier communities. A crowd gathers to witness the effort to extinguish this fire, which burned a block on West Fifth Street in 1924. The Main Street Garage is near the middle of the photograph. Madras experienced several fires during its early years.

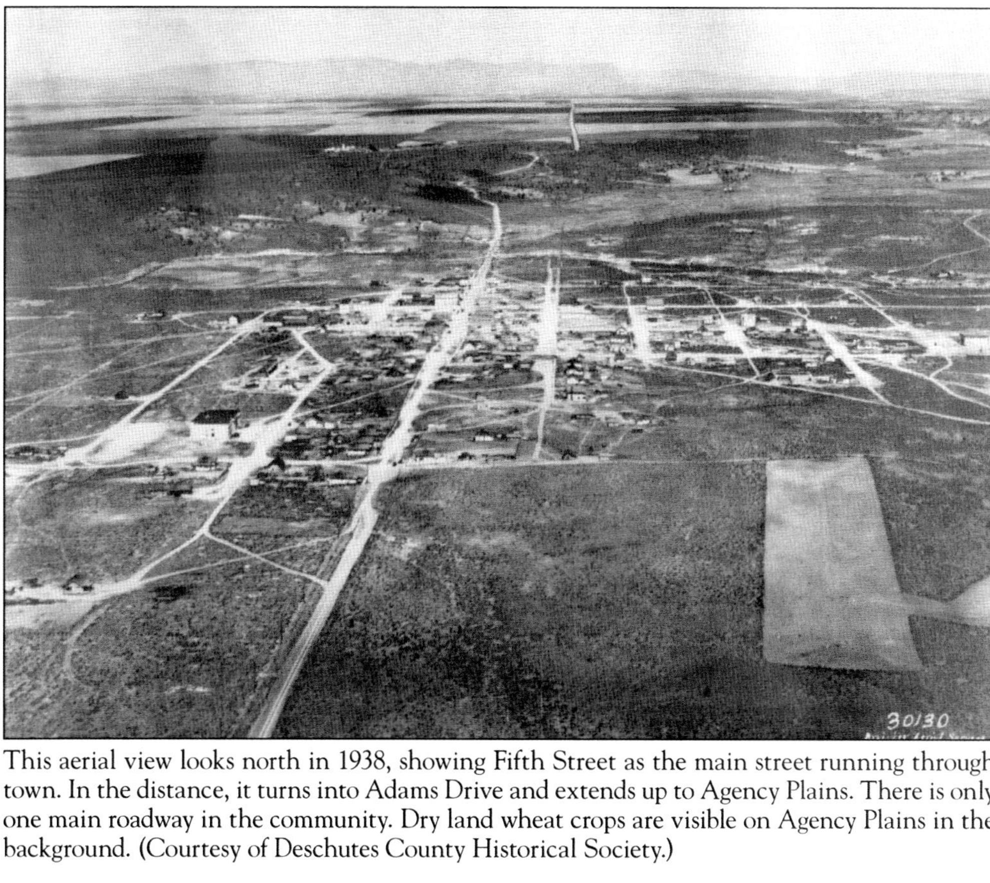

This aerial view looks north in 1938, showing Fifth Street as the main street running through town. In the distance, it turns into Adams Drive and extends up to Agency Plains. There is only one main roadway in the community. Dry land wheat crops are visible on Agency Plains in the background. (Courtesy of Deschutes County Historical Society.)

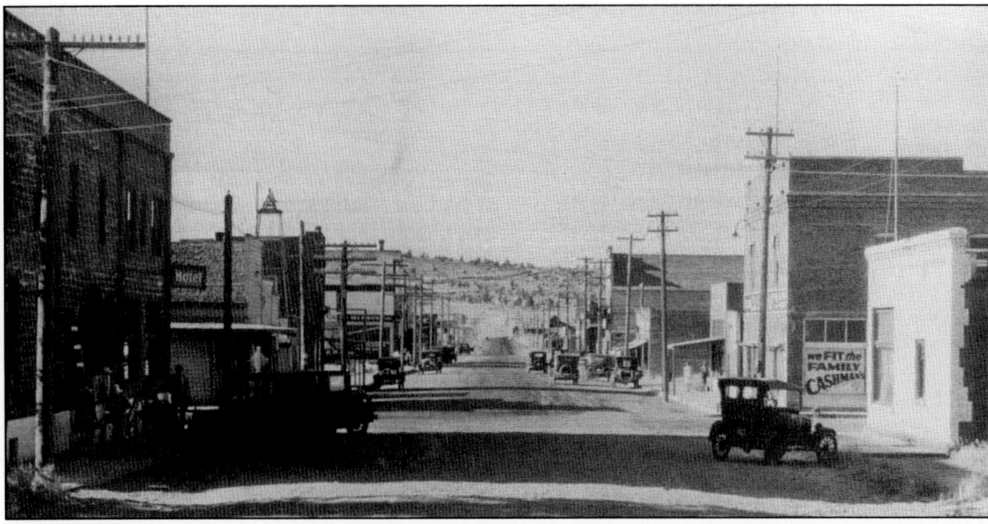

Power poles lined both sides of Fifth Street in 1930. An advertisement for Cashman's to the right says, "We Fit the Family." The Fisher Hotel is the brick building on the left. The street was still unpaved at the time and vehicle traffic frequently dusted the buildings. Water was occasionally spread on the street to reduce dust.

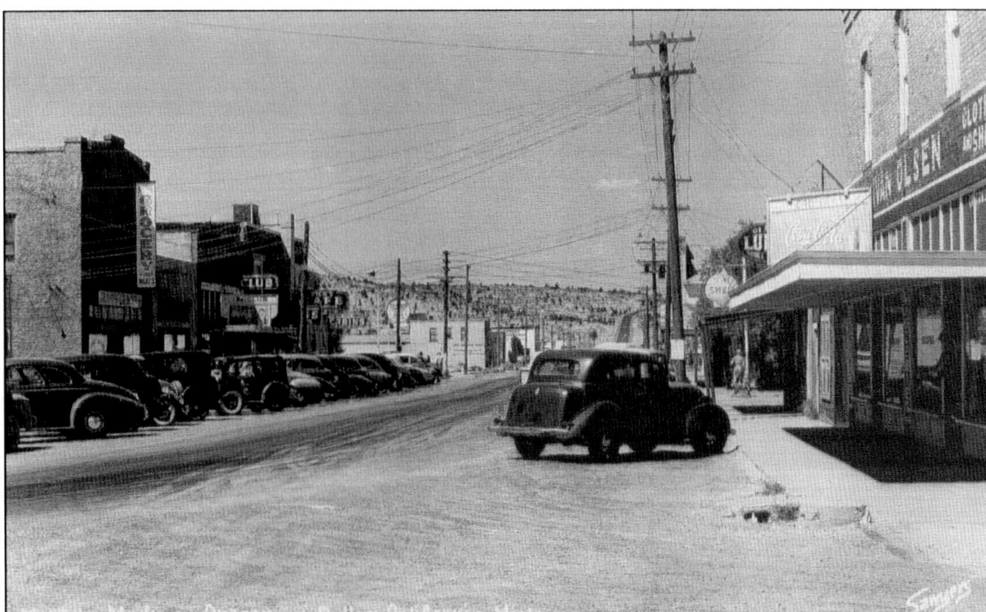

This photograph looks north on Fifth Street around 1938. Ivan Olson Clothing and Shoes is on the right. By then, the street had a couple of gas stations with a Shell station on the right and a Texaco service station a block down on the left. The Safeway Grocery is on the left, followed by The Club tavern and Dick's Café. A much more distinct road ascended up to Agency Plains in the background.

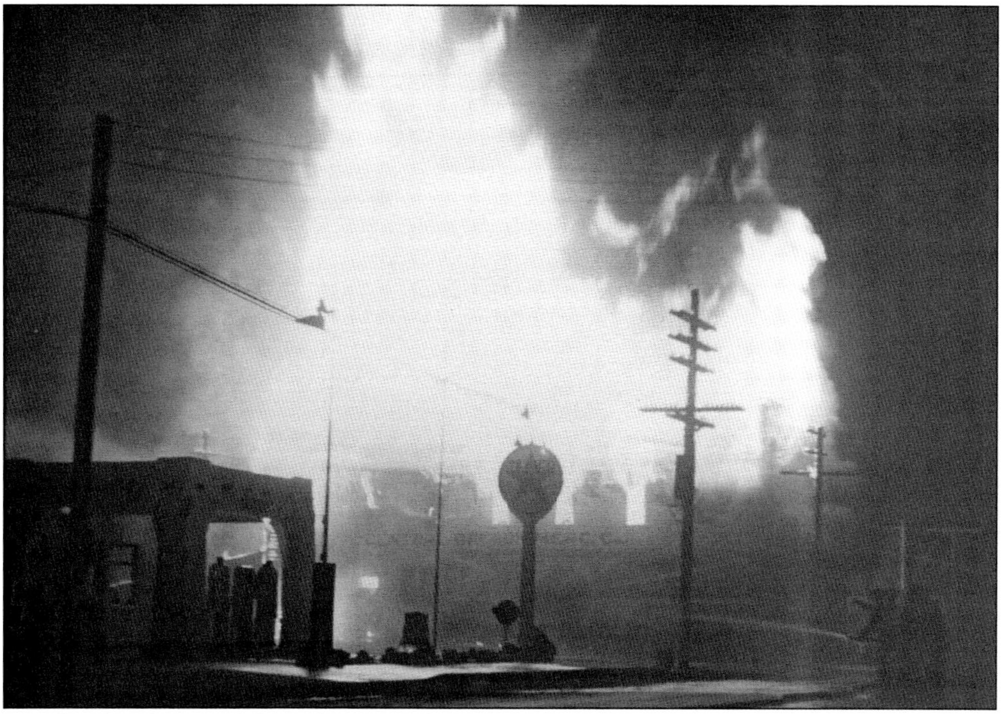

Another fire destroyed these downtown buildings in 1938. The Texaco Station is visible in the left foreground with a raging fire extending flames high into the air behind it.

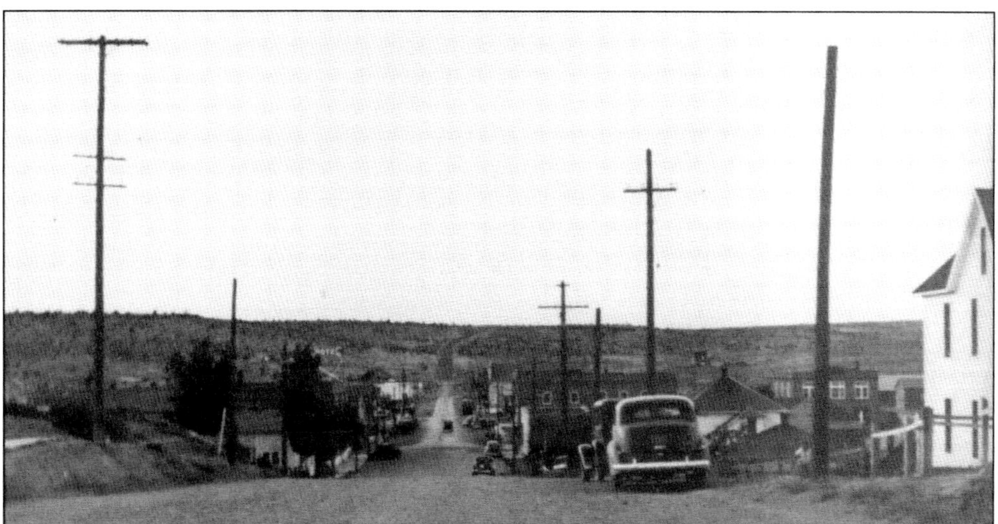

A bus is parked on the right side of still-unpaved Fifth Street in the early 1940s after bus service had begun making regular stops in Madras. The Mason house is the white building on the right.

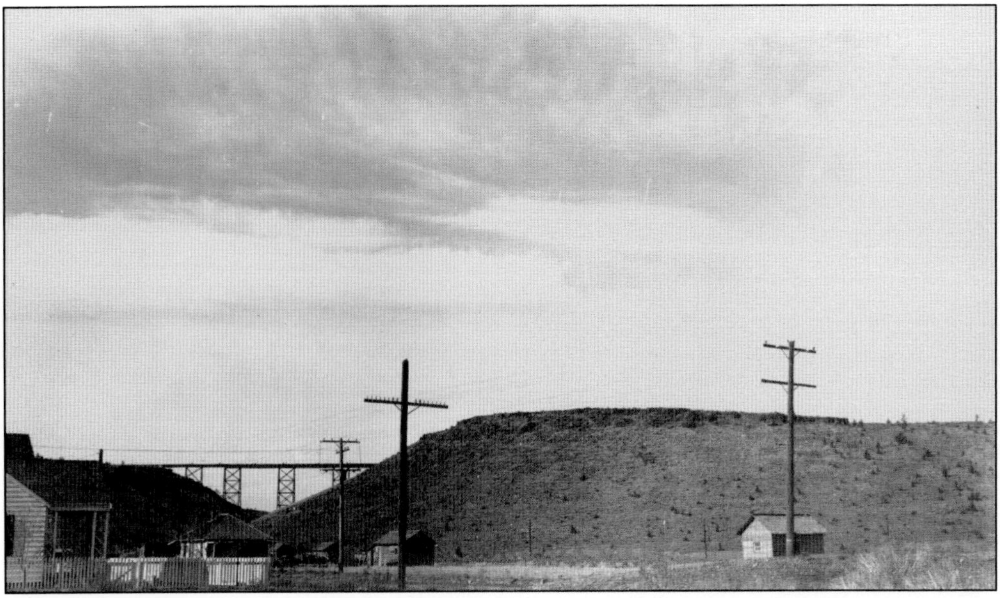

There was still plenty of open space to the west of town in 1930. Louis Johnston's house is on the left with Willow Creek Canyon and the railroad viaduct bridge in the background.

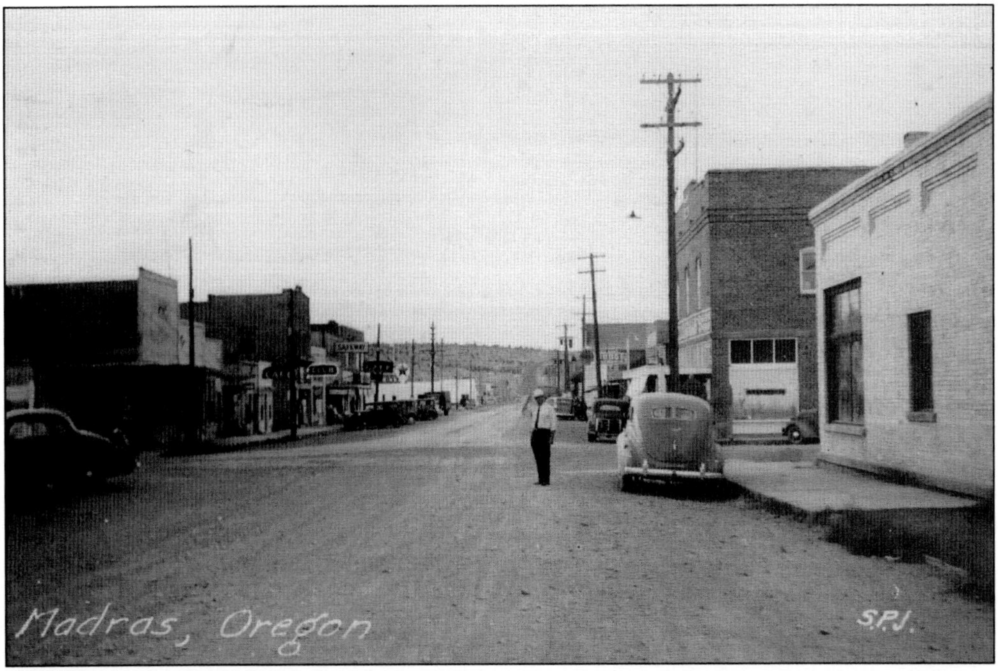

Near the end of World War II in 1945, there were a few more brick buildings and a few new businesses present, but the downtown area remained much as it was after the 1938 fire. There is a vacant lot where the 1938 fire occurred on the middle left. Safeway Grocery is in the middle left on the west side of the street, which has boardwalks on both sides.

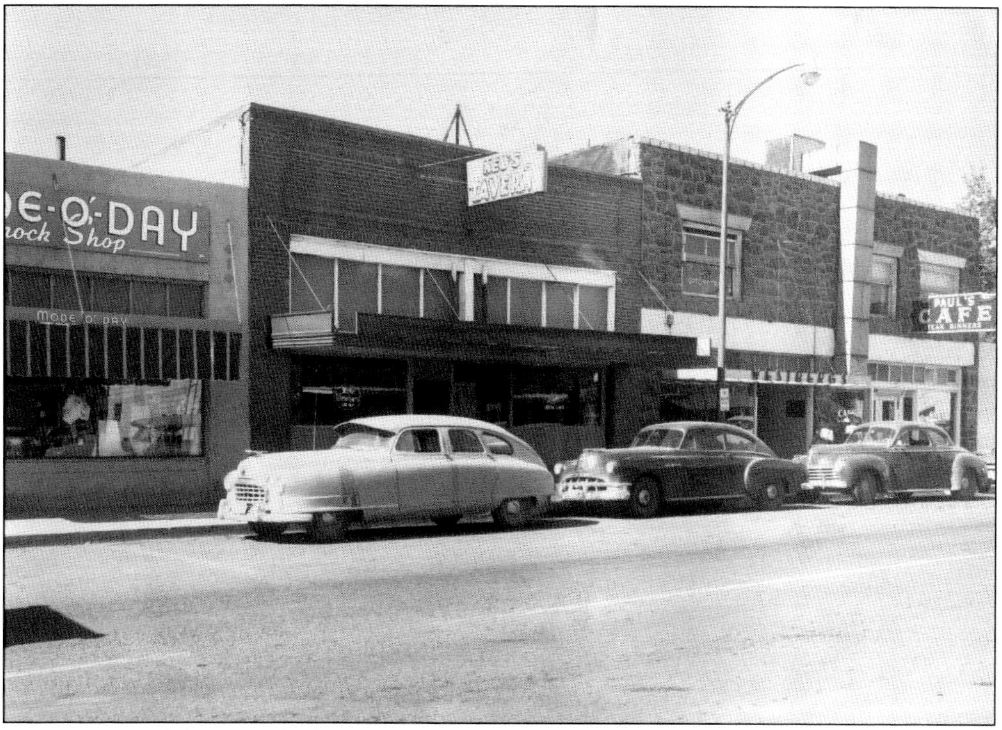

Vintage automobiles are parked along the street in front of Mode-O'- Day, Ned's Tavern, Westbergs, and Paul's Café on Fifth Street in 1952.

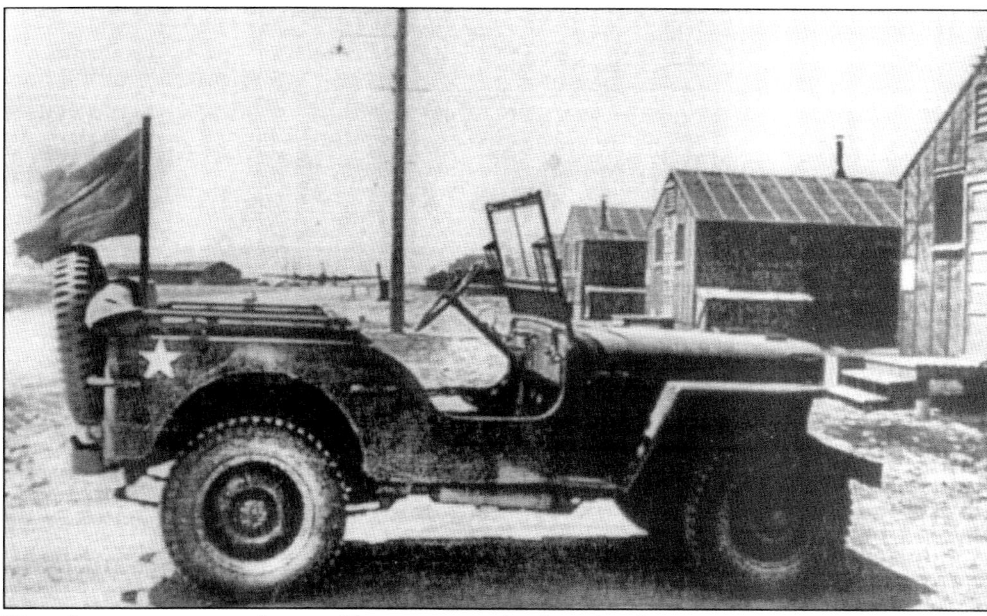

Plans for an airport on Agency Plains just north of Madras began in 1934. Over the next few years, varying degrees of construction created an operable airfield. During World War II, the US Army constructed a new airbase using the site of the civilian airport, bringing several pilots in for flight training on B-17 bombers. Here, a jeep sits in the foreground, and a B-17 bomber is on the tarmac in the background at the airbase.

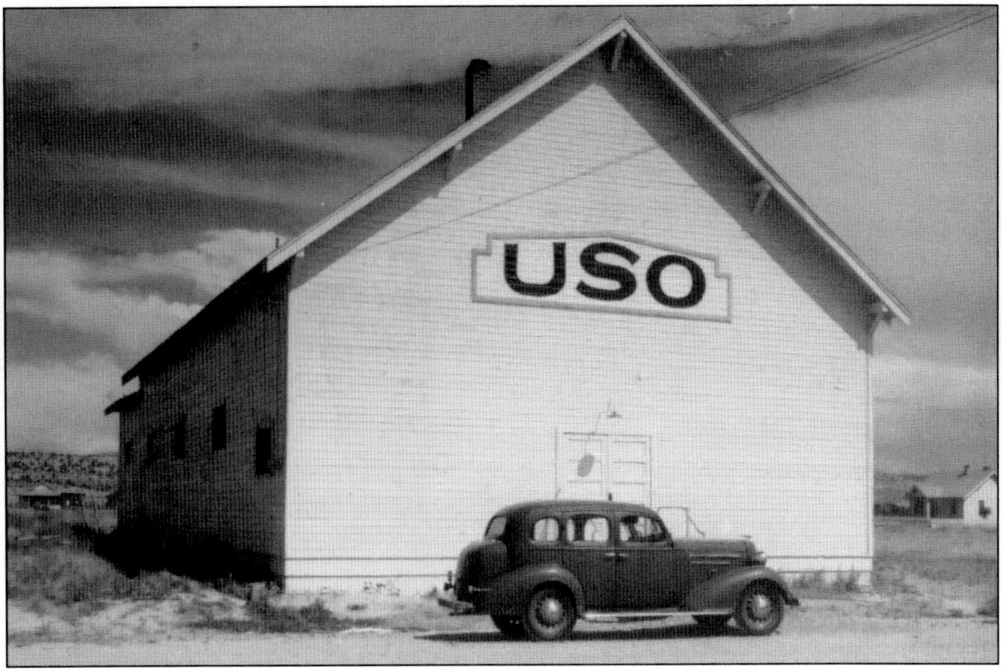

The residents of Madras were eager to support the Army in its operations at the airbase, allowing the Army to use the community hall as a USO facility for trainees stationed at Madras. This building was located where the current county courthouse annex is today. The USO provided opportunities for military men to relax and enjoy recreational pursuits.

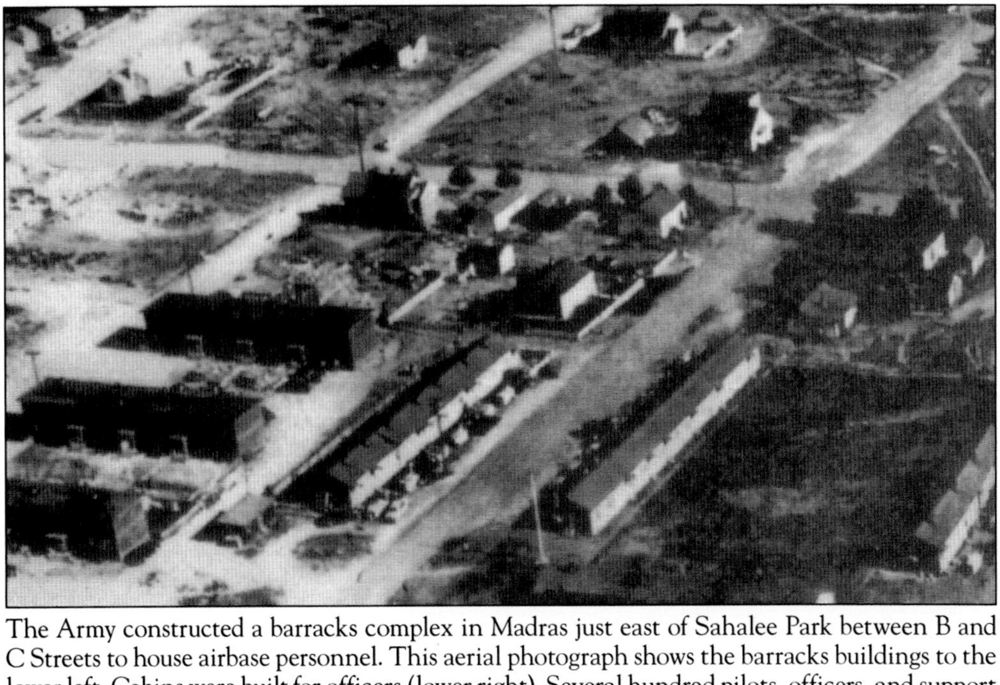

The Army constructed a barracks complex in Madras just east of Sahalee Park between B and C Streets to house airbase personnel. This aerial photograph shows the barracks buildings to the lower left. Cabins were built for officers (lower right). Several hundred pilots, officers, and support personnel were assigned to the base and the large increase in population strained the resources of the community, which had a population of about 450 people.

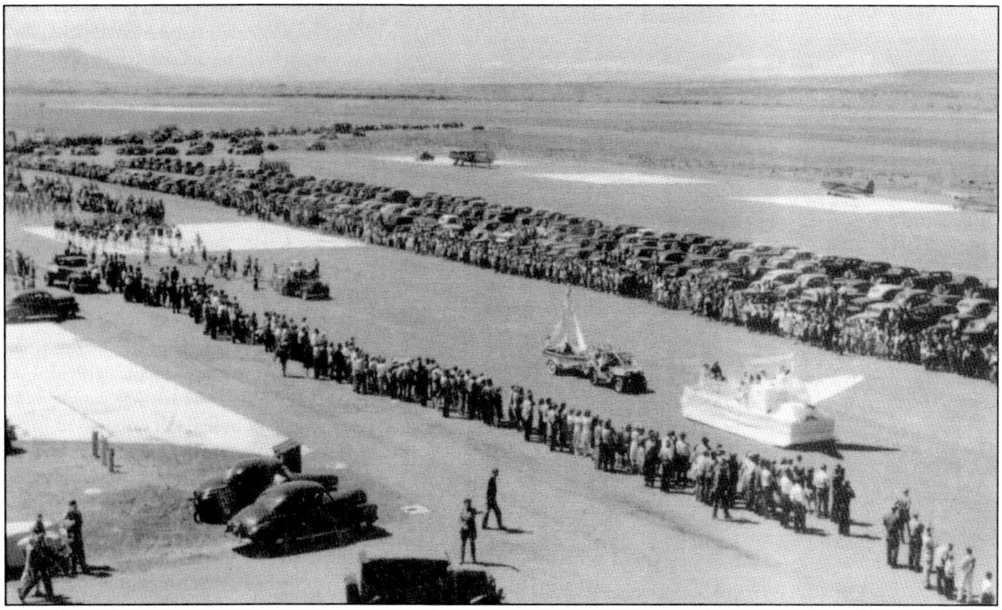

After World War II came to an end, the airbase was abandoned by the military and eventually the City of Madras acquired a large portion of the original base, and it was developed into a civilian airport. The airbase runway was used by the community to celebrate the Madras Water Festival in 1946, seen here.

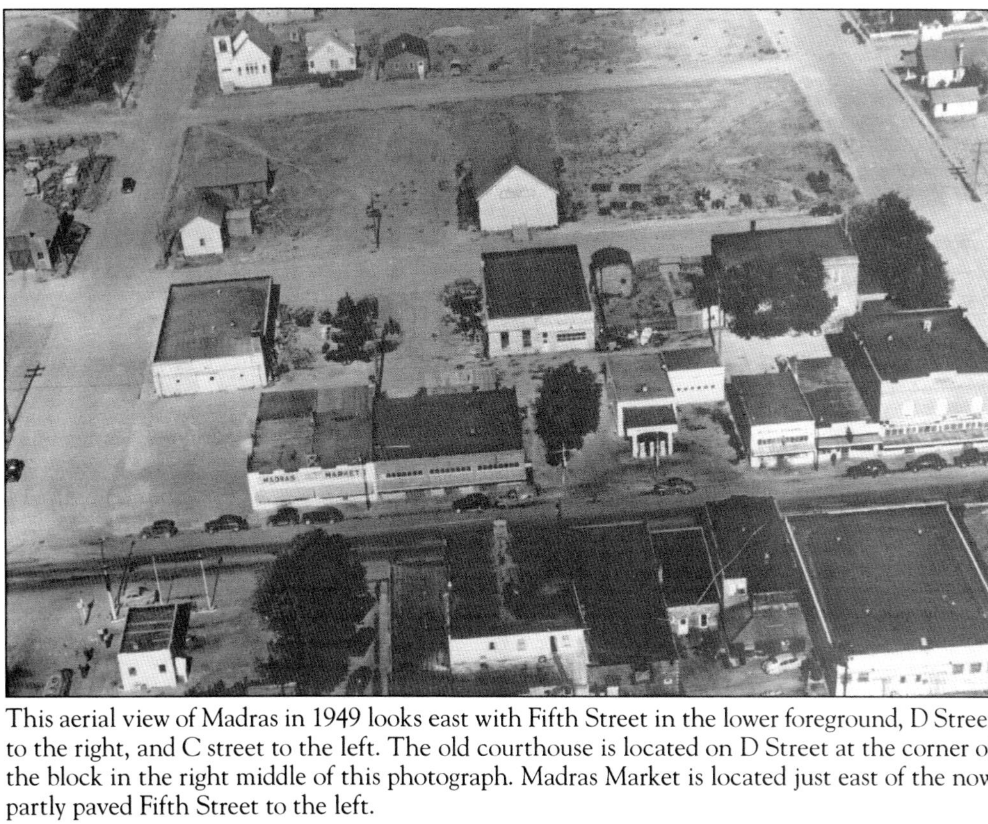

This aerial view of Madras in 1949 looks east with Fifth Street in the lower foreground, D Street to the right, and C street to the left. The old courthouse is located on D Street at the corner of the block in the right middle of this photograph. Madras Market is located just east of the now partly paved Fifth Street to the left.

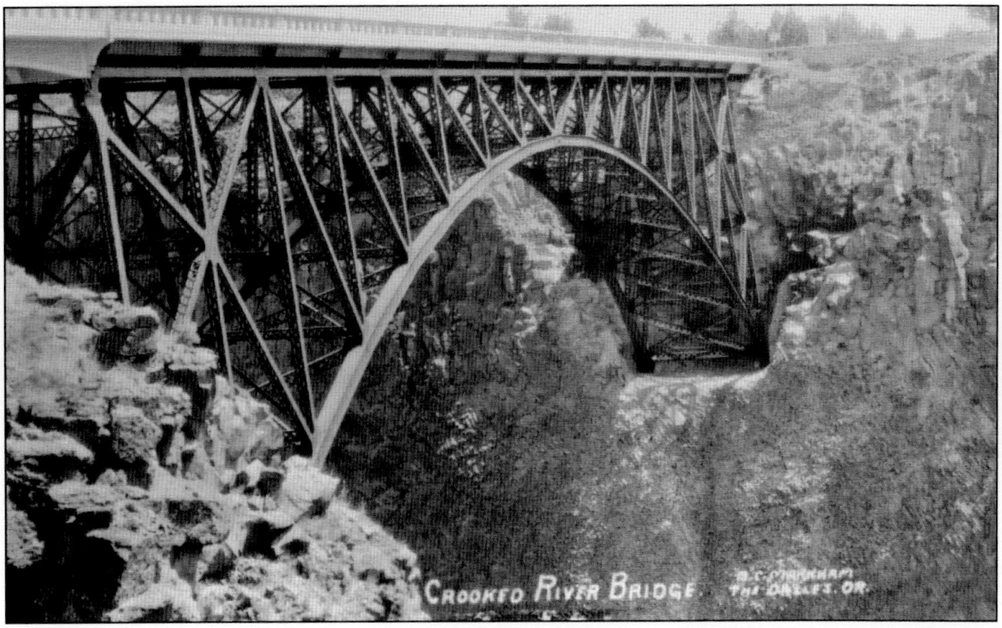

A new era began when highways were constructed, allowing statewide travel into Madras and points south. The Dalles-California Highway was completed late in 1926 with the construction of the bridge over Crooked River Gorge. This bridge eliminated the steep and dangerous route via Trail Crossing just to the east of the bridge. This view looks southeast across the Crooked River Canyon shortly after the bridge was built. The bridge was dedicated early in 1927.

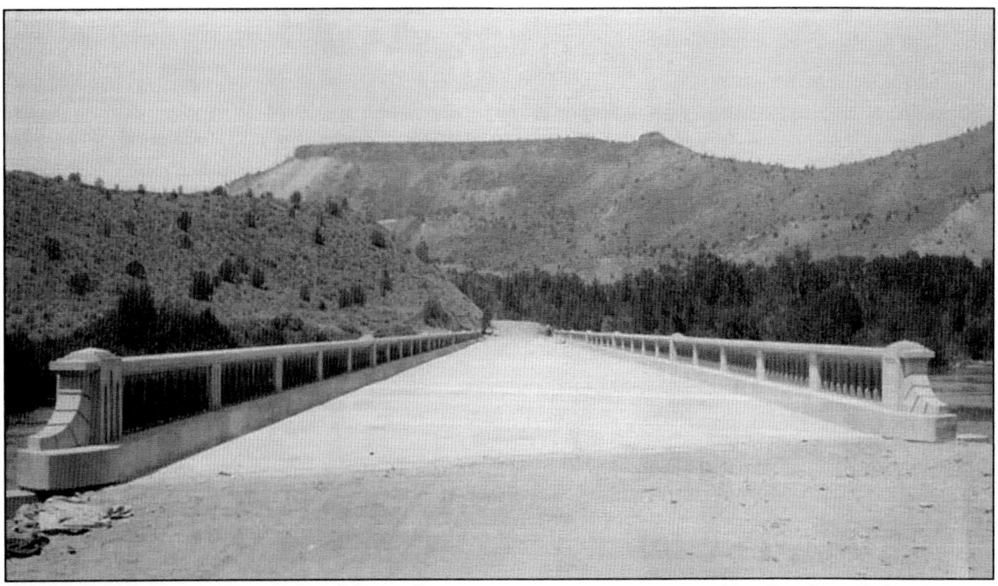

Madras residents had long hoped for a direct transportation route to Portland, and the Oregon Highway Department began plans to construct a highway from Portland to the central part of the state in the early 1930s. Construction was done in segments over several years. One of the links was the Warm Springs Bridge, completed in 1934. It was dedicated as the Duc-Sa-Hi Bridge and crossed the Deschutes River just southeast of the community of Warm Springs. This view shows the bridge at the time of its completion. (Courtesy of Beth Crow.)

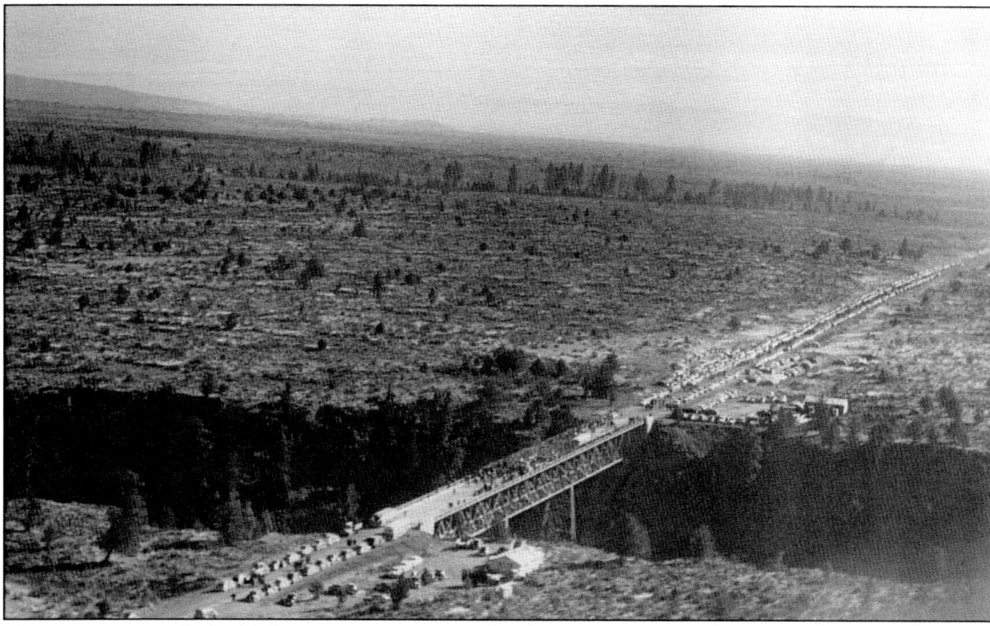

Most segments of the highway connecting central Oregon to Portland had been completed by 1948; the only remaining obstacle was the construction of a bridge over Mill Creek on the Warm Springs Indian Reservation. Final construction of the bridge occurred in 1948, and this aerial view shows the dedication of the bridge early in 1949. Finally, a major highway link was complete from Portland to Madras and beyond. The route would later become Highway 26.

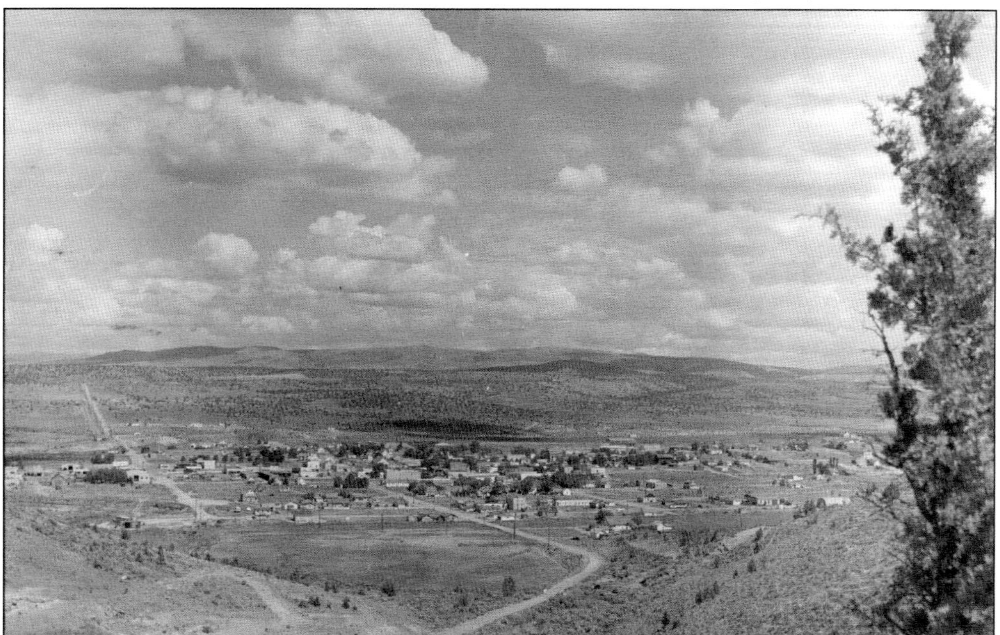

This view looks east toward Baldwin Hills in 1948. The road in the foreground is part of the old Oregon Trunk Railroad bed, which had been converted to a road. By then, the community had two major highways entering the city, and automobile traffic through the community brought another prosperity boom to local businesses.

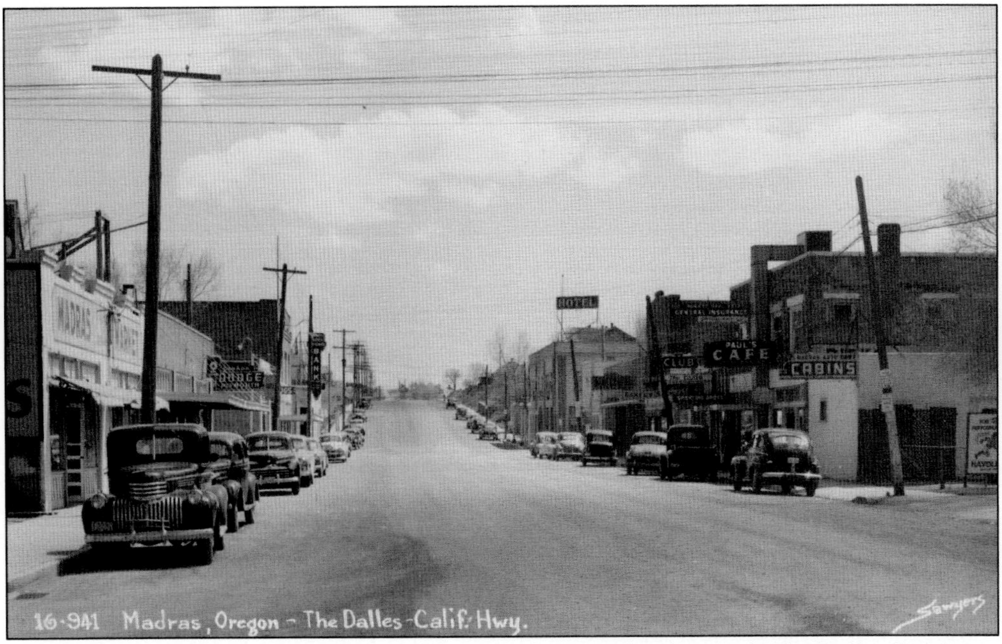

Fifth Street is lined with automobiles in this 1950 photograph, when both The Dalles-California Highway and Highway 26 passed through the town. The Madras Market and the US National Bank are on the left, and several businesses are located on the right.

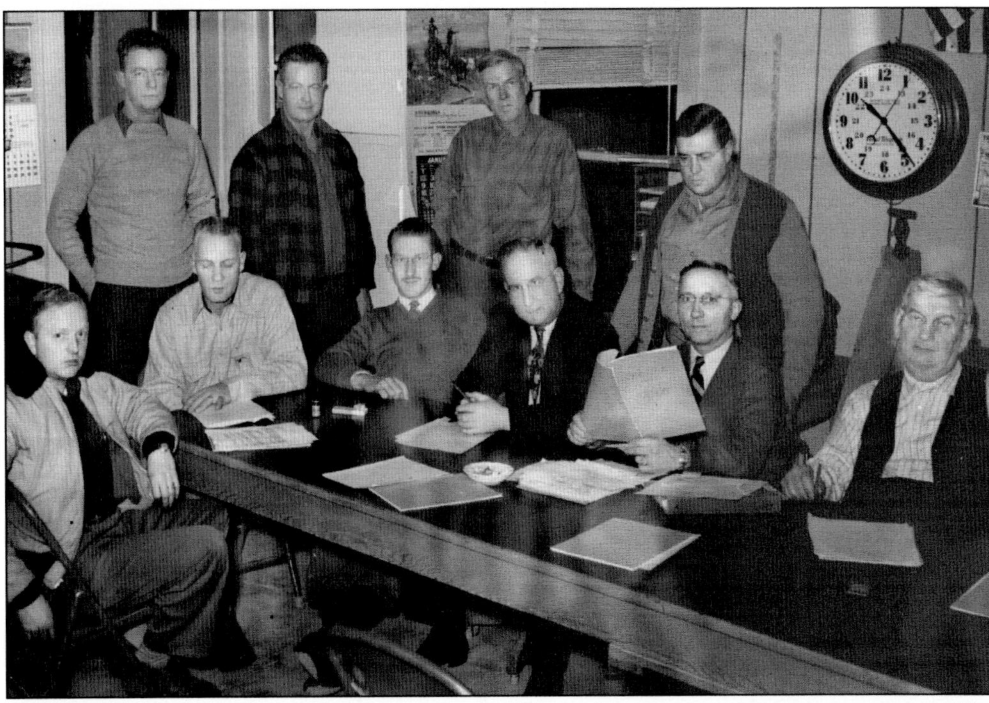

The Madras city council in 1950 had a busy schedule in planning for the future prosperity of the community. Council members are, from left to right, Leonard Conroy, Carl Darrar, Nige Bowers, Walsie Richardson, Howard Kriz, Thad Dizney, unidentified, Paul Dwignas, Adrian Smith, and Nestor Seaman.

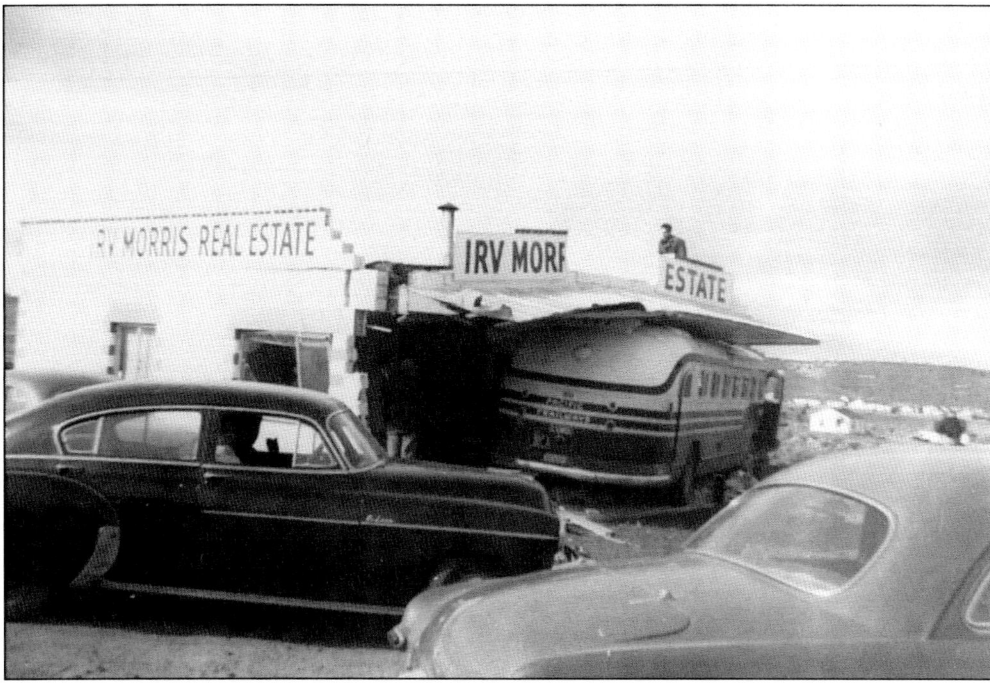

Mt. Hood Stages, Inc., was established in 1931, and by 1943, it was part of the National Trailways Bus system, operating as Pacific Trailways. In 1955, this Pacific Trailways bus made an unscheduled stop in the Irv Morris Real Estate office when the driver had to swerve to avoid a inattentive motorist.

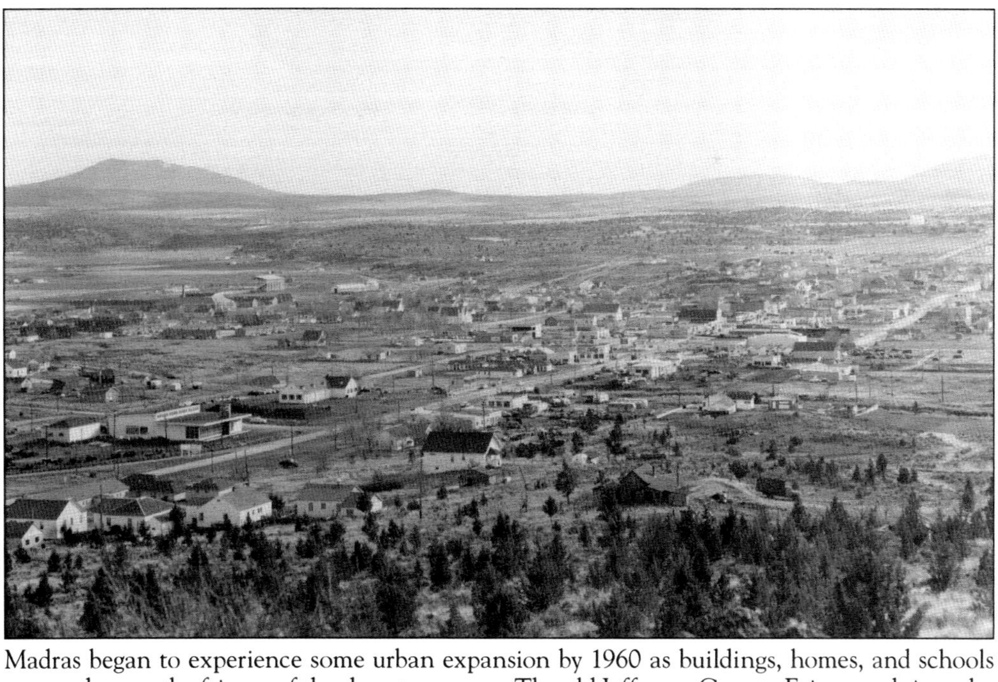
Madras began to experience some urban expansion by 1960 as buildings, homes, and schools sprouted up on the fringes of the downtown core. The old Jefferson County Fairgrounds is to the east in the left background. The Bone Implement Company is located on the left.

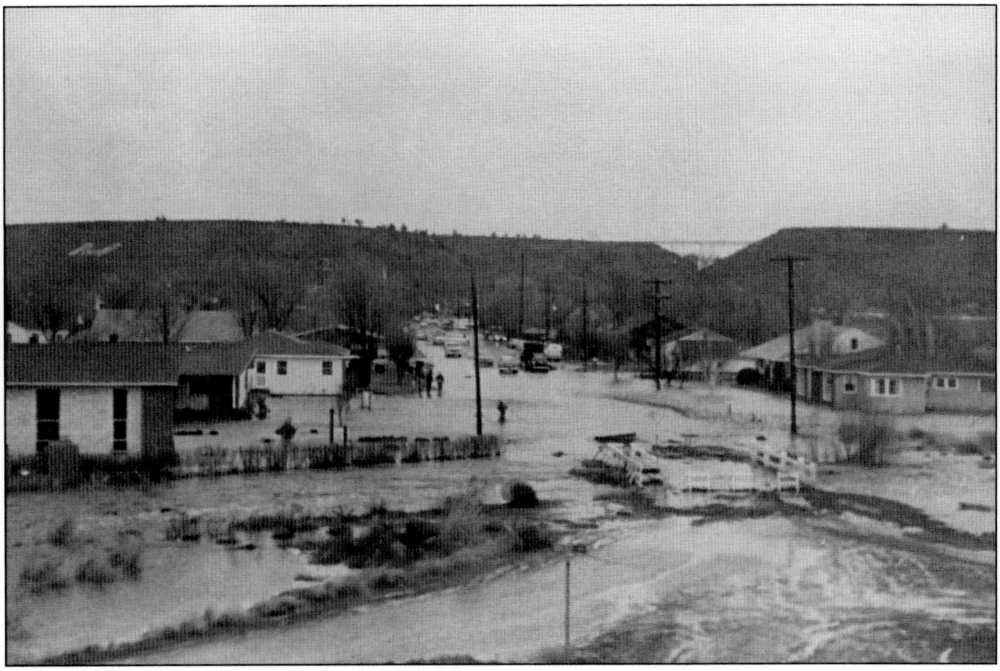

Willow Creek is normally a gentle stream with minimal flow, but around Christmas in 1964, the creek overflowed its banks with a combination of snow and rain, resulting in major flooding throughout central Oregon. This photograph shows Willow Creek's overflow at the C Street Bridge.

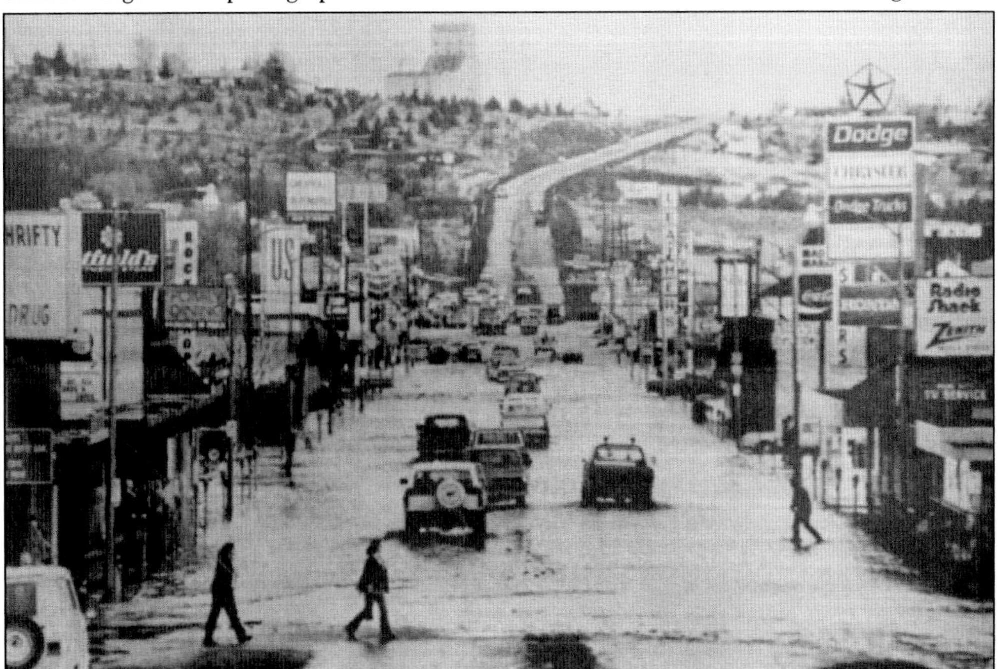

This view of Fifth Street looking north shows traffic and pedestrians braving the water flowing through the center of town in the 1964 flood, which extensively damaged drain systems and buildings.

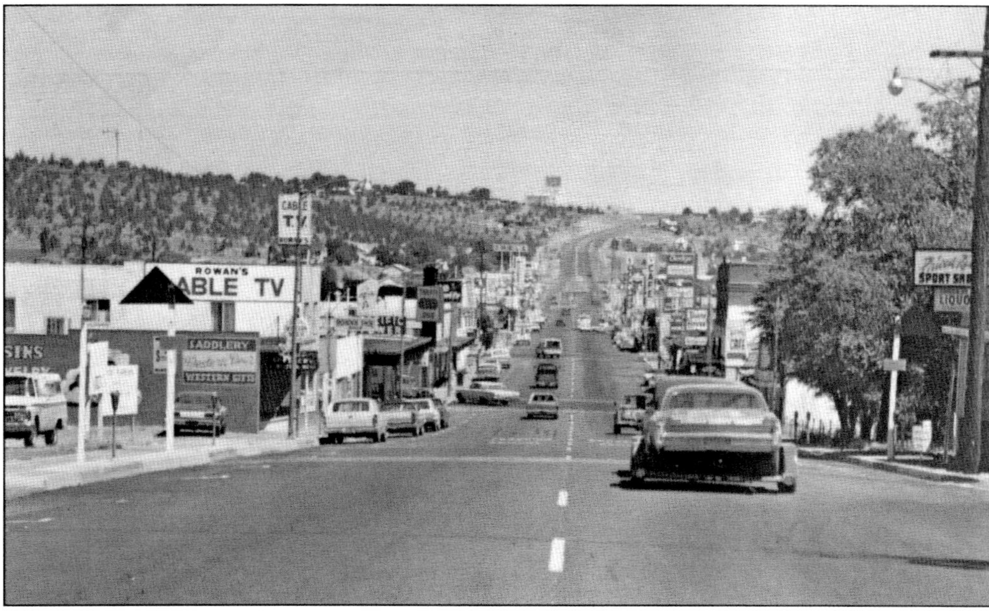

One year after the Christmas flood of 1964, traffic was separated by two one-way streets through town, with Fifth Street traveling north and Fourth Street traveling south. The grain elevator building is to the north in the background of the skyline.

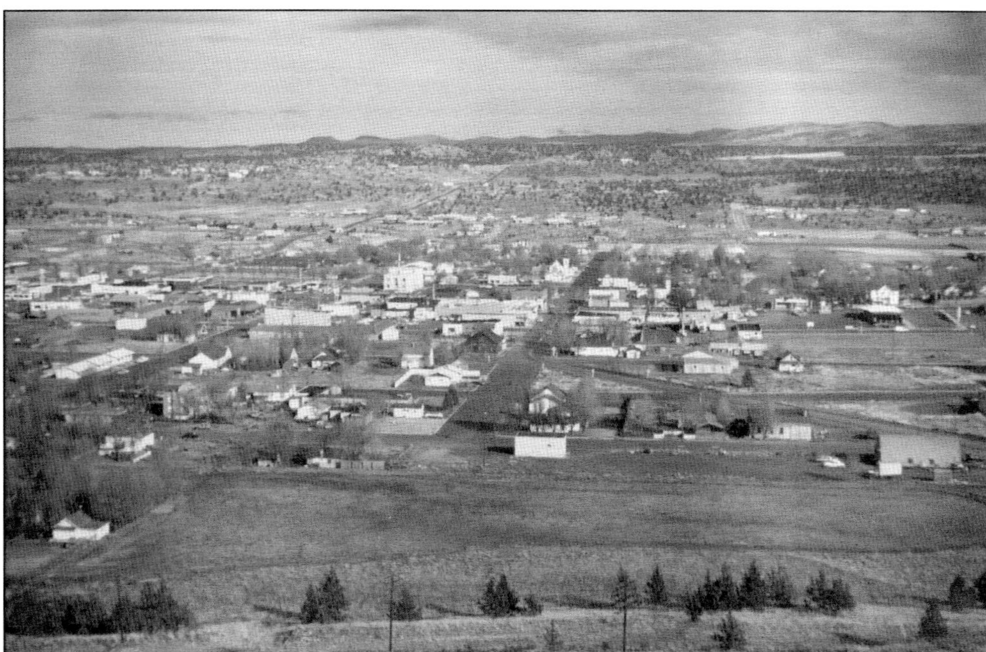

This photograph was taken from the ridge west of town looking northeast in 1961. The population of the community had expanded to about 900.

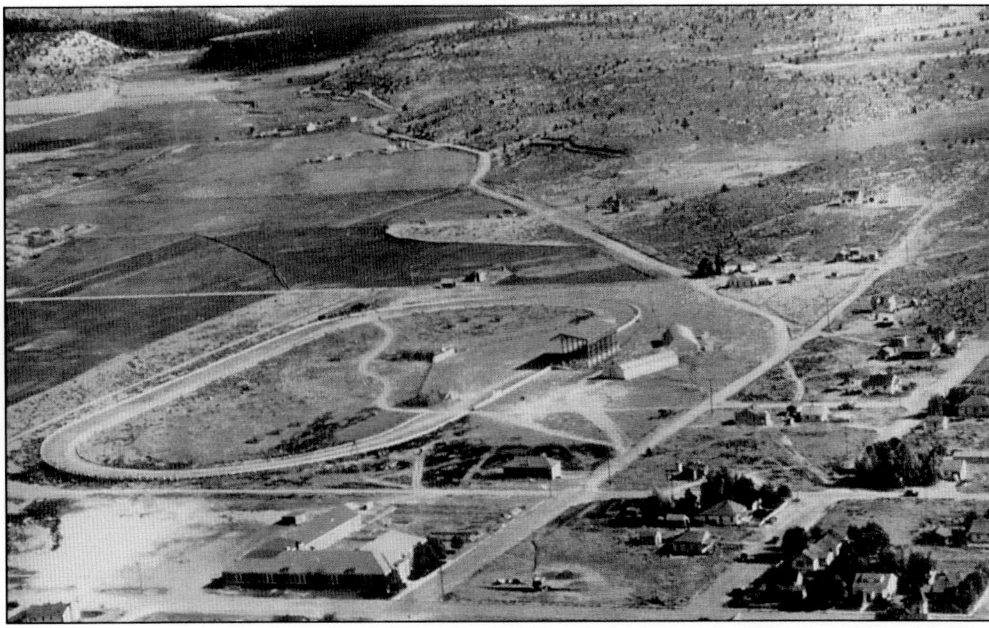

The first site of the Jefferson County Fairgrounds was on the east side of the community, where the high school is now. The beginnings of the Jefferson County Fair took place in the early 1920s when local farm produce and crafts were displayed in buildings in Madras. The first official fair took place in 1930 with more than 1,500 people in attendance.

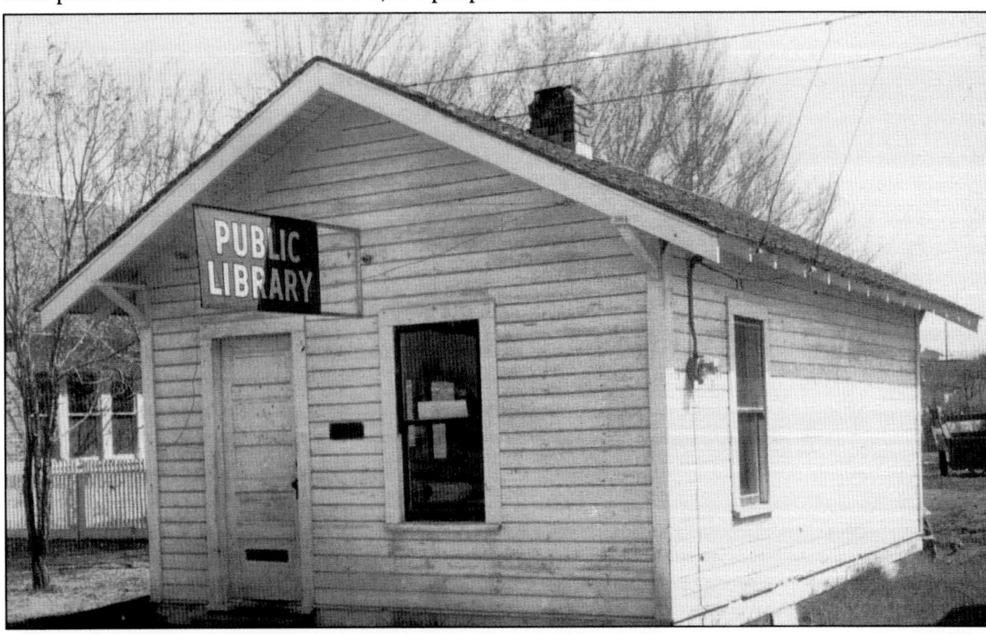

Efforts were made to establish a public library in Madras in 1916. The library was first located in the old Odd Fellows Hall and later in a space provided in the Madras City Hall, which later became the county courthouse. The Jefferson County Library Association purchased a small frame building in 1920 across the street from the old Jefferson County Courthouse. The land was sold in 1944, and the building was moved to Southeast D Street, where this photograph was taken in 1955.

Four

Let the Good Times Roll

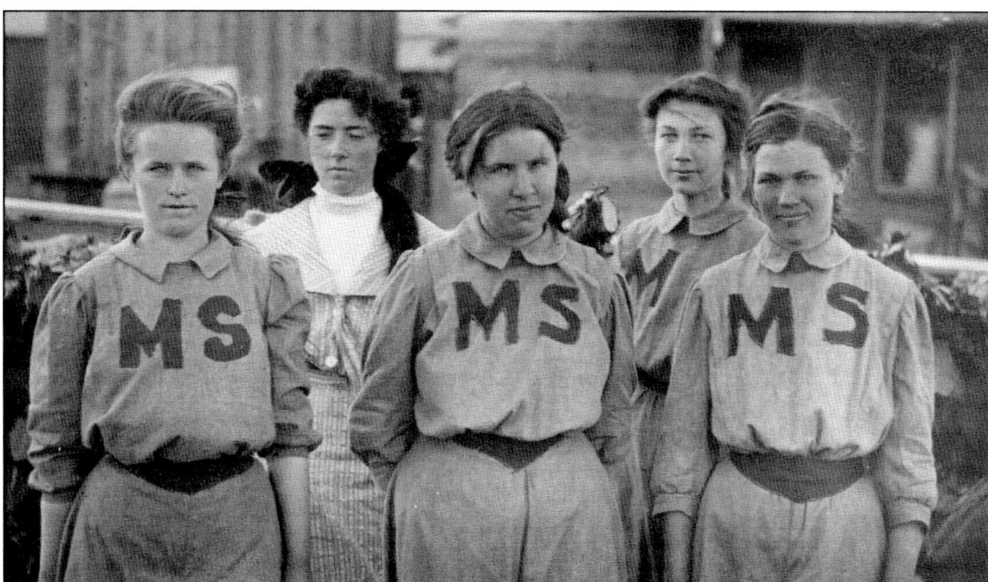

The first girls' basketball team at Madras High School, in 1914, included, from left to right, unidentified, Nora Livingston, Jenny Harper, Ethel Klann, and May Campbell. The uniforms were probably considered appropriate for young ladies of the time but certainly did not provide for comfort and versatility in athletic pursuits.

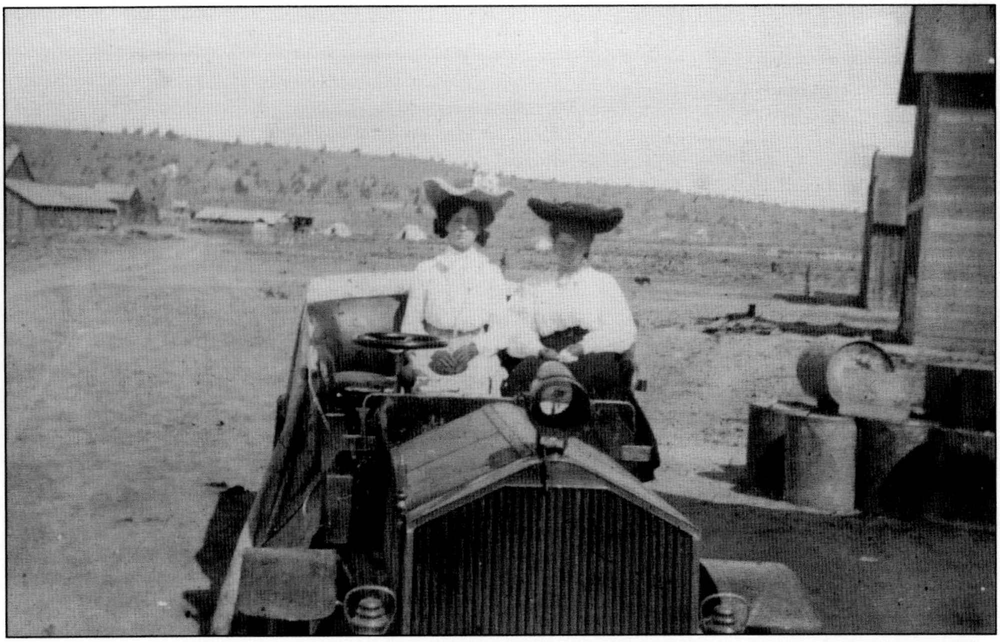

The novelty of automobiles attracted much attention in Madras in the early 1900s. This is the first automobile in Madras in 1905, with Ona Hering (left) and Marie Dizney seated in the back waiting for a ride. Note the fuel barrels and cans to the right. Most fuel had to be shipped by freight wagons, and there was very limited availability.

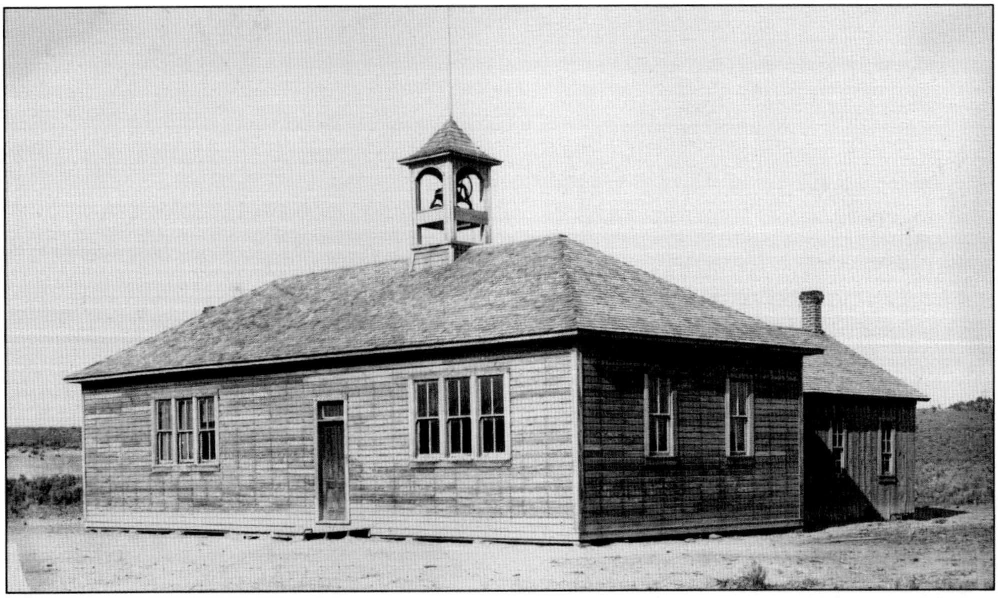

The second schoolhouse in Madras was built in 1904, with the first school attached to the back and used for additional space. The building, which features a bell tower and a bell, was at first not painted but was later painted white. The stove for heating the school was in the old school addition. The building was located at the east end of E Street and was used until 1908.

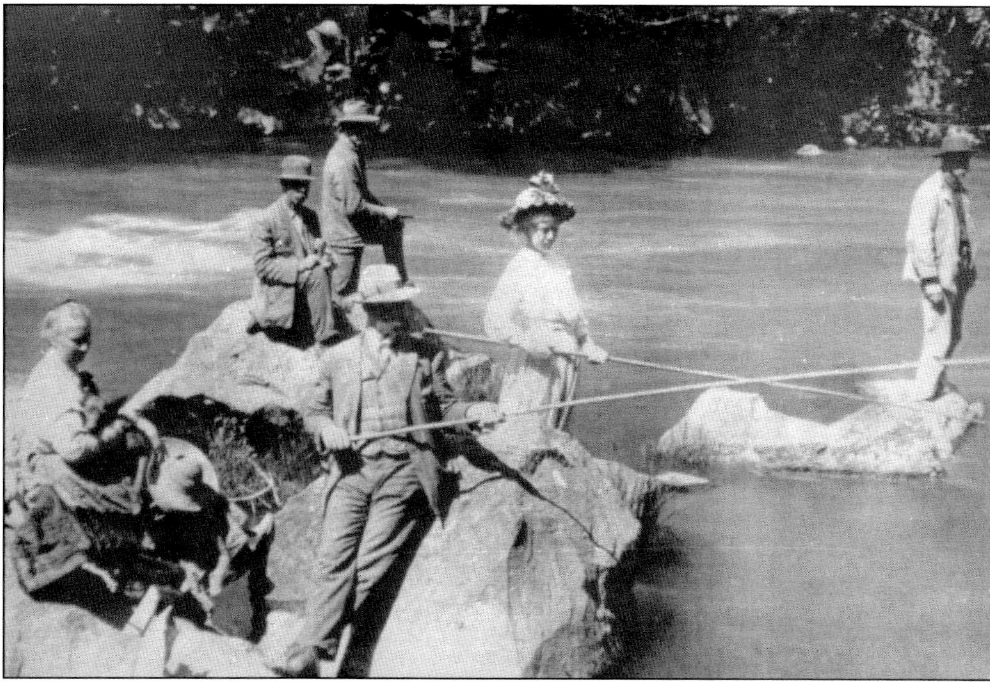

Madras residents frequently made trips to the Crooked River near Opal Springs for recreational pursuits. This group spends a pleasant afternoon fishing the Crooked River around 1900. It was a steep hike down to the river and was usually an all-day event with a picnic lunch. Another pastime was gathering "opals" from Opal Springs.

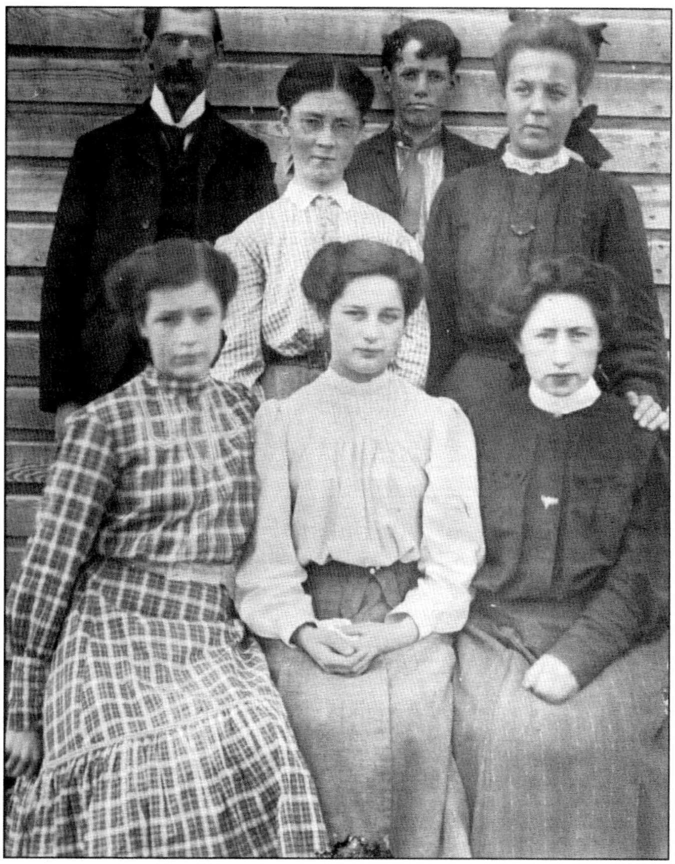

The first graduating eighth-grade class in Madras included, from left to right, (seated) unidentified, Myrtle Harvey, and Martha Conroy; (standing) teacher Pinkney "Pink" Fulton, Suzie Cowhard, Charlie Craig, and Jenny Harper.

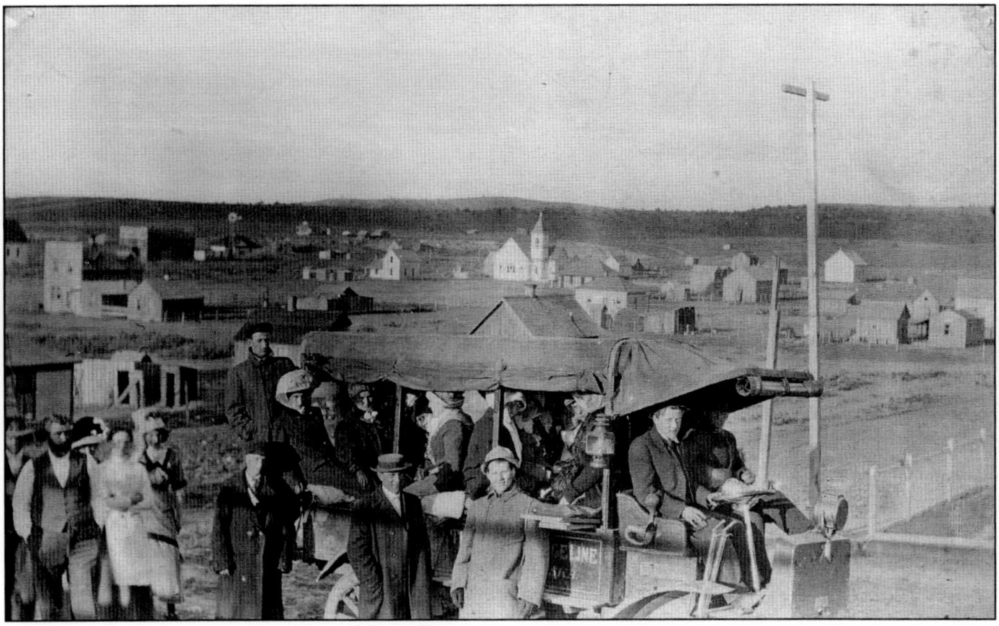

The Epworth League was a group of youths associated with the Methodist Church who provided entertainment and opportunities for socializing in the community. Frequently, groups from neighboring communities would visit like this group of young adults from Prineville in 1909. They are seated in one of the first auto stages to travel between local communities in central Oregon. The Methodist church is located in the middle background. (Courtesy of Bowman Museum.)

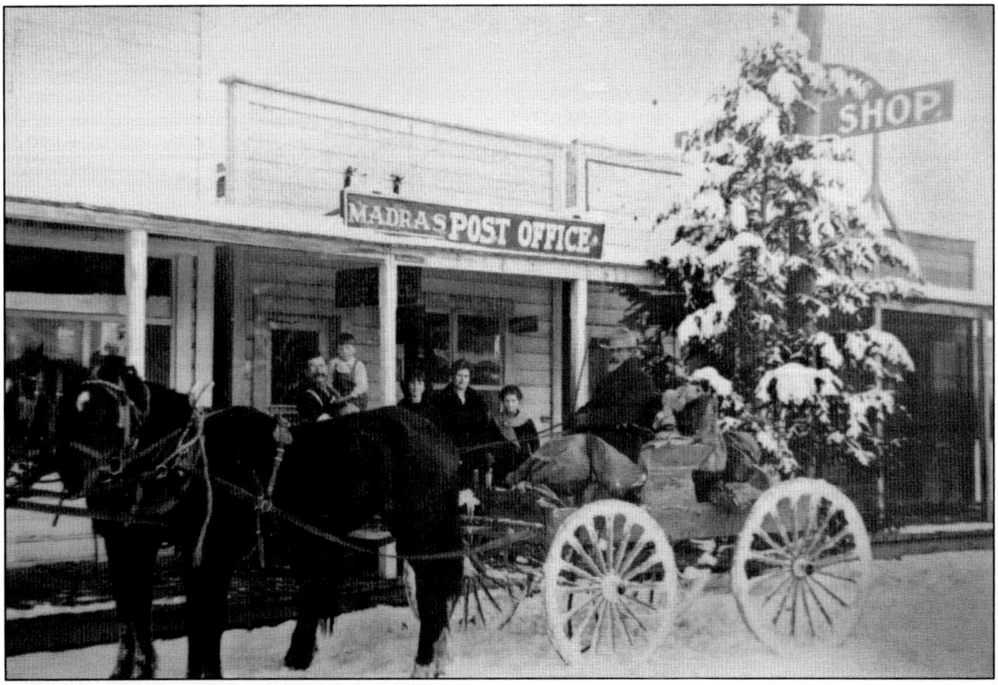

A well-bundled John Lockwood pulls his mail wagon up in front of the Madras Post Office in 1910 as the Davis family eagerly awaits their mail in the snow.

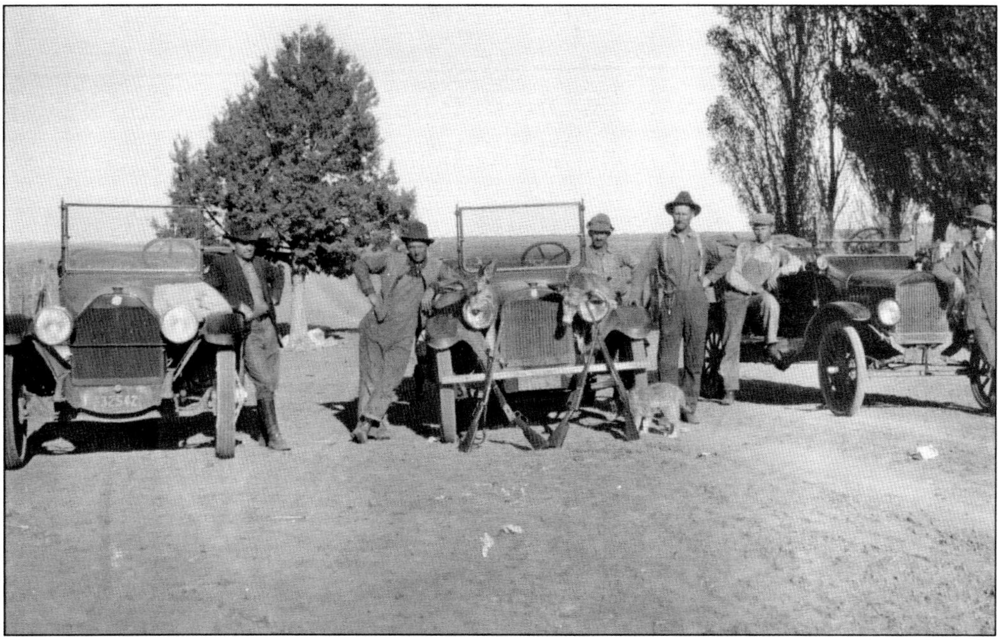

A group of Madras hunters proudly display the success of a recent hunt with the carcasses of two deer on the fender of an automobile in 1912. Hunting has long been a favorite sport for local residents.

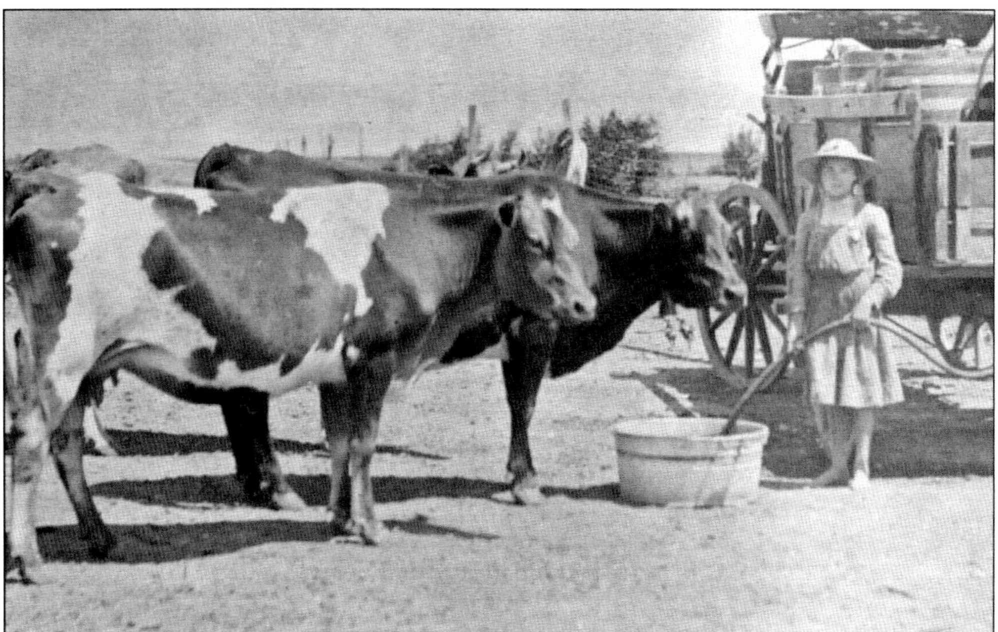

Young Ellen Luelling fills a tub with water for dairy cows on Agency Plains in 1911. Water mostly had to be hauled from wells or springs, and the wagon in the right background has five barrels filled at the railroad water tank.

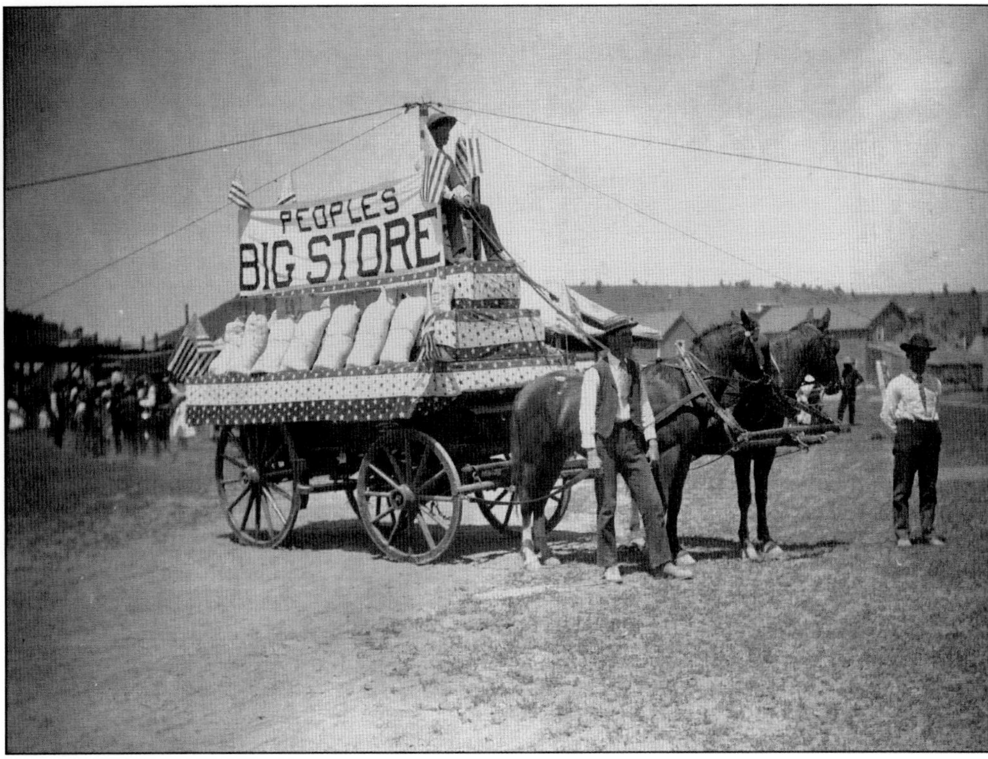

Parades were popular events in the frontier town. Here, a wagon float for the 1910 Fourth of July parade displays an advertisement for Peoples Big Store. Willow Creek Canyon is visible in the background. Most members of the community would line up along Fifth Street to watch parades.

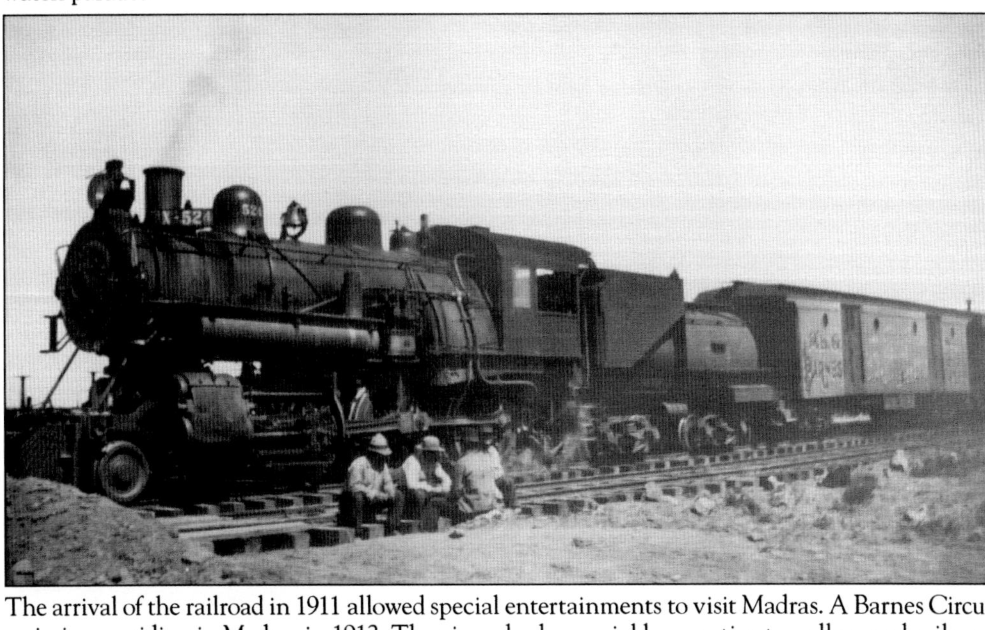

The arrival of the railroad in 1911 allowed special entertainments to visit Madras. A Barnes Circus train is on a siding in Madras in 1912. The circus had a special locomotive to pull several railcars. It was a highly anticipated event as most citizens had never seen a circus before.

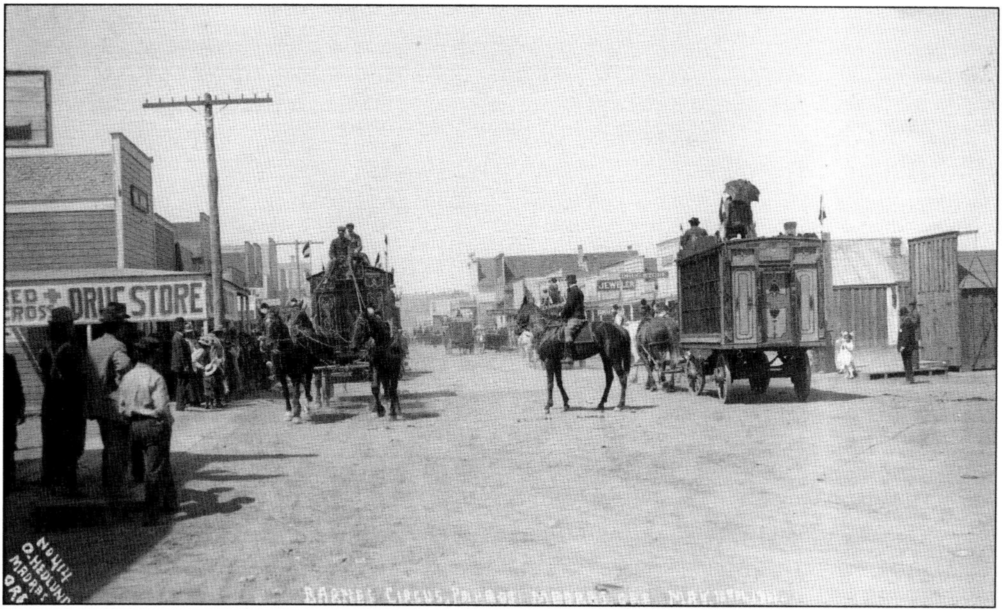

Horse-drawn circus wagons have been unloaded from railcars and parade through the streets of Madras in 1912, promoting the big event to be held in a large tent on the outskirts of town. A crowd of people lines the streets to view the wagons.

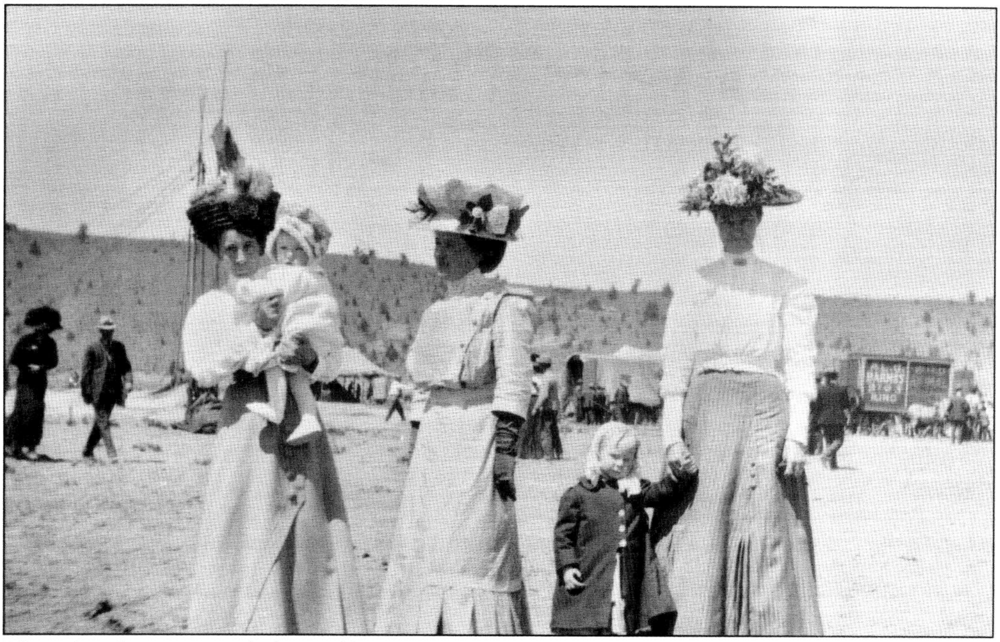

Three local women, including Lillie May Read Turner (center), brought their children to see the circus being set up near the outer boundaries of Madras in 1912.

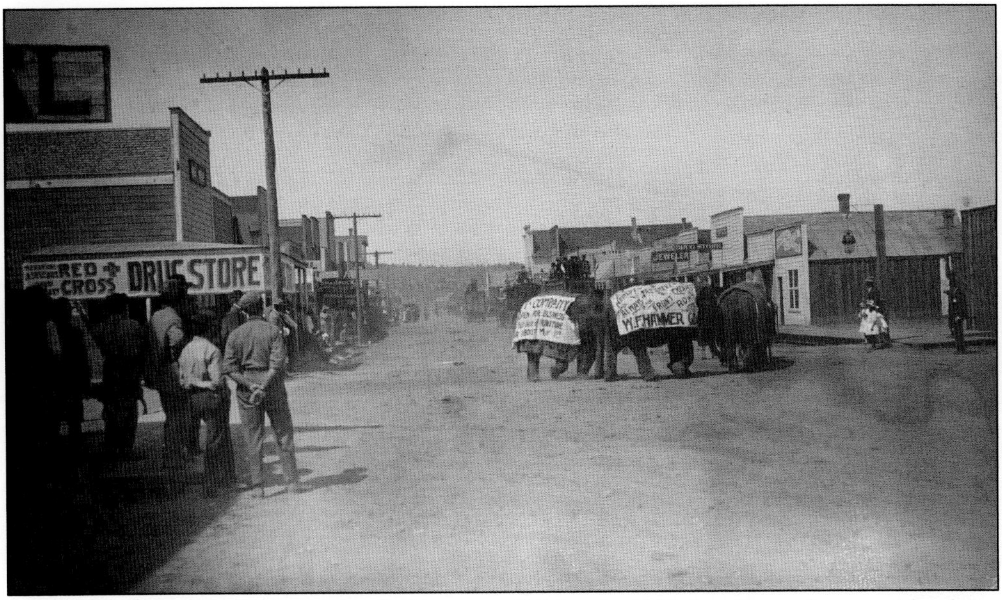

Circus elephants are paraded through downtown Madras in 1912. Local merchants paid to have advertisement signs placed on the animals in hopes of attracting customers. Many people rest along the boardwalk on the left after picnicking and watching the circus wagons and animals march up and down the street. (Courtesy of Loyd Vincent.)

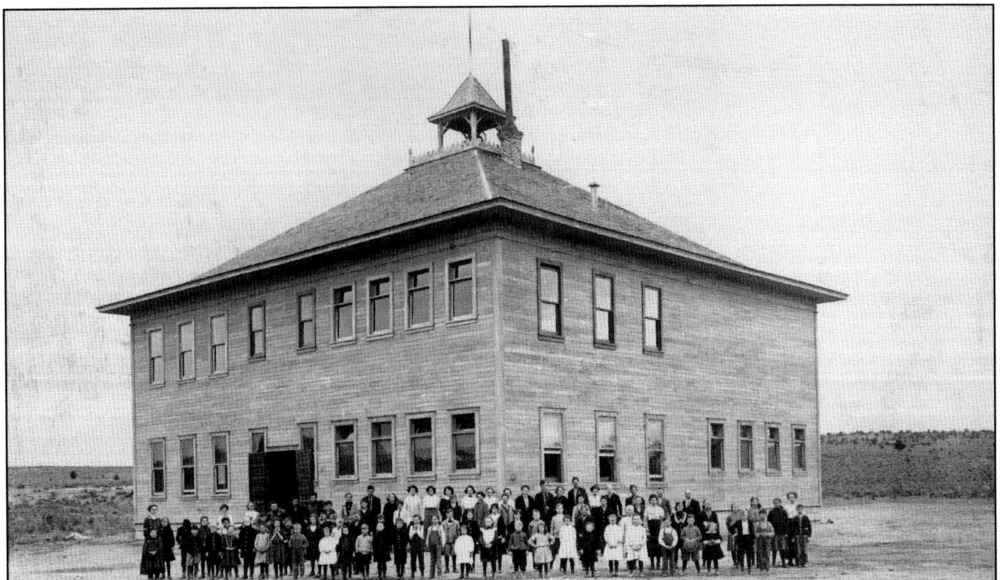

A new two-story public school was built in 1908 on the eastern end of E Street at the intersection with Tenth Street, replacing an earlier schoolhouse. The community was proud of its new school. Grade school was held on the lower floor and high school classes were held on the upper floor. The school utilized the bell that was used at the earlier school. Students proudly pose for a photograph in front of the school in 1912. After several years, the upper floor was closed for safety reasons.

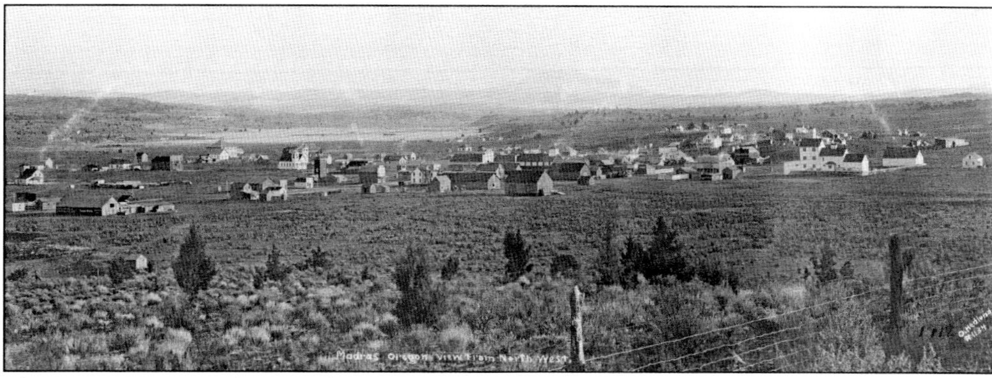

This is a panoramic photograph of Madras from around 1912 looking east toward the town. It was taken by local photographer Ole Hedlund. Several prominent buildings are visible, including the school and the churches in the left middle and the flour mill on the right.

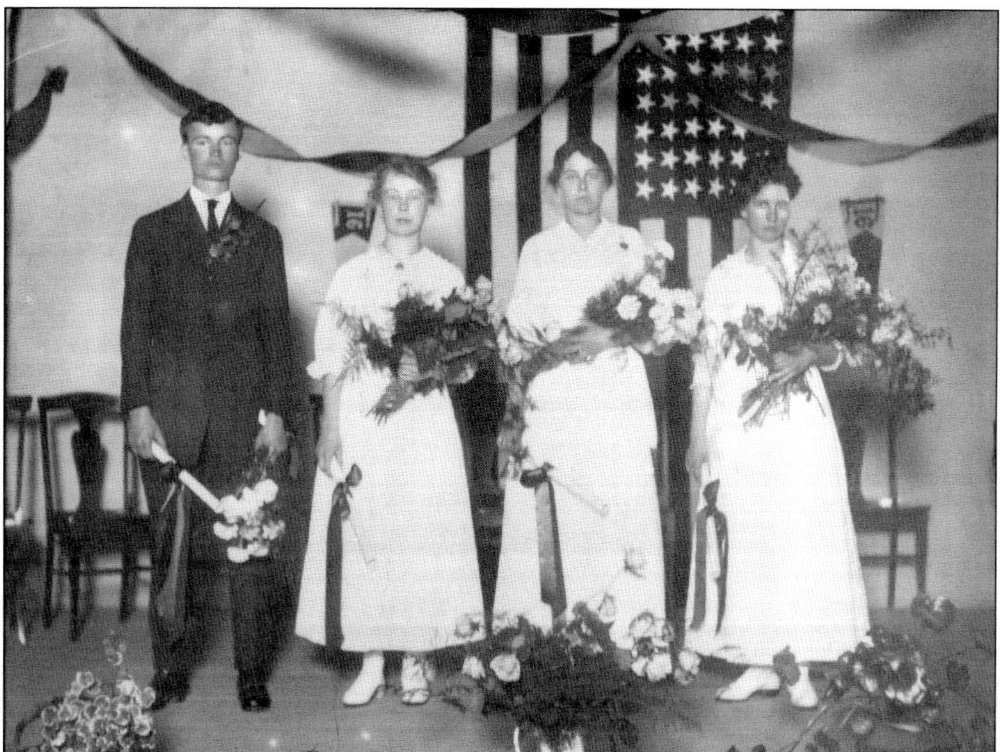

These four students were the first to graduate from Madras High School in 1916 in a proud moment for the students and for the entire community. They are, from left to right, Guy Powell, Beatrice Olson, Bessie U'ren, and Aurel Moore.

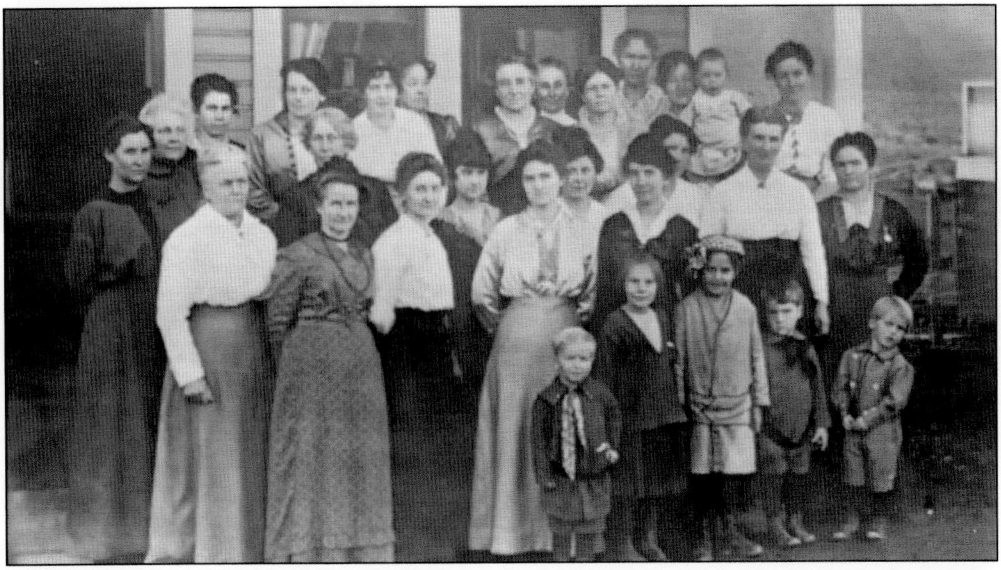

The Ladies Society of the Christian Church posed for this photograph in 1911 at the Ashley home in Madras. Members and children in the photograph include Louise Pearce, Lucille Snook, Joe Siler, Andrew Morrow, Grandma Siler, Mary King, Lillie Turner, Grandma Martha Percival, Mrs. L. Newell, Mrs. Hatfield, Mrs. McWilliams, Mrs. Ashley, Martha Snook, Hattie Read, D. Sweeting, Marie Dizney, Ezra Clark, Emily Morrow, and Robert and Viola Gray.

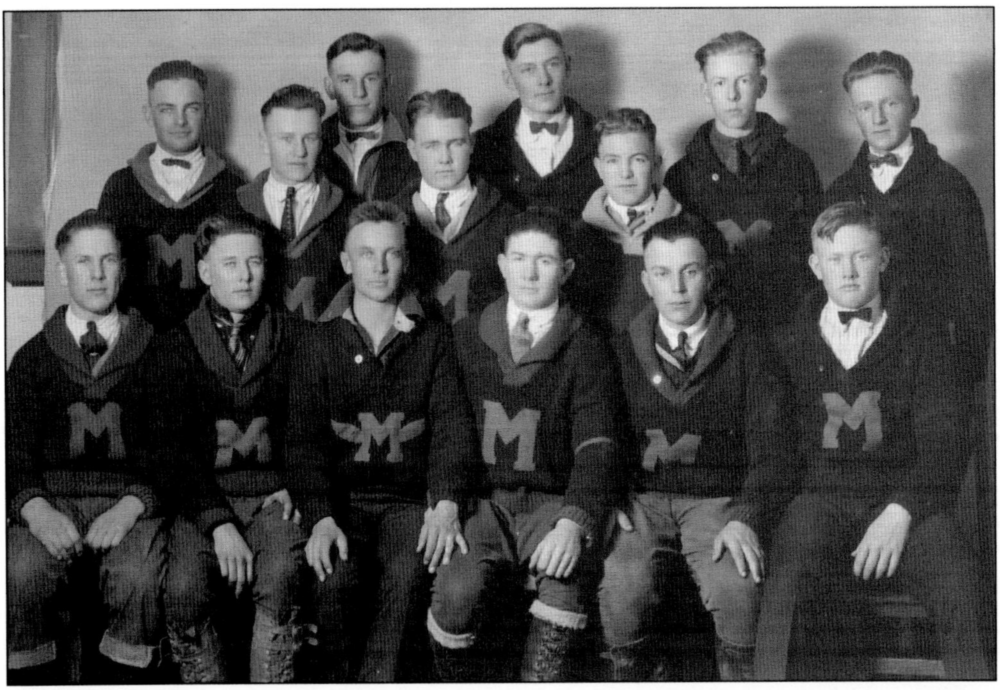

The Letterman Club of Madras High School is seen here around 1921. Large crowds supported local school teams, although the sports were limited in the early years with mostly baseball, basketball, football, and some track and field as the main activities. These young men proudly wear the "M" emblem signifying their accomplishments.

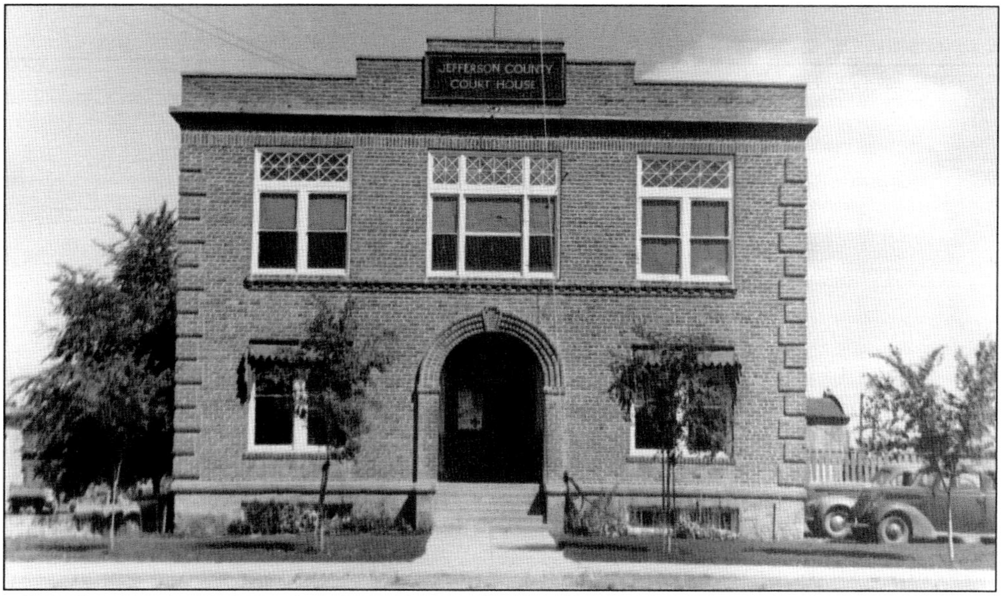

The Jefferson County Courthouse, on the north side of D Street between Fifth and Sixth Streets, was a gathering place for local events. A new courthouse was later constructed, and this building housed the Jefferson County Historical Society Museum for many years. It was condemned in 2011 and is now vacant.

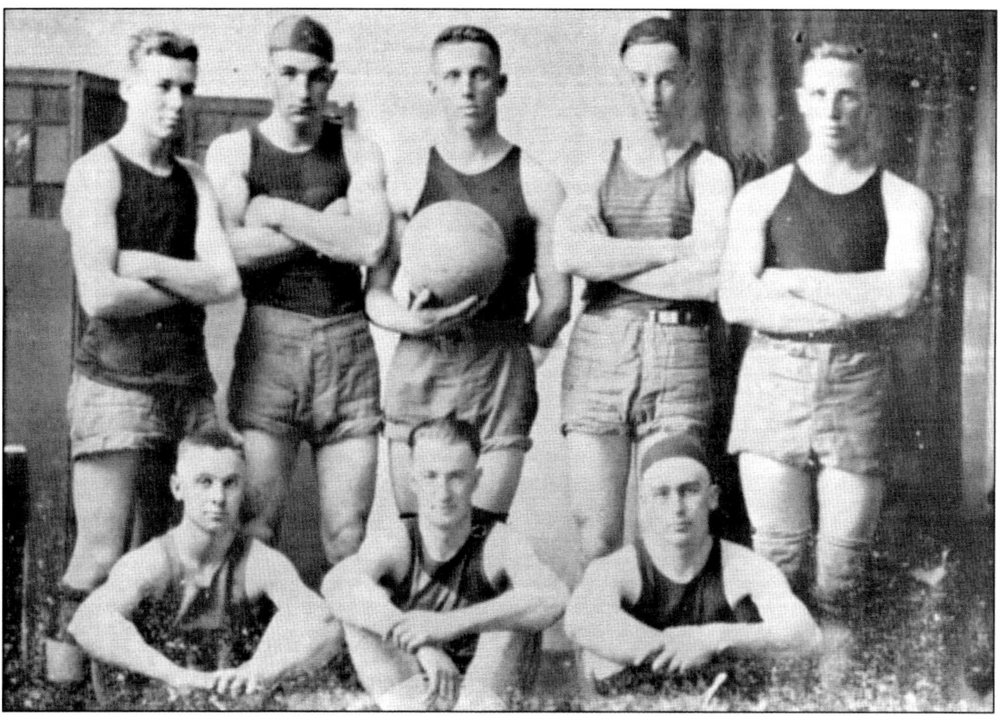

The 1920 Madras boys' basketball team included, from left to right, (seated) Cecil Moore, George Farquarson, and Harold Johnson; (standing) Jesse Gard, Clarence Crosswhite, John Young, Boyd Stangland, and Dick Young. The team was invited to the Oregon State High School Basketball Tournament, the first team from Madras to play in the state championship playoffs.

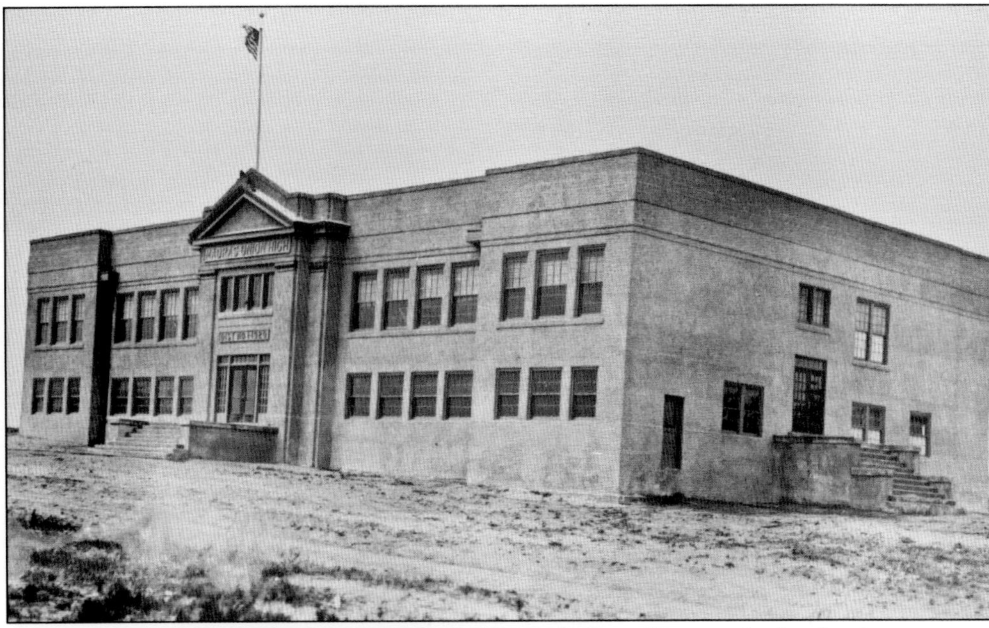

The new high school in Madras is seen here shortly after its construction in 1920. A new building was needed because the old public school had become overcrowded. Bond issues were passed to spend $44,000 for building the school. This building was used as the high school until it was destroyed by fire in 1937.

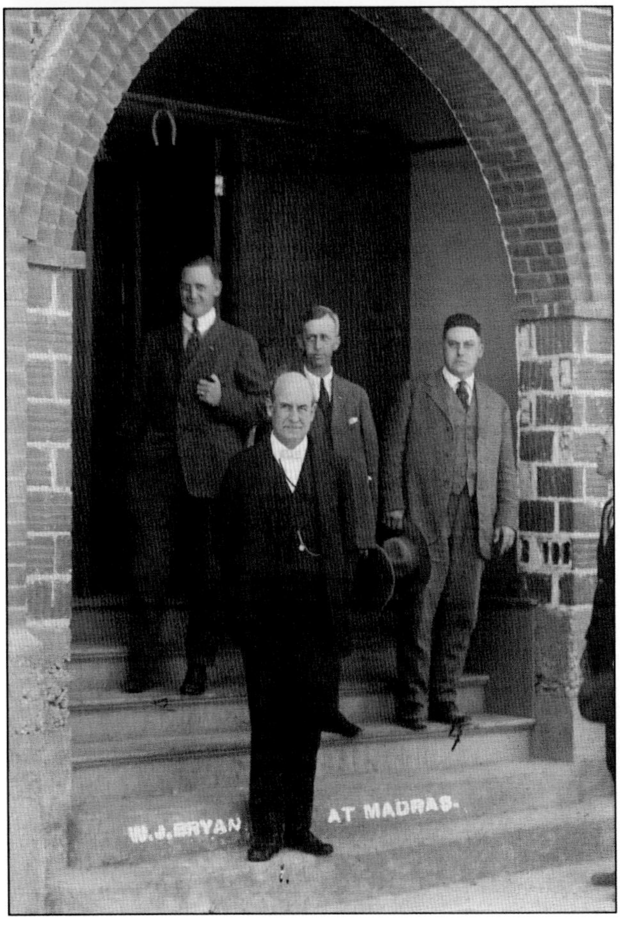

Madras proudly hosted politician William Jennings Bryant, photographed on the steps of the Jefferson County Courthouse, in 1920. Behind him are, from left to right, Lewis Irving, Mr. Wiley, and John Henderson. Bryant toured the nation to promote his presidential aspirations and to participate in Chautauqua programs.

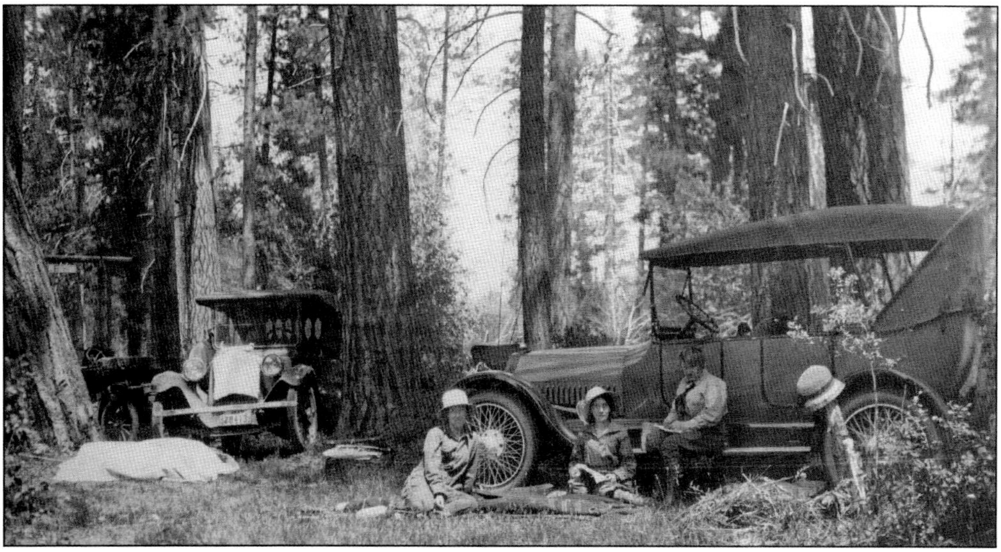

Madras residents often traveled to Suttle Lake or Camp Sherman for recreational visits. These cars are at Camp Sherman on a camping trip, and the woman to the left is Lillie May Read Turner, the wife of Howard Turner, one of the more prominent men in Madras.

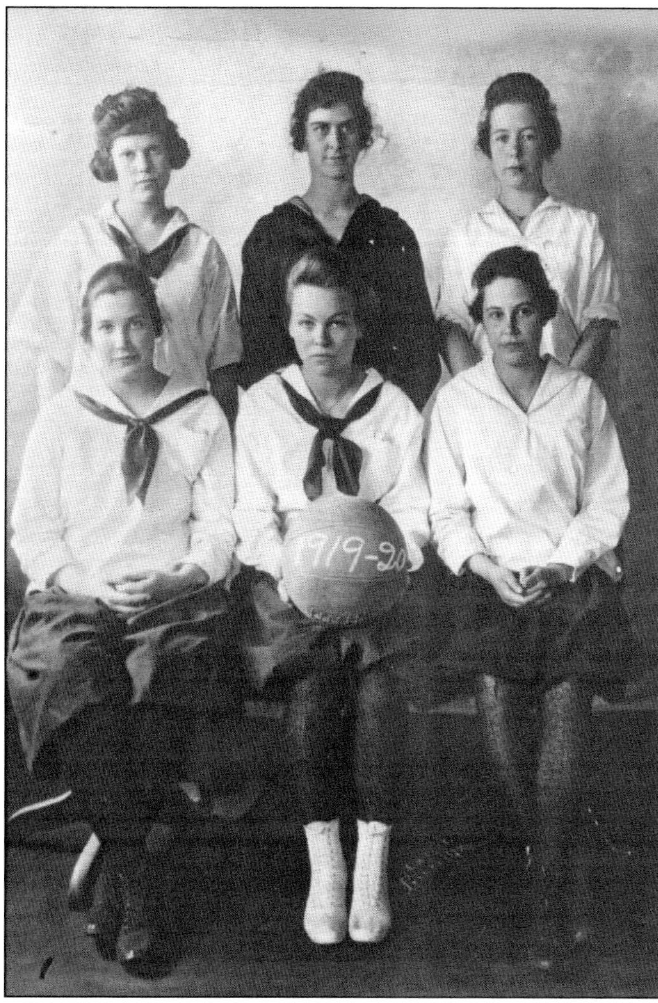

The 1920 Madras girls' basketball team included, from left to right, (first row) Nellie Shutt, Margaret U'ren, and Lovetta Shutt; (second row) Lavelle Grag, coach Erma Laird, and Leda Ramsey. Women often played other women's teams at the same school, occasionally traveling to other communities.

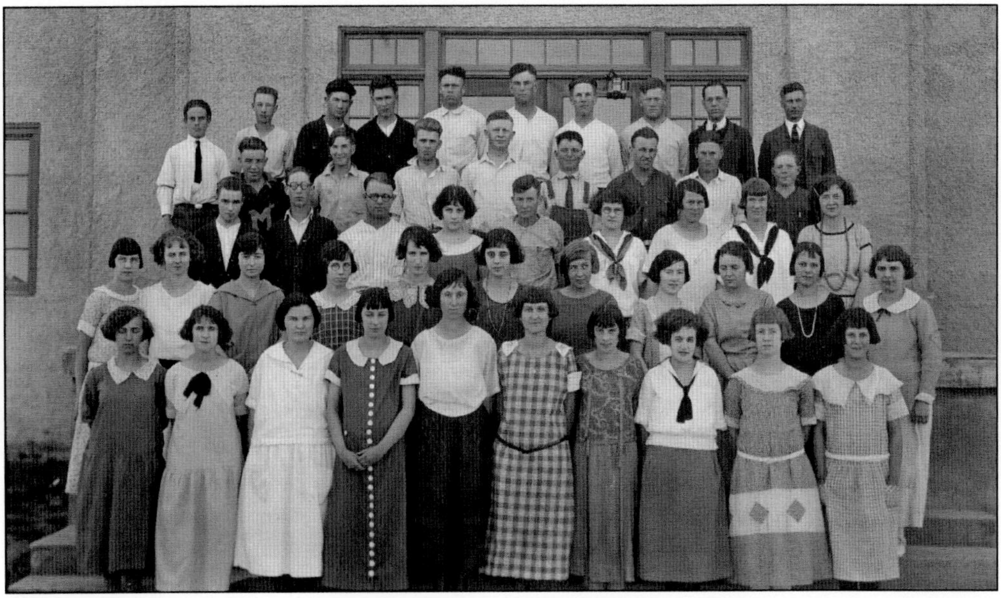

The student body of Madras High School in 1924 included, from left to right, (first row) Camilla Percival, Dorothy Dley, ? Robertson, ? Klann, unidentified, ? Jones, Louise Pierce, Lucille Snook, Alice Evick, and unidentified; (second row) Helen Klann, four unidentified, Hazel Mason, Betty Johnson, Edna Watts, Jesse May Johnson, and two unidentified; (third row) Dwight Gard, Van McTaggert, Pat Houston, Bea Ramsey, Harl VanNoy, Juanita Fox, Roberta Campbell, and two unidentified; (fourth row) Wally Hannon, Dean Toly, unidentified, Lawrence Evick, unidentified, ? Mason, George Campbell, and Kenneth Green; (fifth row) Willis Warren, Ted Gunderson, ? McTaggert, Dewey Dee, George Southman, Gus Ramsey, Gene Cook, two unidentified, and ? Gabriel.

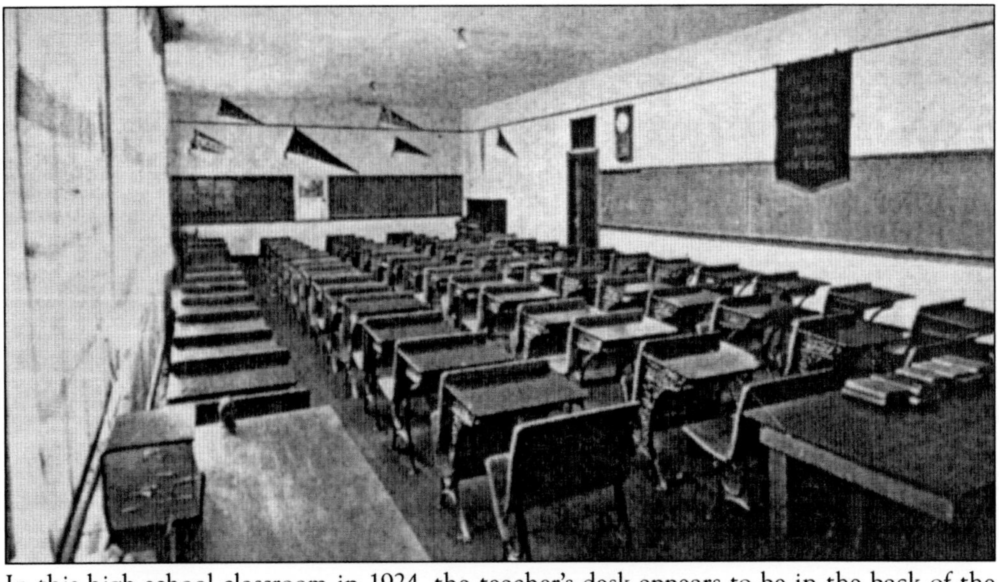

In this high school classroom in 1924, the teacher's desk appears to be in the back of the room and there are several desks facing the chalkboard. A piano is in the front right of the classroom, and pennants and banners are on the wall. A large dictionary is also on the table in the left forefront.

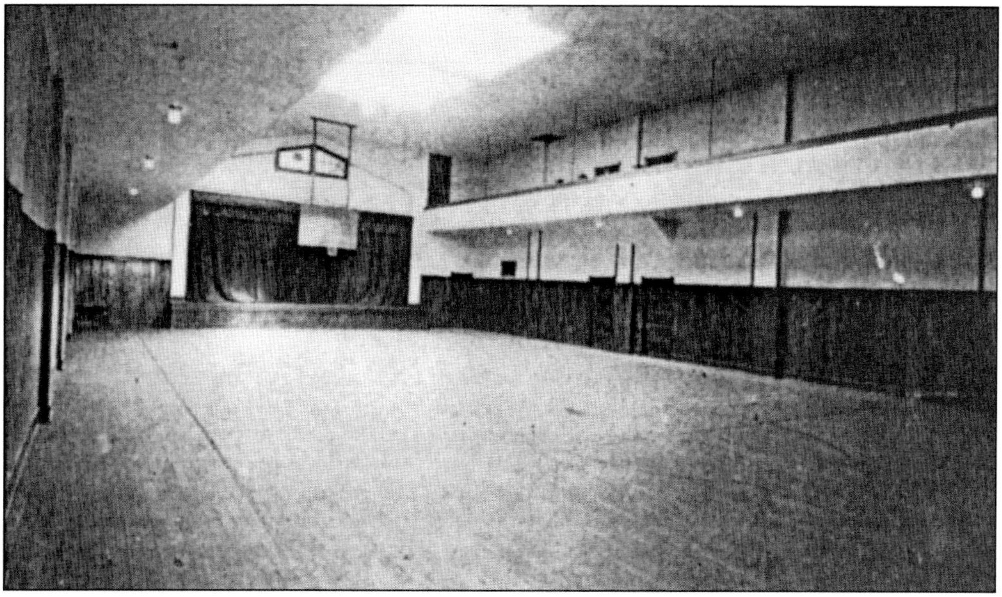

There is a stage at the far end of the gymnasium, seen here in 1924, with one basketball backboard in front of it and a small balcony on the right for spectators.

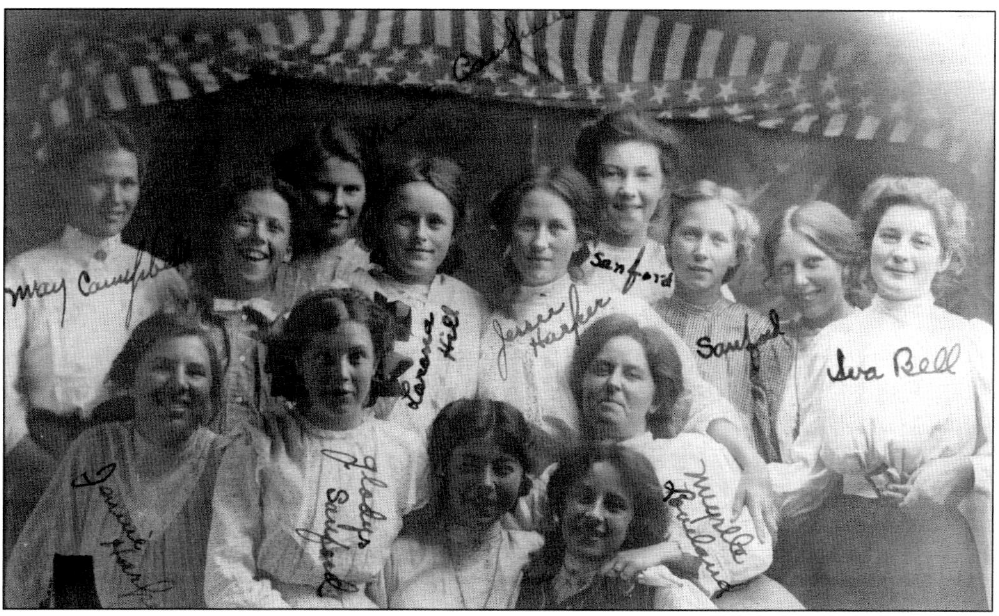

This joyful group of Madras High School students poses during the Fourth of July festivities in 1916. They are, from left to right, (seated) Jennie Harper, Gladys Sanford, Nora Livingston, unidentified, and Myrtle Loveland; (standing) May Campbell, unidentified, M. Campbell, Larena Hill, Jessie Harper, two unnamed Sanford sisters, unidentified, and Iva Bell.

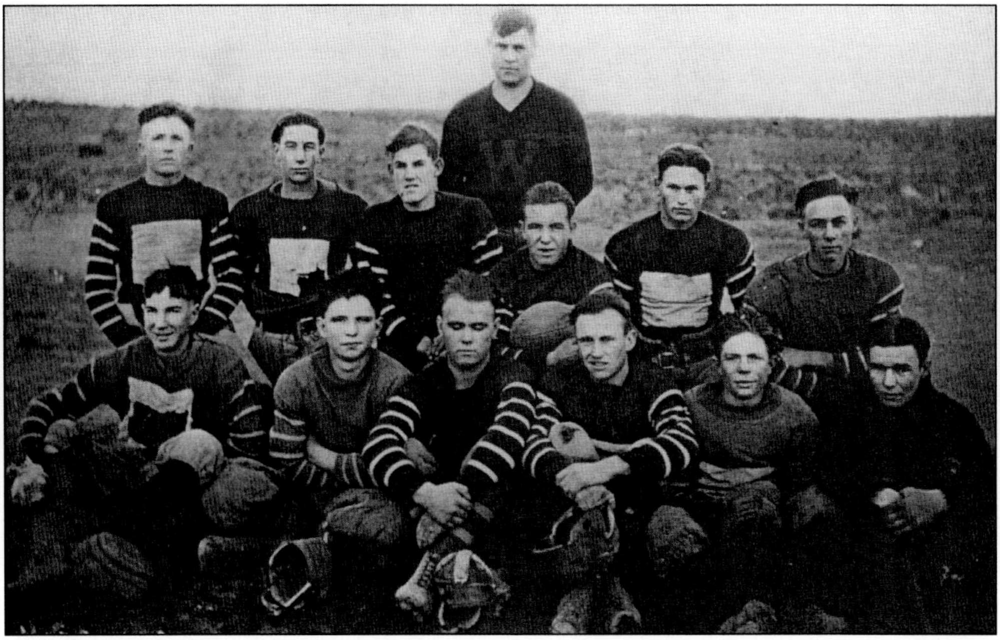

The 1924 Madras Union High School football team was affectionately known as the Fighting Fools. Pictured from left to right are (first row) ? Trolan, T. Wilkes, H. Hannon, ? Mason, ? Green, and ? Gard; (second row) ? Evick, ? McTaggert, ? Endicott, W. Hannon, ? Campbell, and ? Corwin. Coach Bernard Ramsey stands behind the team.

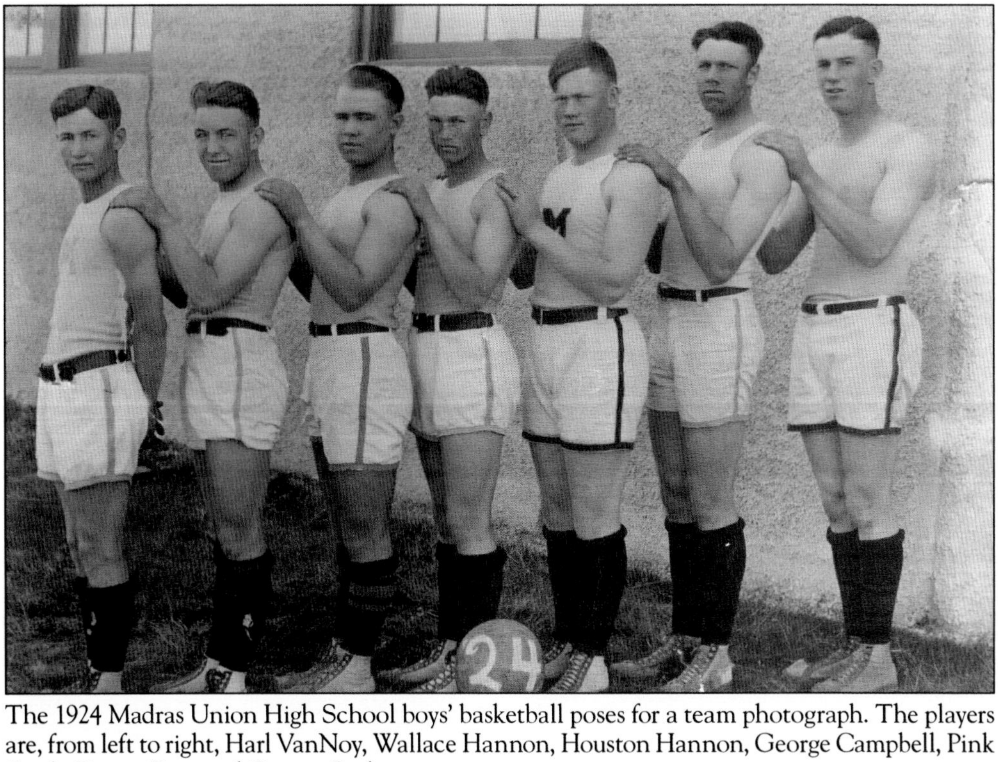

The 1924 Madras Union High School boys' basketball poses for a team photograph. The players are, from left to right, Harl VanNoy, Wallace Hannon, Houston Hannon, George Campbell, Pink Cook, Dewey Dee, and George Sothman.

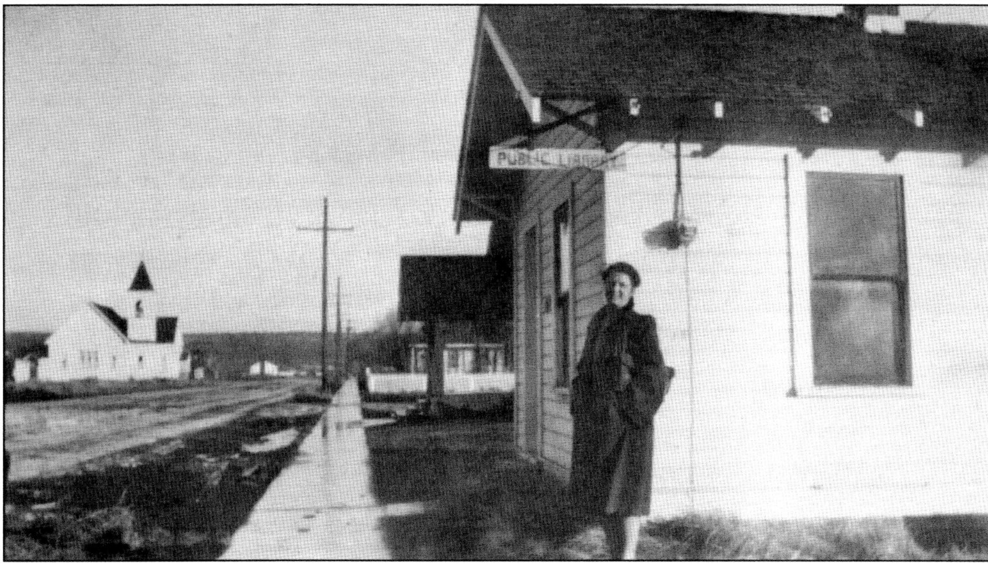

An unidentified woman poses in front of the Madras Public Library after it looks like a rain has made the street and sidewalks wet. In the corner is the Methodist church at the corner of Eighth and D Streets, which was built in 1907.

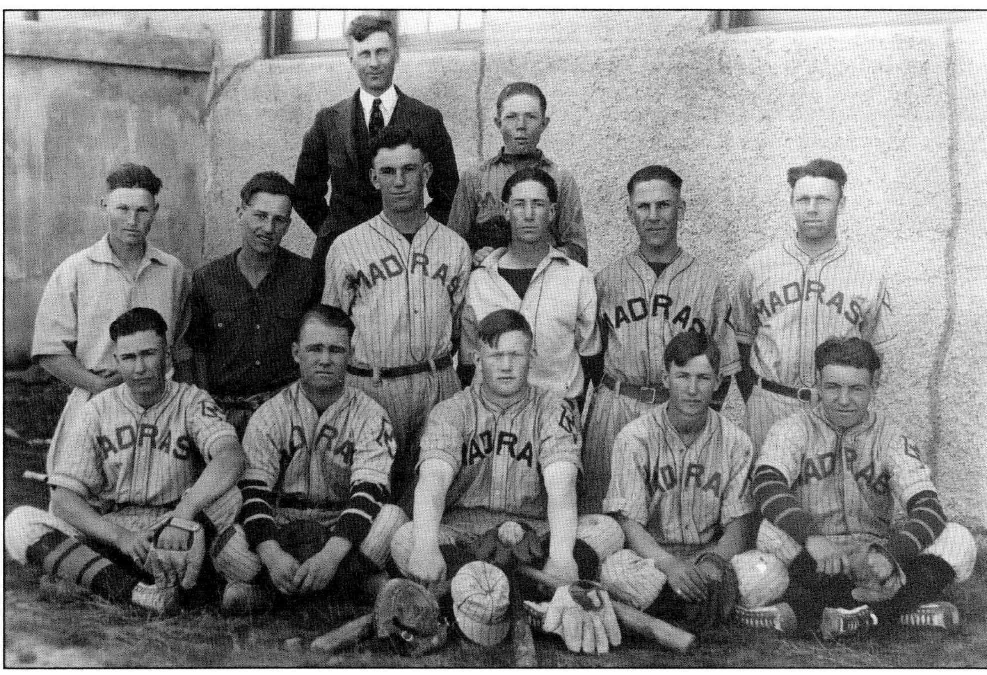

The 1924 Madras Union High School baseball team included, from left to right, (first row) Dean Sherrod, Houston Hannon, Pink Cook, Harl VanNoy, and Wallace Hannon; (second row) George Campbell, Wayne Mason, George Sothman, Van McTaggert, Gus Ramsey, and Dewey Dee; (third row) coach and principal George Gabreil and Kenneth Green.

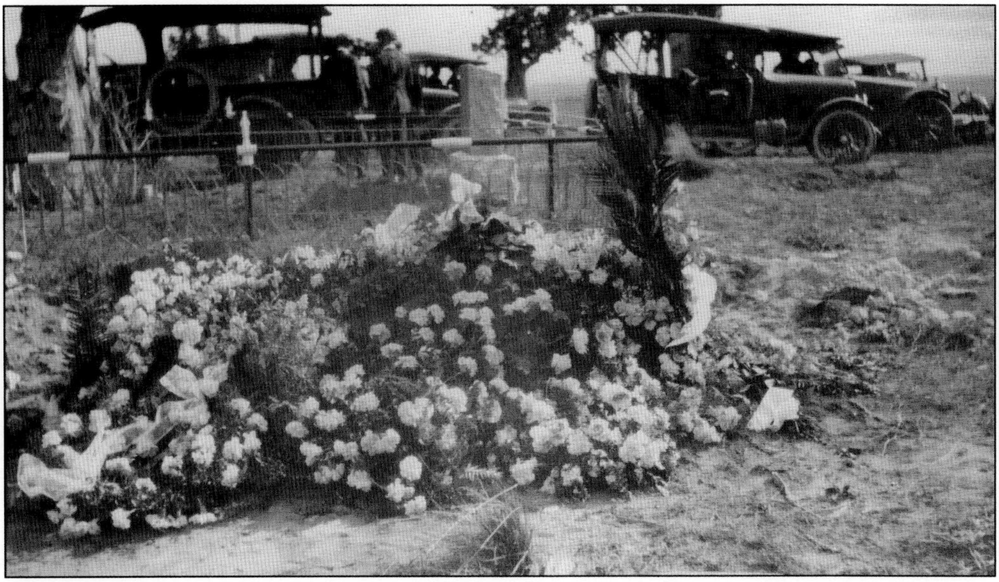

The cemetery in Madras, seen here in 1917, was established in 1904 on the homestead of Nannie Holt, who died that year and was the first person buried in the cemetery. The cemetery was later operated by the Order of Odd Fellows until 1982, when it was handed over to Jefferson County. The cemetery is now known as the Mt. Jefferson Memorial Park.

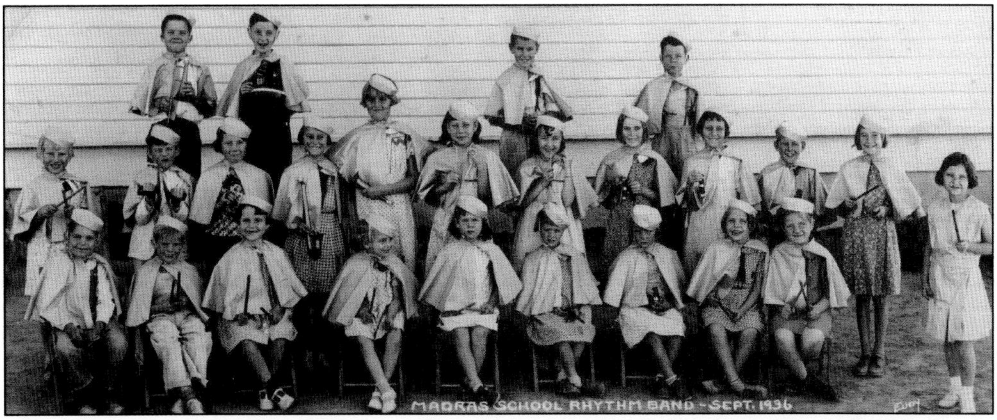

The 1936 Madras School Rhythm Band included, from left to right, (first row) unidentified, Billy Ramsey, Caryl Ann Watts, Patty Percival, Madeline Kelley, Wilma Edwards, Mary Edwards, Patty Ramsey, Mary Jay Overhulse, and leader Darlene Doil; (second row) Arleene Fox, Harold Darron, Mary Doyle, Thelma Haberstich, Laverne Lytle, Evelyn Keeney, June Hering, Doris Mason, Marjorie Haberstich, Homer Haberstich, and Mona Crews; (third row) Eldon King, Jack Thomas, Morris Mason, and Bill Kelley.

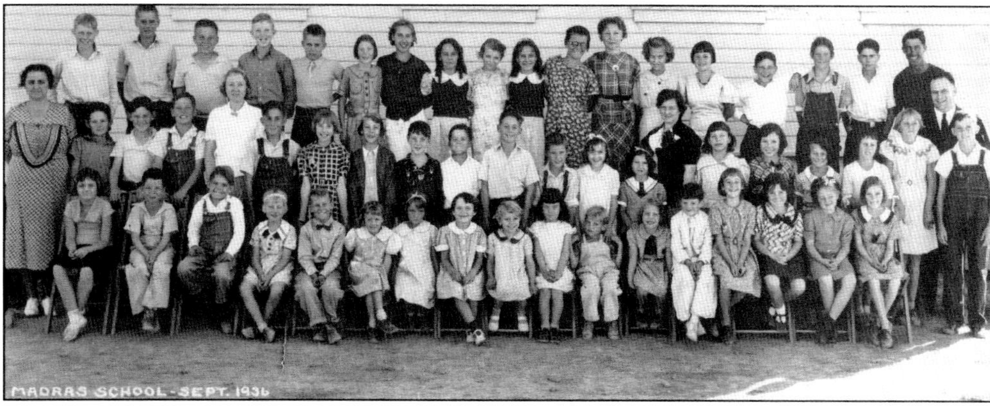

The entire Madras Grade School—grades one through eight—posed for this photograph in 1936.

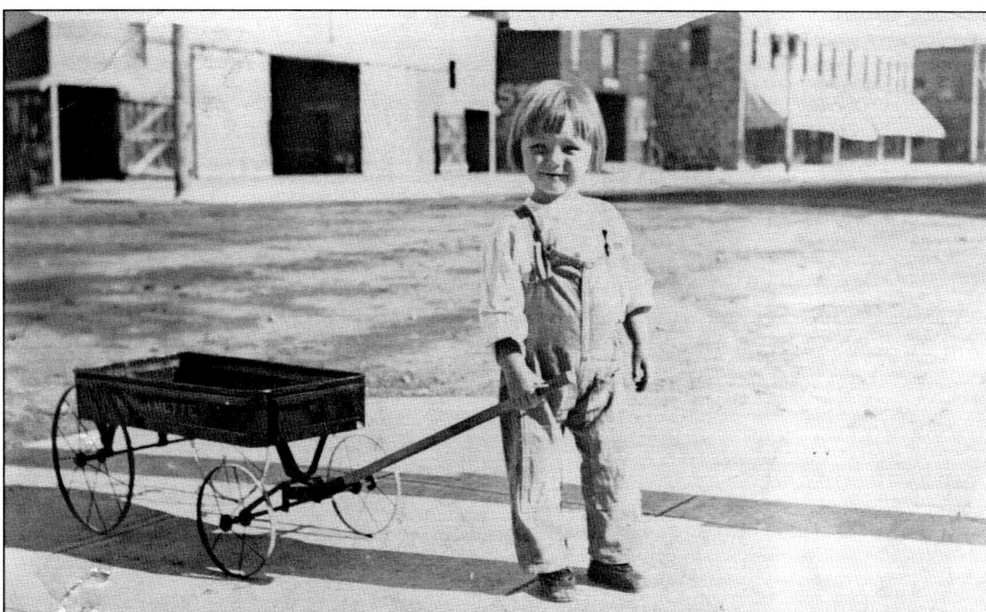
Young Arthur Jones plays with his wagon on the streets of Madras around 1938. Unpaved side streets were common until the early 1950s.

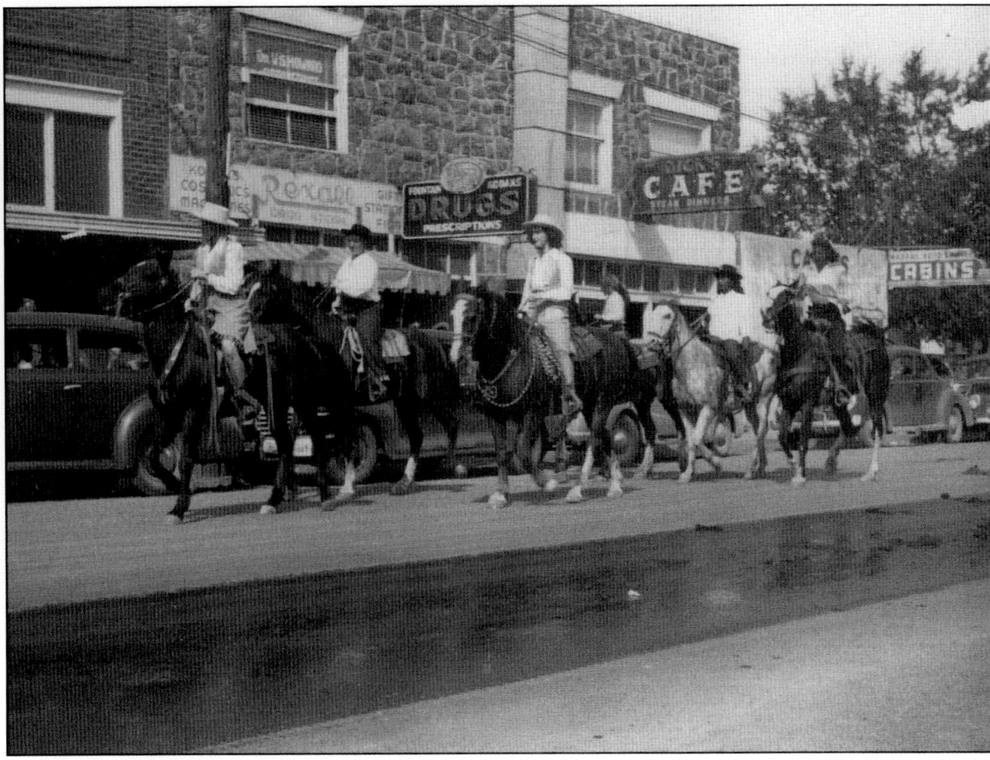

A parade marched down the now-paved Fifth Street for the Jefferson County Fair in 1947. In the background on the west side of the street is the Rexall Drug Store, Dick's Café, and the Madras Auto Lawn Cabins.

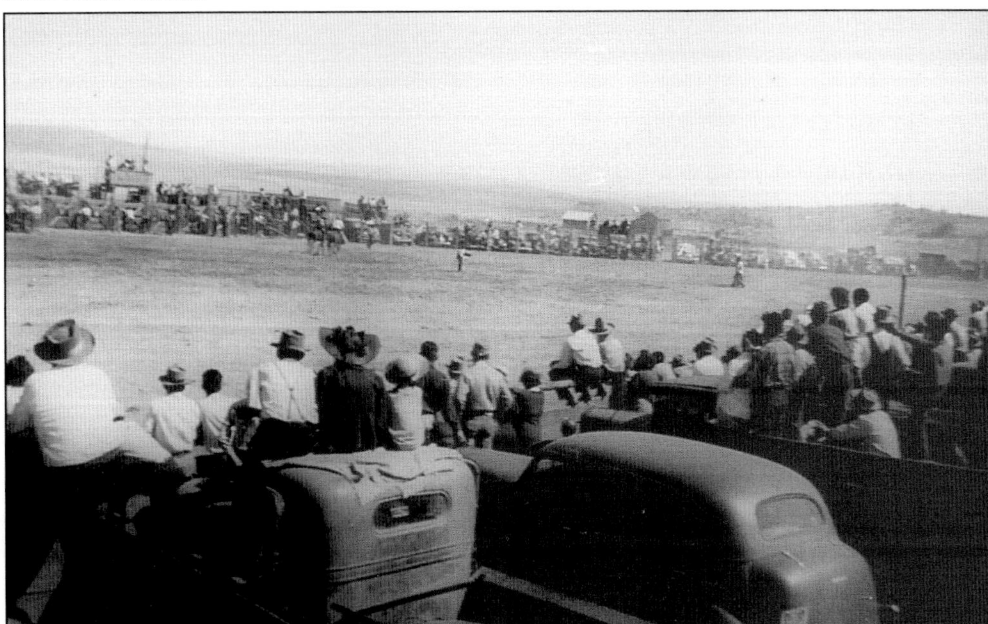

Automobiles surround the Jefferson County Fair arena in 1947 as spectators watch the rodeo, a major part of the fair.

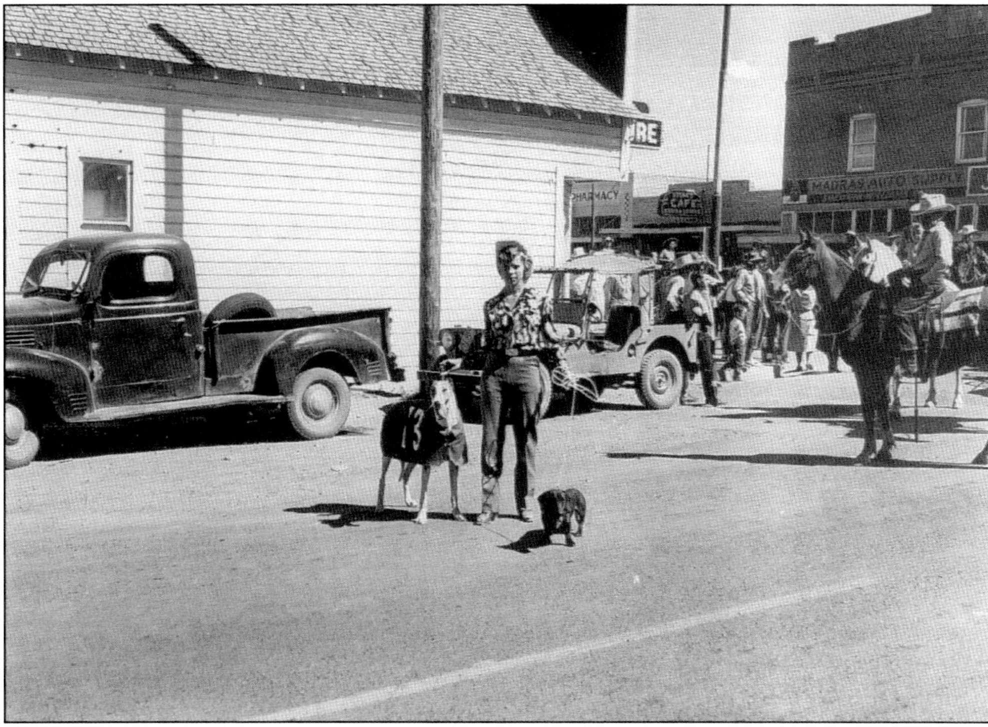

Lala DeLude poses with her two dogs at the Jefferson County Fair parade in 1947. Stone's Café and Madras Auto Supply are on the far side of the street.

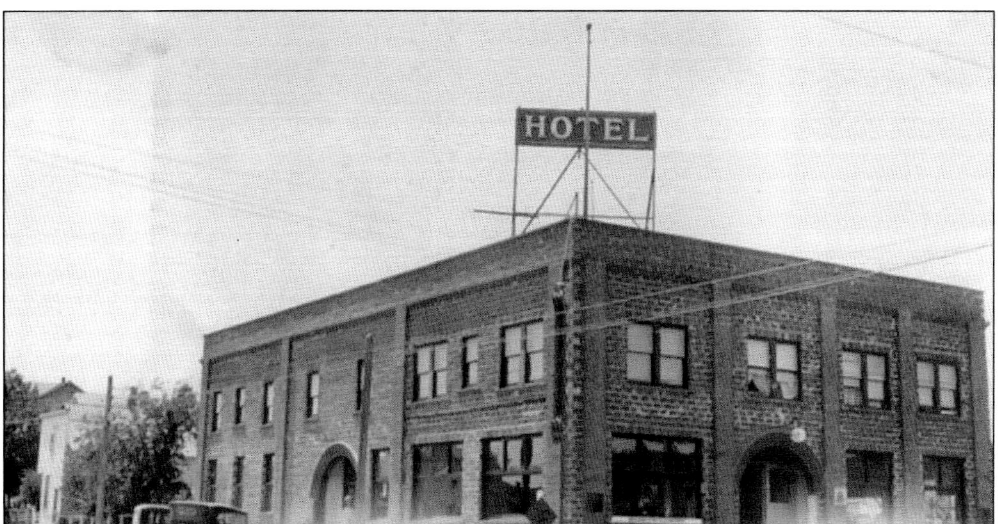

The Bellamy Hotel was known by several names. It was first the Fisher Hotel, then the Bellamy Hotel, and eventually Madras Hotel. It was located at what is now known as Sunshine Corner. While not the first hotel in Madras, it was utilized for many years.

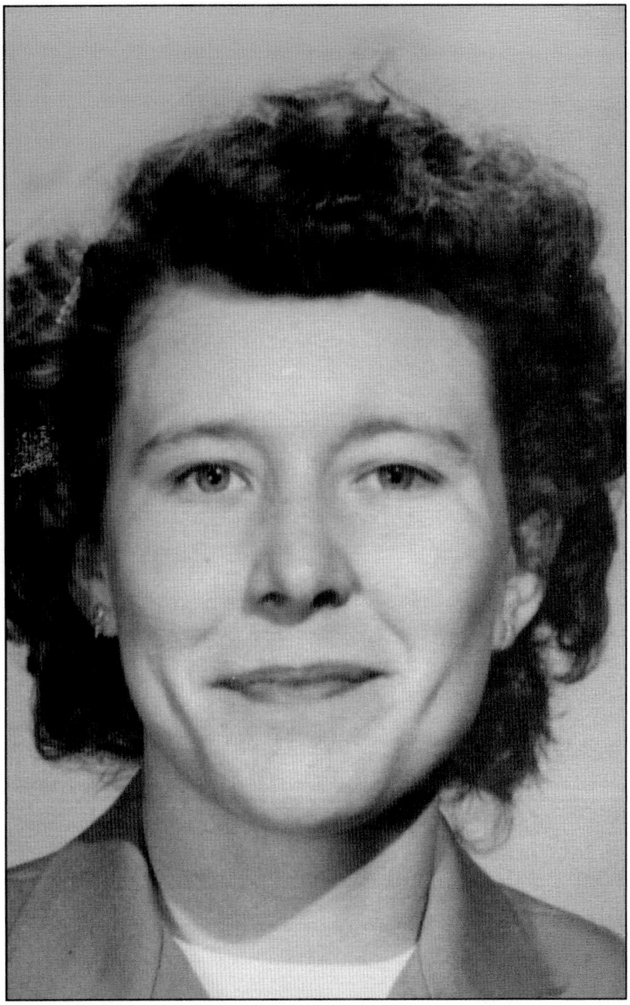

Beth Chapin attended Eastern Oregon College, and after graduating, she began her long teaching career in Madras. She taught at Madras schools from 1949 to 1985, leaving a legacy of education to several generations of students. She married fellow Madras teacher Tom Crow, and since her retirement from teaching, she has become known as the "unofficial" Jefferson County historian.

Beth Chapin's first class of second-graders in 1949–1950 included, by number, 1. Charles Bell, 4. Delmar Davis, 5. Robert Earl, 6. Stephens Hart, 9. Kenneth Lydy, 10. Kelly McGreer, 11. Bruce Naugher, 12. Clarence Reese, 13. Richard Ridgway, 15. Fabion Sutterlee, 18. William Wanker, 21. Larry Currier, 22. Steve Olson, 26. Carol Franklin, 28. Julie Ginther, 29. Lorna Glass, 30. Patricia Jasa, 31. Patricia Olson, 33. Sharon Schmidt, 34. Margaret Ann Williams, and 36. Valorie Fivecoat.

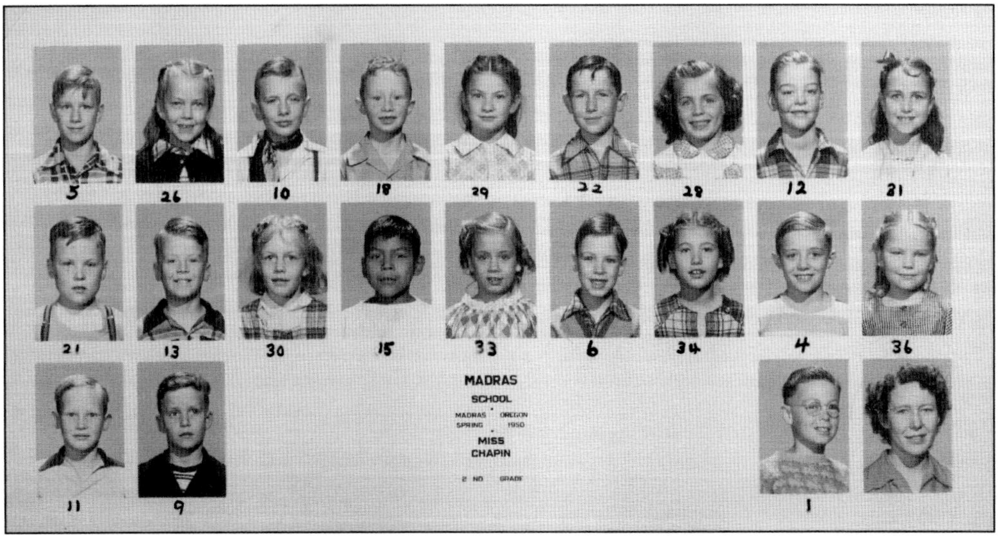

Beth Chapin Crow is seen here at the time of her retirement from teaching in 1985. Many teachers have served long terms teaching in the Madras school system, but Crow has taken on a much larger role after her retirement, painstakingly preserving the history of the community since her retirement.

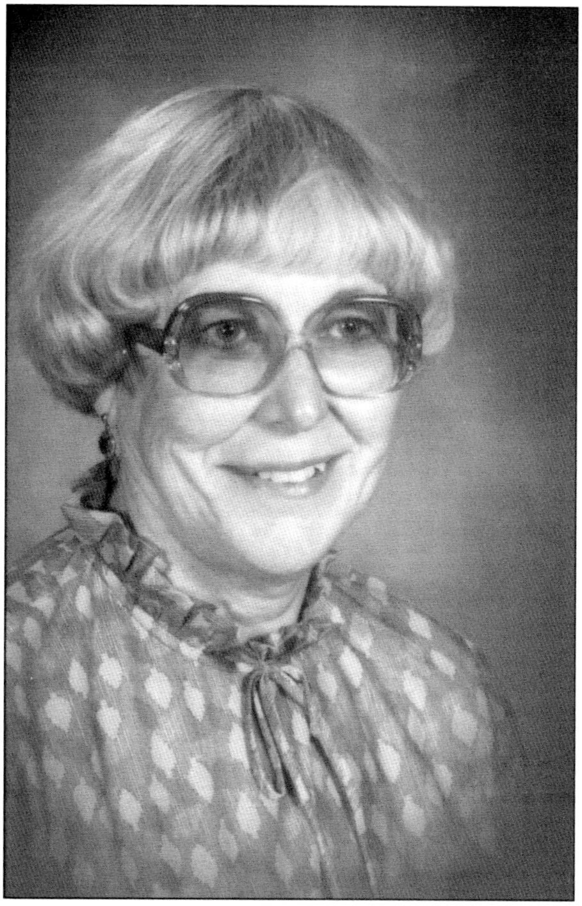

Beth Chapin Crow's last class of students in 1985 included, from left to right, (first row) Raelynn Waldow, Angela Gaul, Jason Potampa, Jennifer Runge, Gary King, Kevin Hopps, Tammy Teal, Jamie Sites, Chad Casady, and Shane Bush; (second row) Emily Ray, Shawn Phifer, Firle Estep, Jim Kinslow, Tommy Norton, and Carla Hileman; (third row) Jessica Fox, Reed Grote, Jenny Pack, Elizabeth Wilkerson, Heather Clowers, Jeanne Southern, and Tony Galimore. Not pictured is Molly Archer.

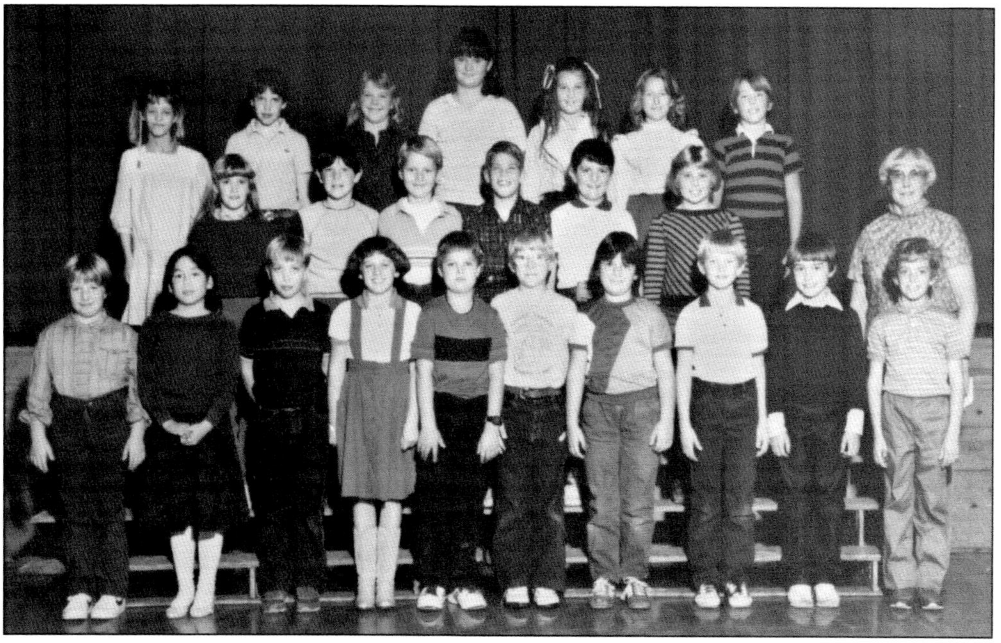

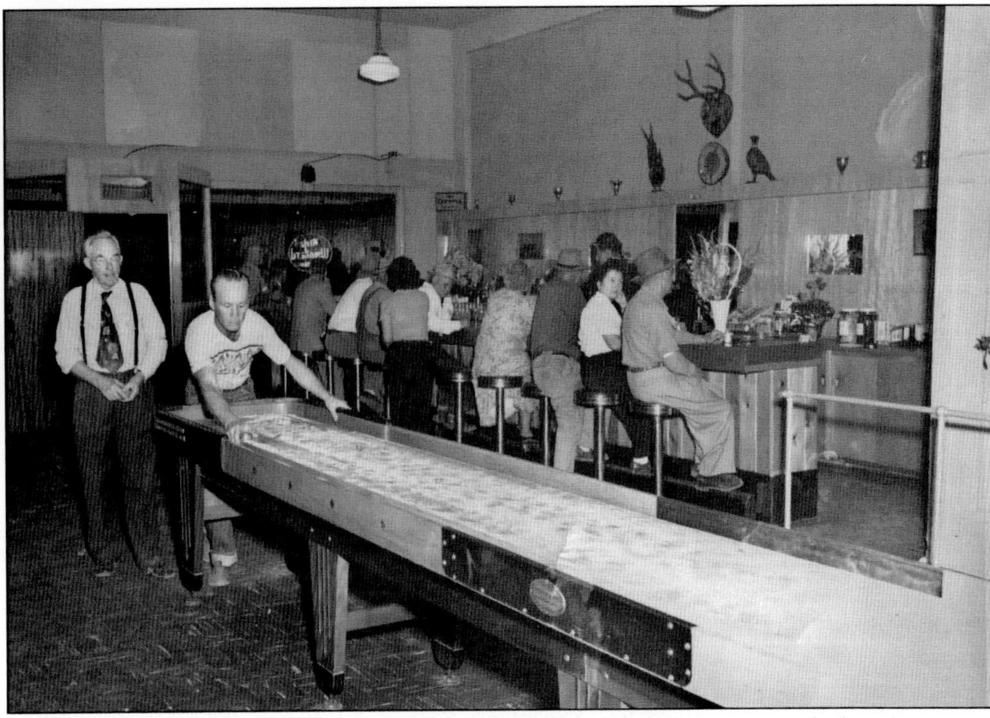

Longtime Madras doctor Victor Howard plays shuffleboard with an unidentified young man in the Nugget Pool Hall in Madras in the early 1950s. The bar was a popular local hangout.

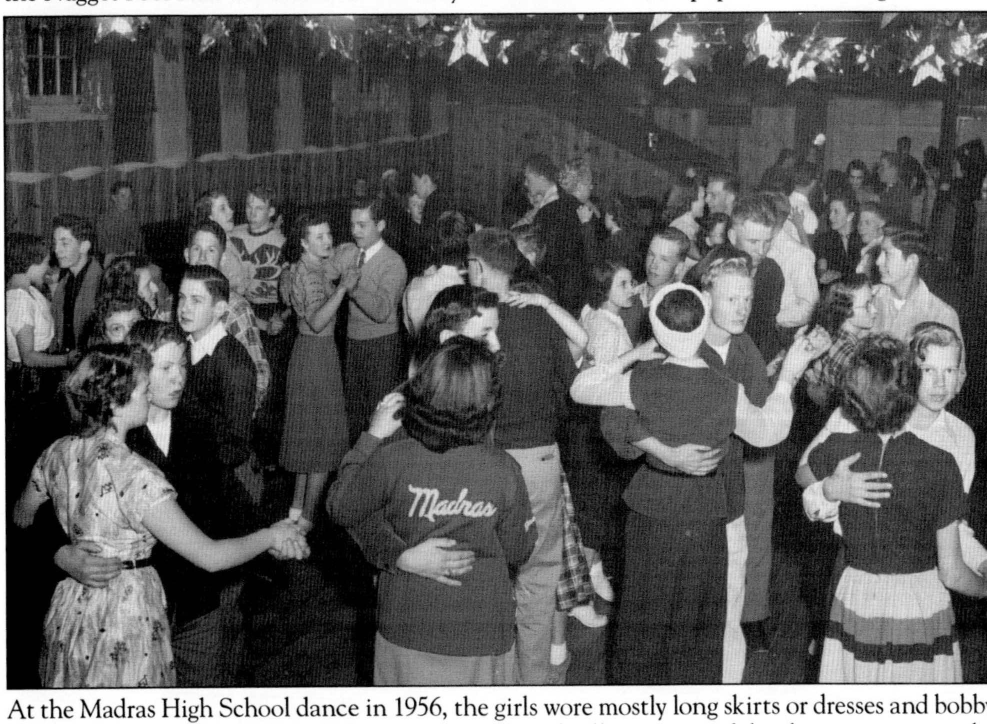

At the Madras High School dance in 1956, the girls wore mostly long skirts or dresses and bobby sox. Although this was the beginning of the rock-and-roll era, most of the dancers appear to be enjoying a slow dance while holding their partners.

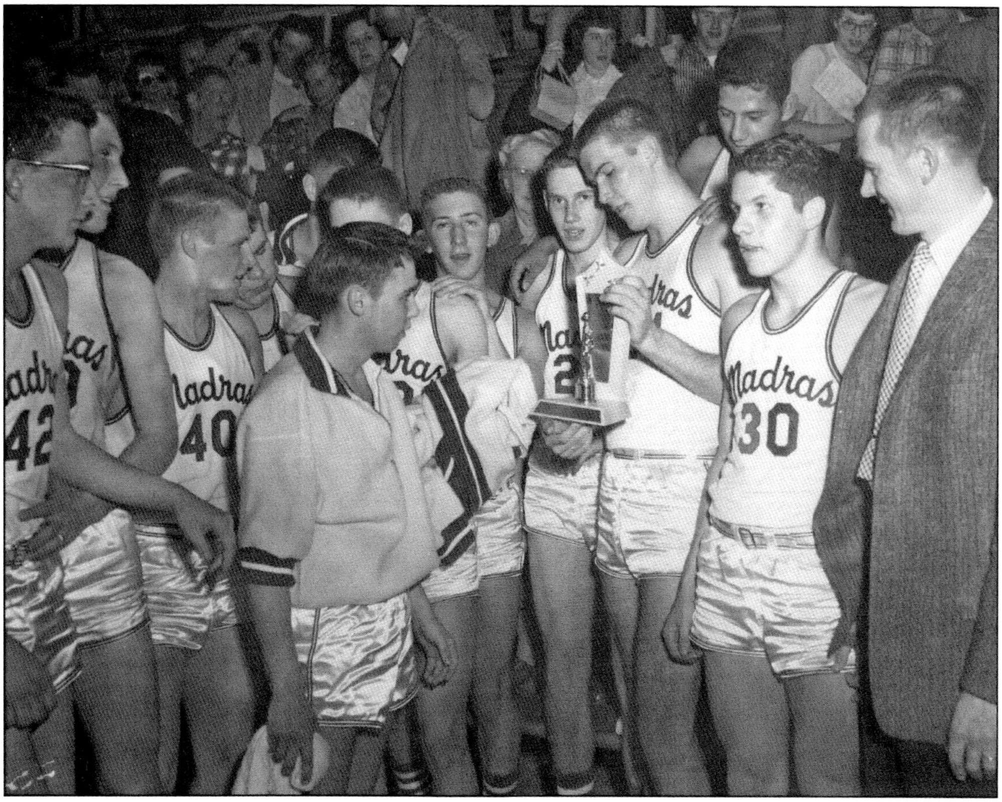

When the Madras High School basketball team won the district championship in 1957, it was a celebratory event for the whole community. The team included Mike VanWirt, Paul Stine, Bill Davis, Gary Bynsor, Al Neiman, Murray Webstor, Dick Winsor, Satch Miller, Richard Weigand, and Ole Johnson.

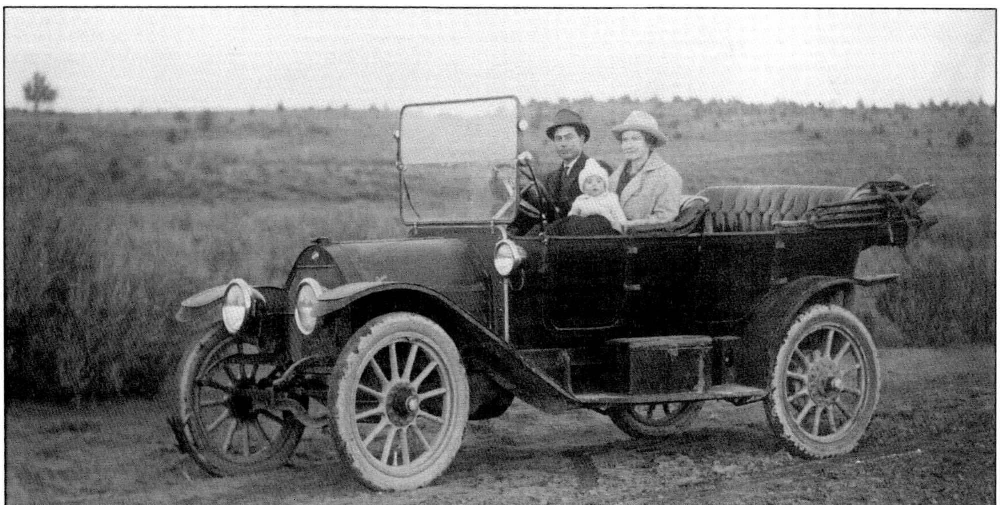

Mr. and Mrs. Robert Lowe go for a Sunday outing in their automobile in 1915. The Lowes owned the Sugar Bowl Café in Madras. Mrs. Lowe is holding their child. Automobile travel was an adventure at the time, as roads were primitive, and spare tires were essential.

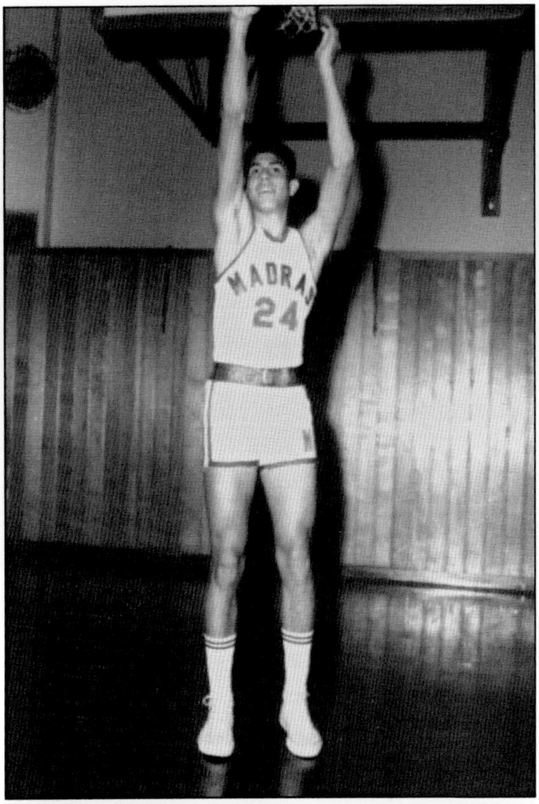

Basketball has always been a very popular sport in the Madras community. In 1970, a special run through the state tournament saw Madras crowned state champions. Nearly the entire town traveled to see the championship game. Ron Jones was the star of the team and is seen here scoring a basket in one of the playoff games. He was selected to the all-state team and went on to play for Oregon State University.

The 1970 state championship basketball team included, from left to right, Craig Weigand, Ron Jones, Ron Yaw, Phil Utter, Ken Shafer, Danny Martinez, Gary Snow, Shannon Ahern, Bill Cram, and Barry Hatfield. Team members Rick Souers and Willie Stacona are not pictured.

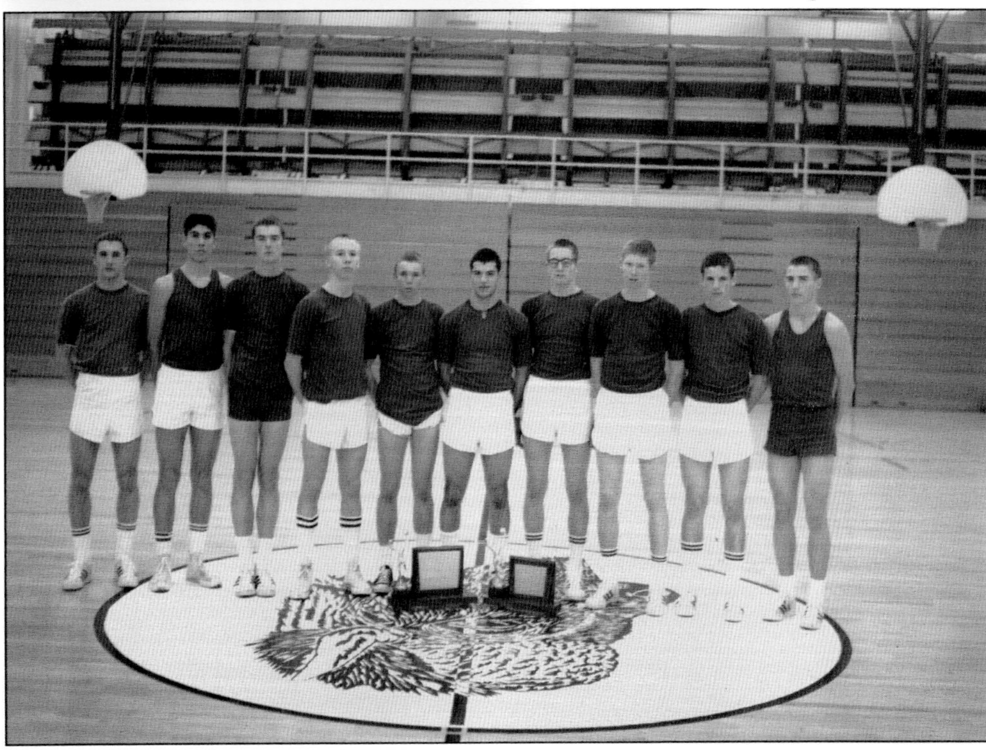

Five

The Rise of Business and Industry

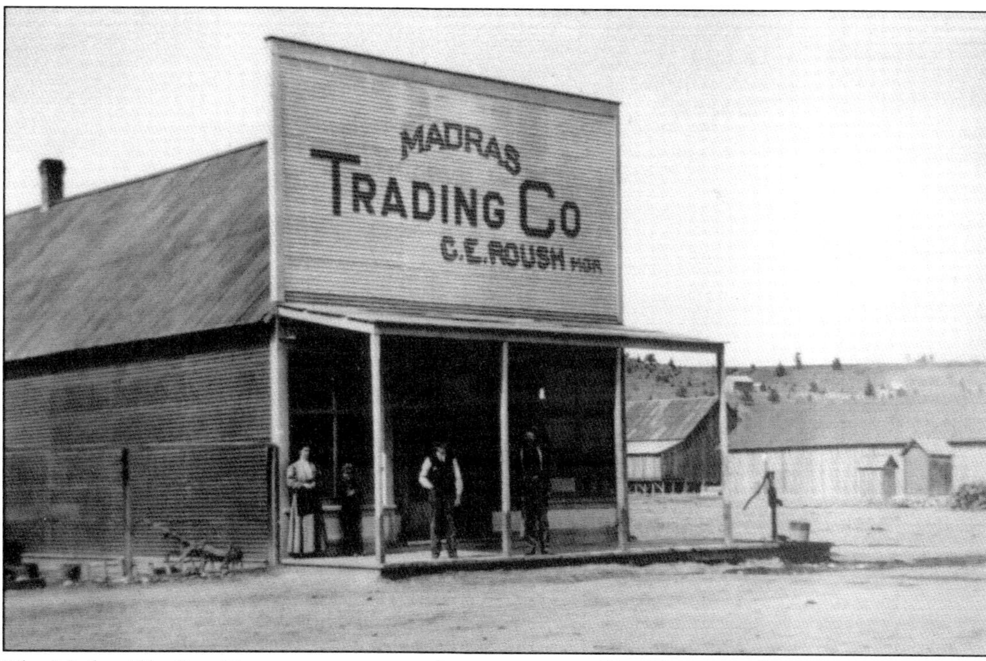

The Madras Trading Company, a mercantile store operated by Chester and Katherine Roush, was established in 1907 on the west side of Fifth Street between B and C Streets. Chester operated the business until 1926. From left to right on the porch are Katherine, son Chester, unidentified, and Chester Roush. Note the water pump to the right of the boardwalk.

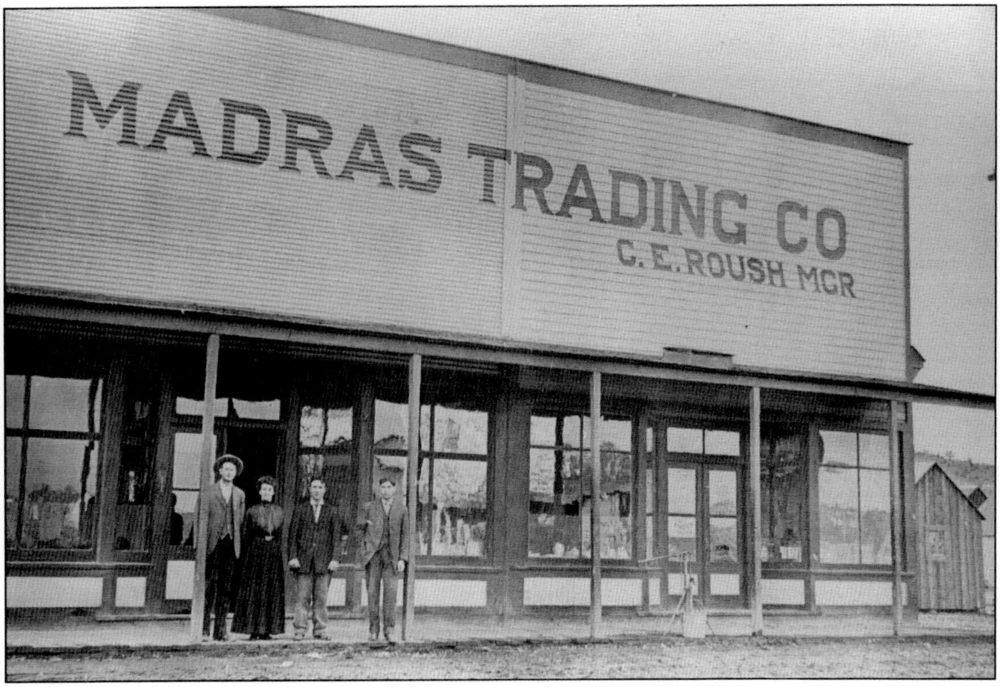

The Roushs expanded their Madras Trading Company store in 1909. Here, they pose in front of it. The photograph includes, from left to right, Chester Roush, Katherine Roush, Milton Pilette, and store employee Samuel Gray.

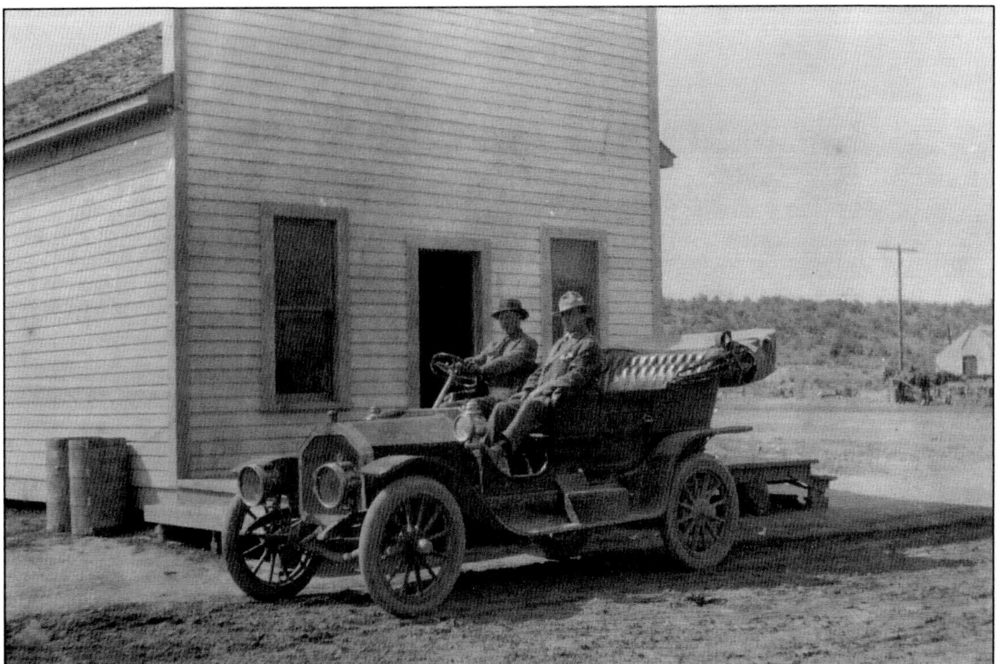

John Moore (driving) and Howard Turner drive past the *Madras Pioneer* newspaper office in 1909, the year Turner bought the building. The building was constructed in 1904 by Max Luddeman on the south side of D Street between Fourth and Fifth Streets.

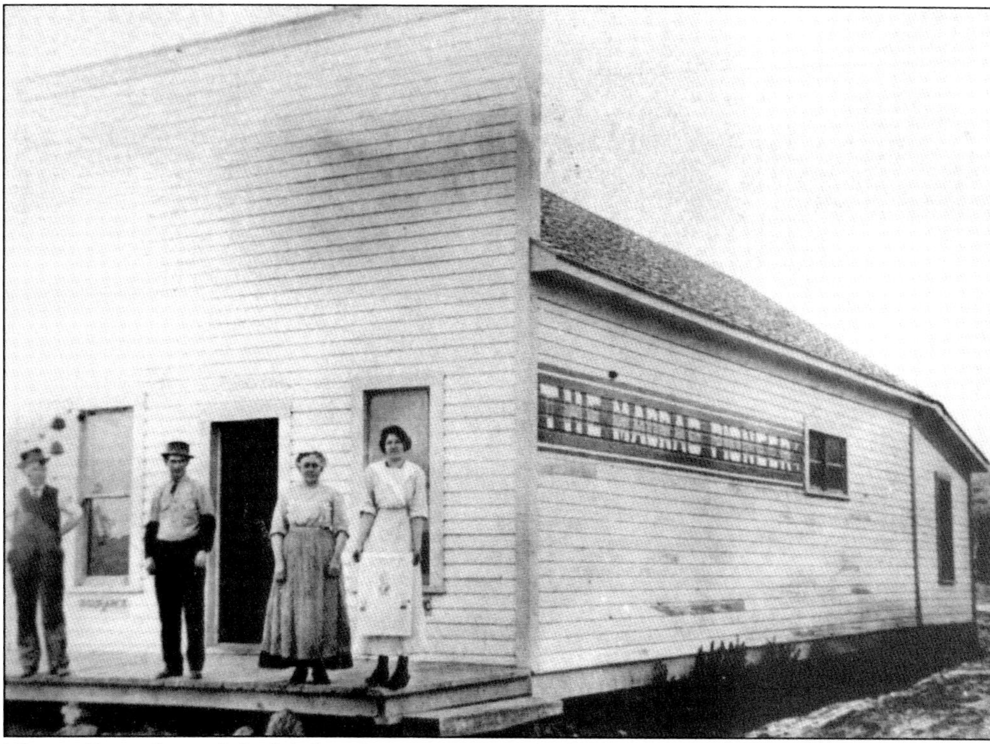

The staff members of the *Madras Pioneer* pose on the boardwalk in front of the office in 1908.

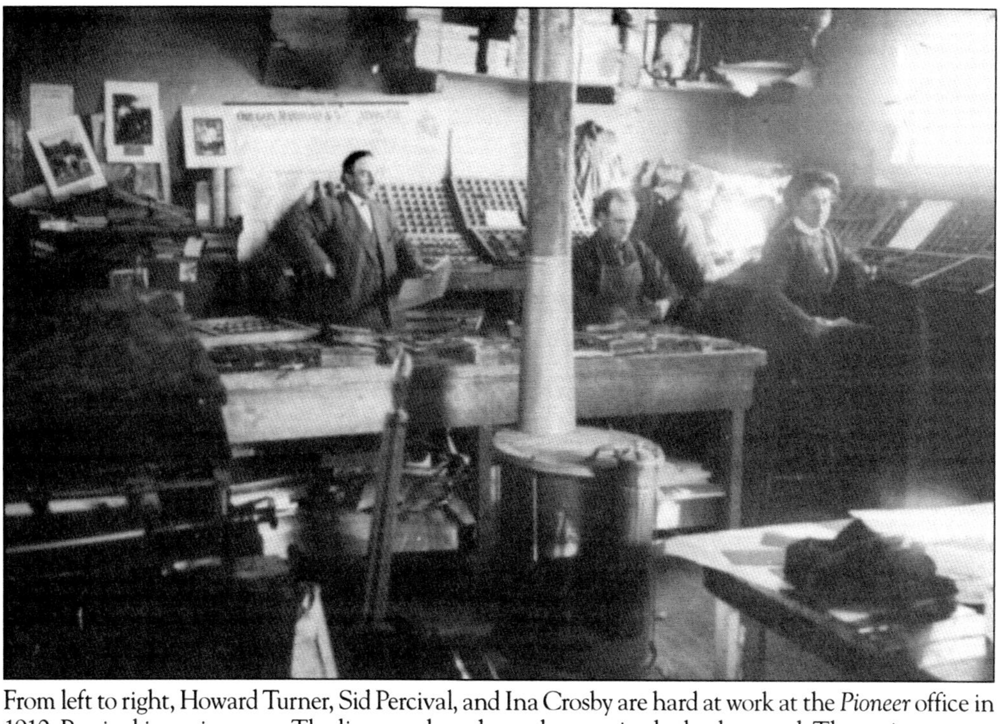

From left to right, Howard Turner, Sid Percival, and Ina Crosby are hard at work at the *Pioneer* office in 1910. Percival is setting type. The linotype boards can be seen in the background. The main revenue sources for the paper at this time were homestead land claim notices and advertisements.

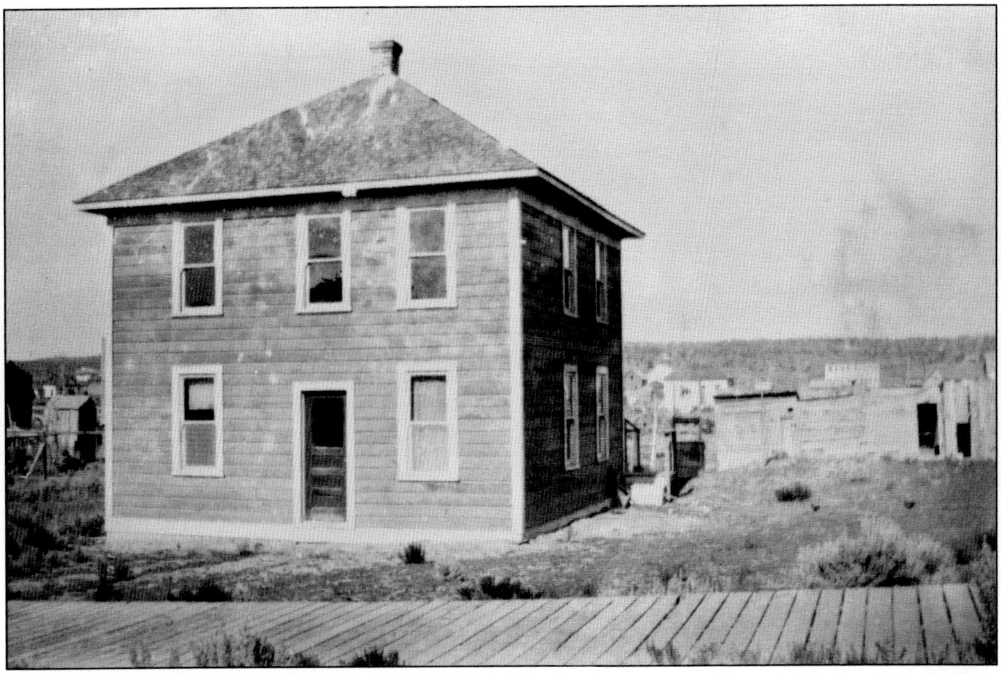

Keys Business School, seen here in 1909, was operated to instruct students in business and office management. The school only occupied one floor of this building and was not in operation long. In 1915, this building served as a hospital.

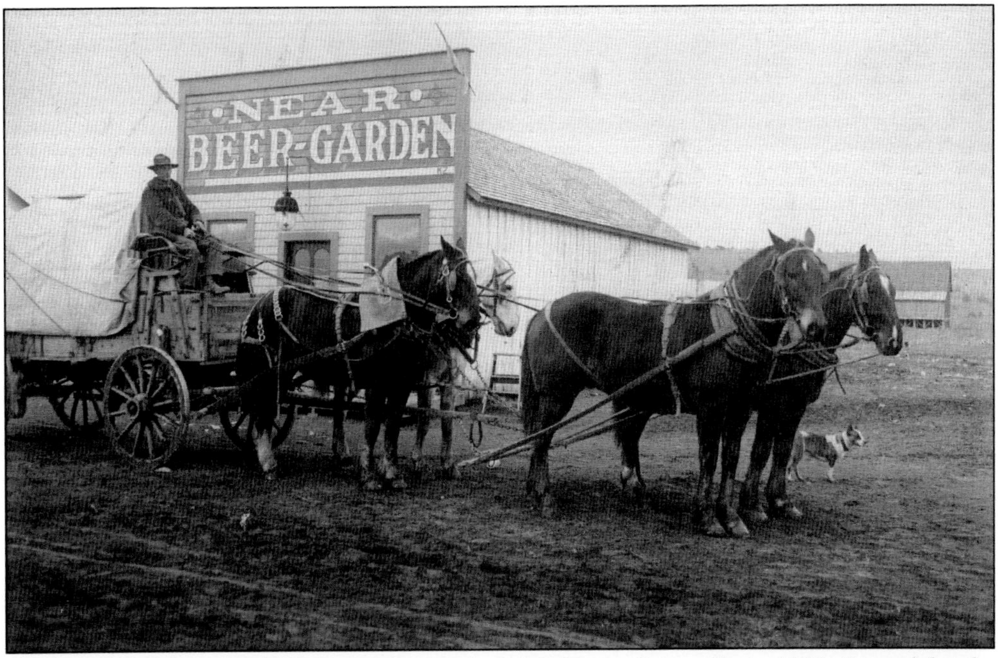

John Evick drives a freight wagon en route from Madras to Prineville in 1908. Several freight lines operated through Madras, and many local homesteaders supplemented their income by working for freight companies or hauling freight on their own. The Near Beer-Garden is behind the freight wagon.

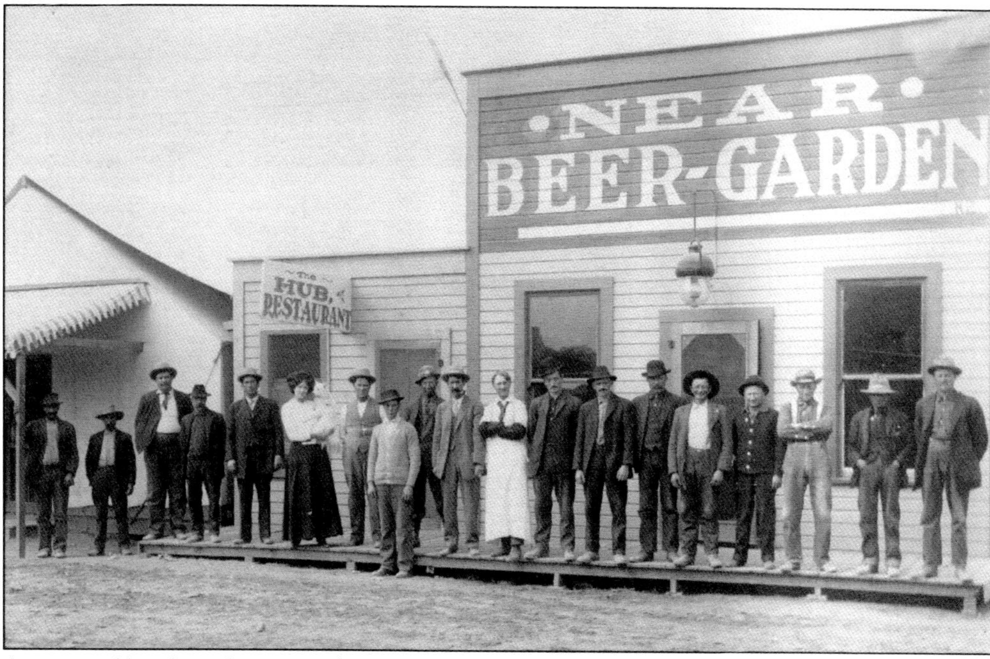

A group of local residents stands along the boardwalk in front of the Hub Restaurant and the Near Beer-Garden about 1909. The Near Beer-Garden was operated by Dave Burden.

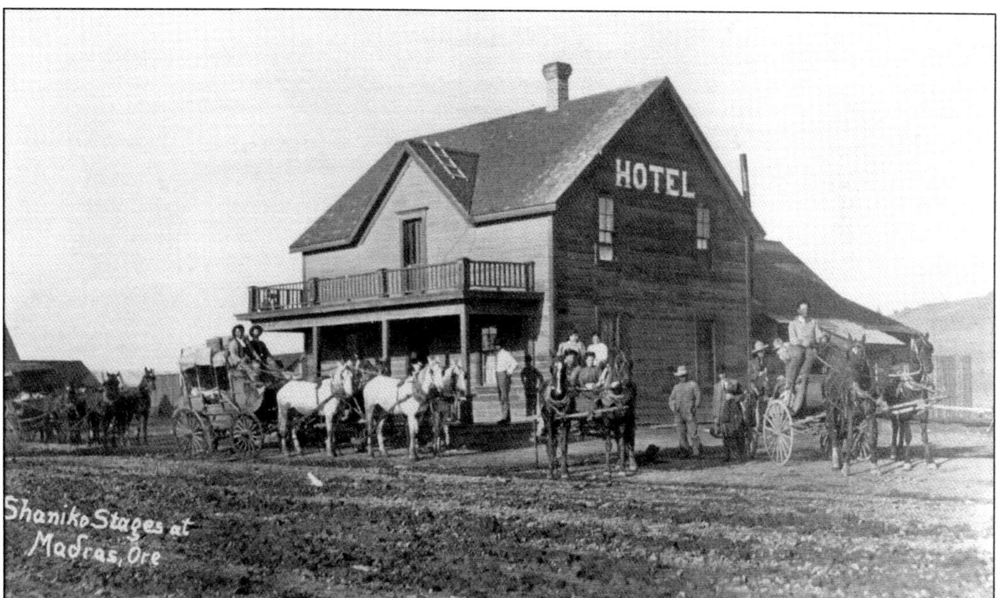

Several stages are in front of the Green Hotel in Madras in 1908. The hotel was located on Fifth Street between A and B Streets. The stages operated between Prineville and Shaniko with various stops along the route including Madras.

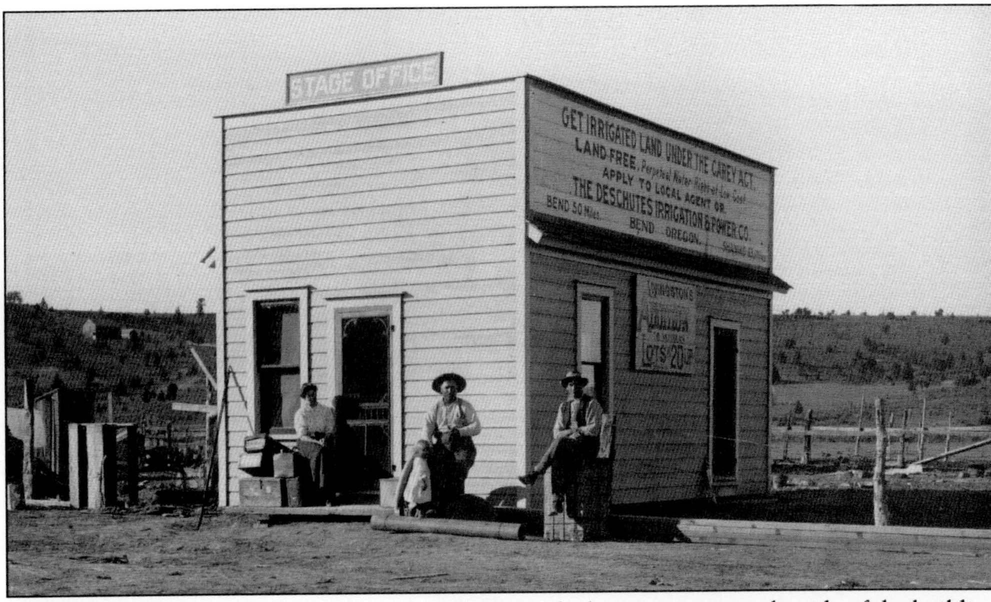

The Madras Stage station is seen here in 1909. Painted advertisements on the side of the building promote the Deschutes Irrigation and Power Company in Bend and the opportunity to purchase Carey Act lands with irrigation water available. Also, lots in the Livingston Addition in Madras are advertised for $20 and up. From left to right are Marie Dizney, Lester Mineor, and driver James Sears.

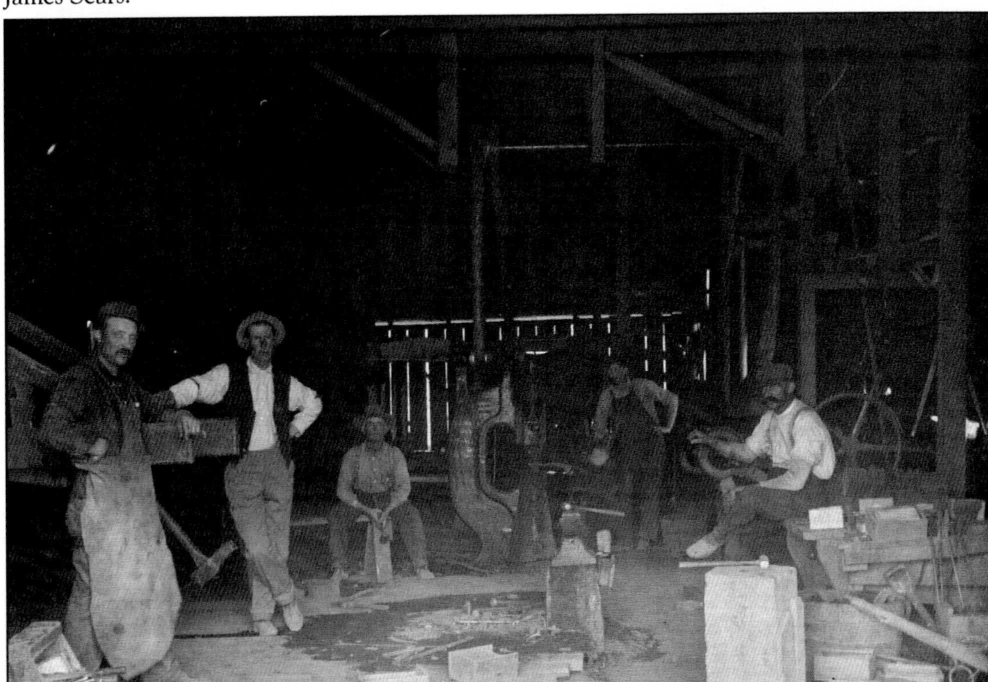

A.W. Culp (second from left) stands with other unidentified men in the Tucker blacksmith shop in 1905. The shop was owned by Tom Tucker, who drowned in 1918 while fishing on the Deschutes River near Vanora.

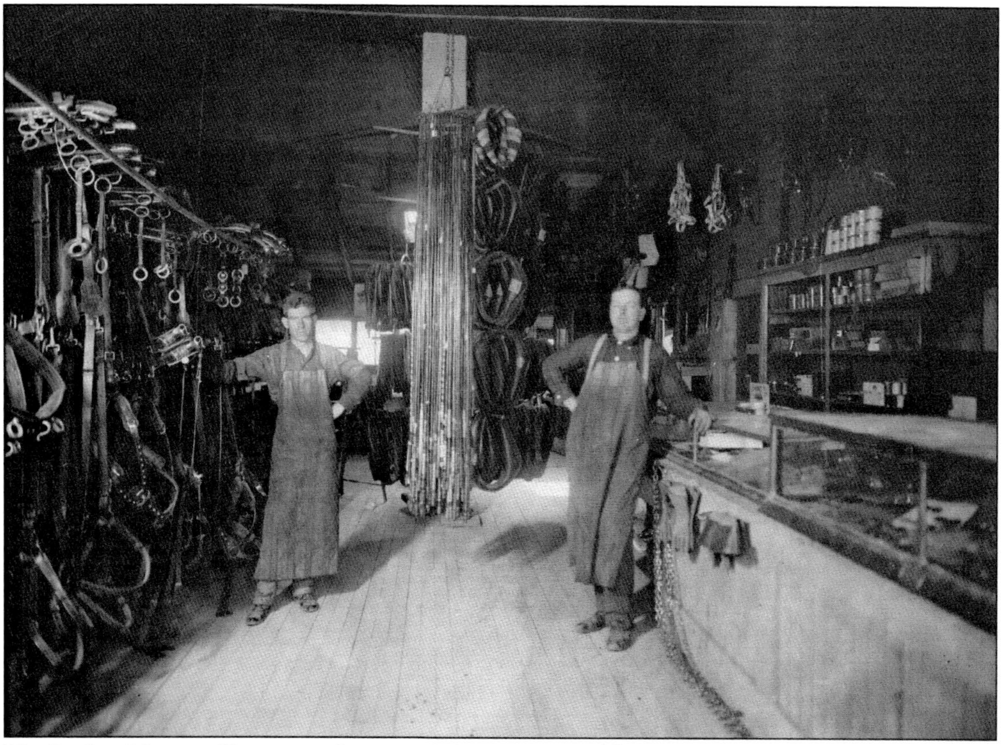

The Larkin Harness Shop, seen here in 1910, was operated by Benjamin Larkin, who established his shop on the corner of Fourth and C Streets. The harness shop sold most accessories needed for horses, included harnesses, bridles, and horse collars. Larkin operated businesses in several locations in Madras. Employee Ed Mason is on the left, and Larkin is on the right.

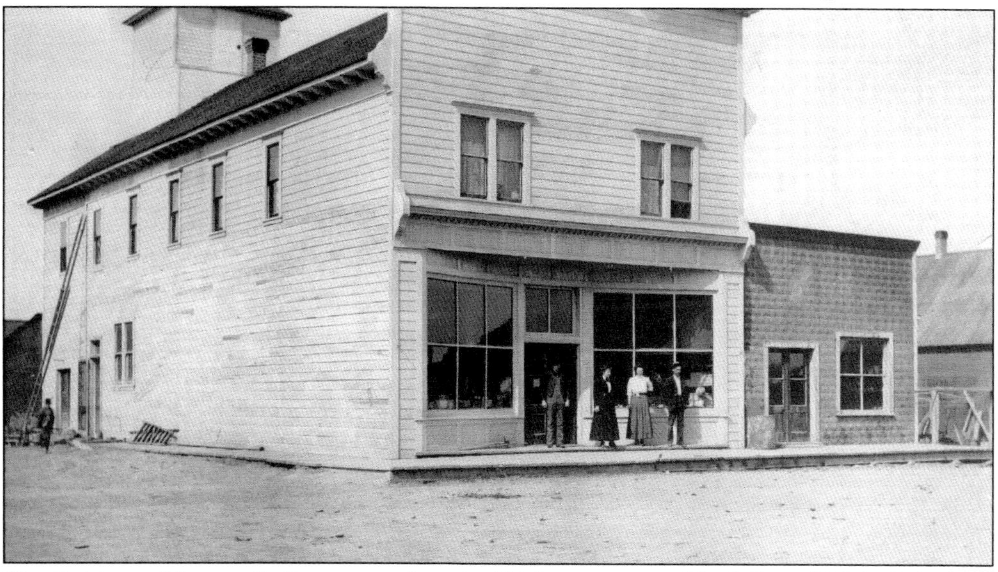

The Robinson Mercantile Store, seen here in 1906, was operated by J.C. and M.A. Robinson. The store, at the corner of Fifth and C Streets, carried a wide variety of merchandise. In 1910, the Robinsons sold the business, and it became known as the Central Oregon Mercantile Company. The building burned in 1939.

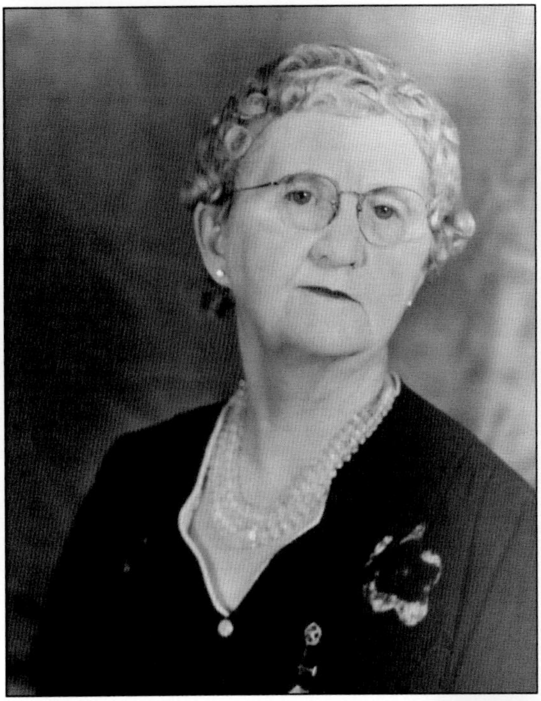

May Benson Johnson, owner of the *Madras Pioneer* newspaper from 1924 to 1947, was an early entrepreneur in Madras who also served as postmaster from 1933 to 1948. Her husband, William F. Johnson, was a cashier in a local bank and an editor of the *Madras Pioneer* who died before she purchased it.

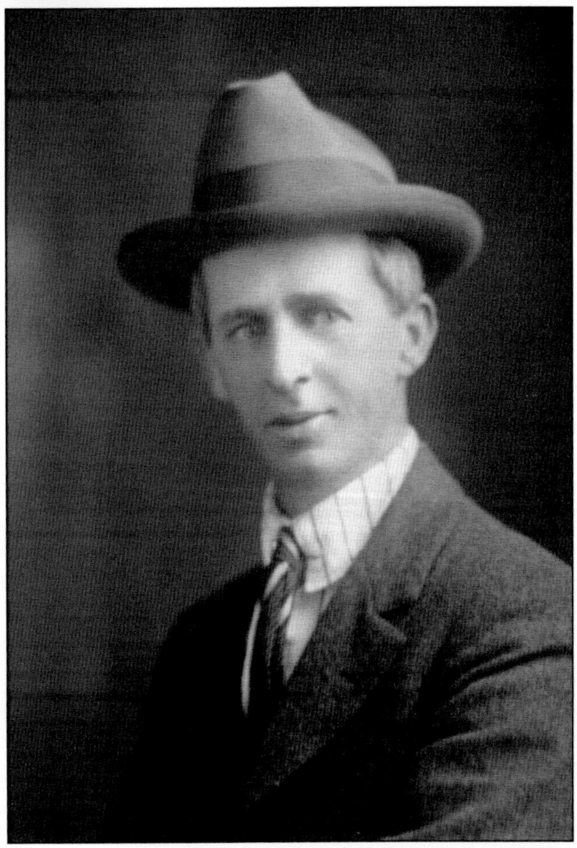

Lewis "Turk" Irving came to Madras in 1910 and established a law office. He later became involved in the grain industry and owned a chain of warehouses as well as Turk's Texaco service station on Fifth Street. He was active in local affairs and served as mayor of Madras during World War I.

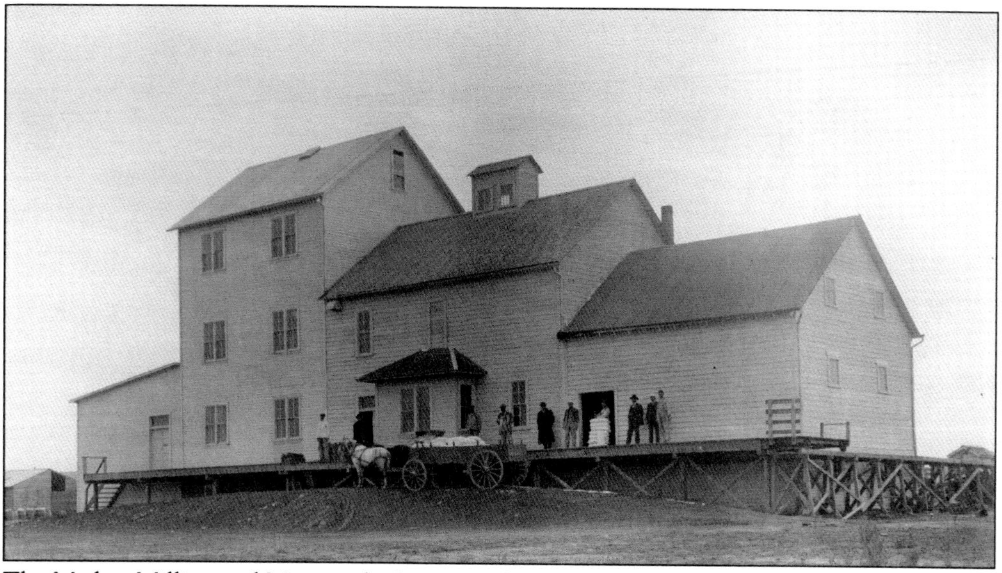

The Madras Milling and Mercantile Company, between Third and Fourth Streets on C Street, is seen here around 1910. The flour mill was first organized in 1904 by Max Putz, Henry Dietzel, and Simon Conroy and was one of the largest industries in central Oregon for several years. It was destroyed by fire in 1924.

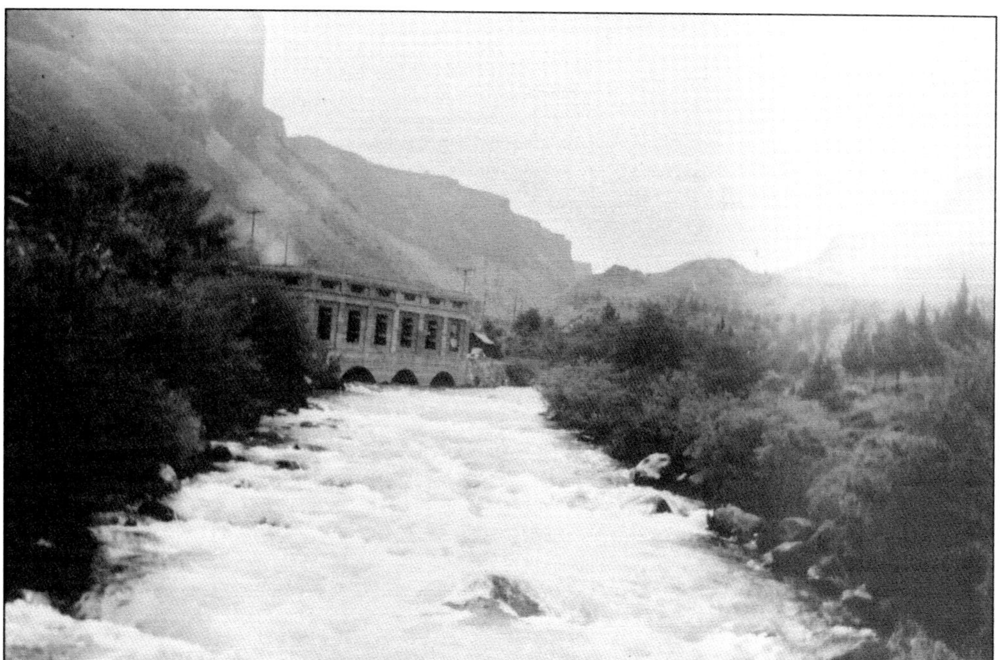

The Cove Power Plant on Crooked River, built by the Deschutes Power Company in 1913, is seen here about 1915. It provided the first electric power to Madras on April 15, 1913. The facility was later obtained by Pacific Power Company, and its capacity was increased. It operated until Round Butte Dam was constructed; it is now under the waters of Lake Billy Chinook.

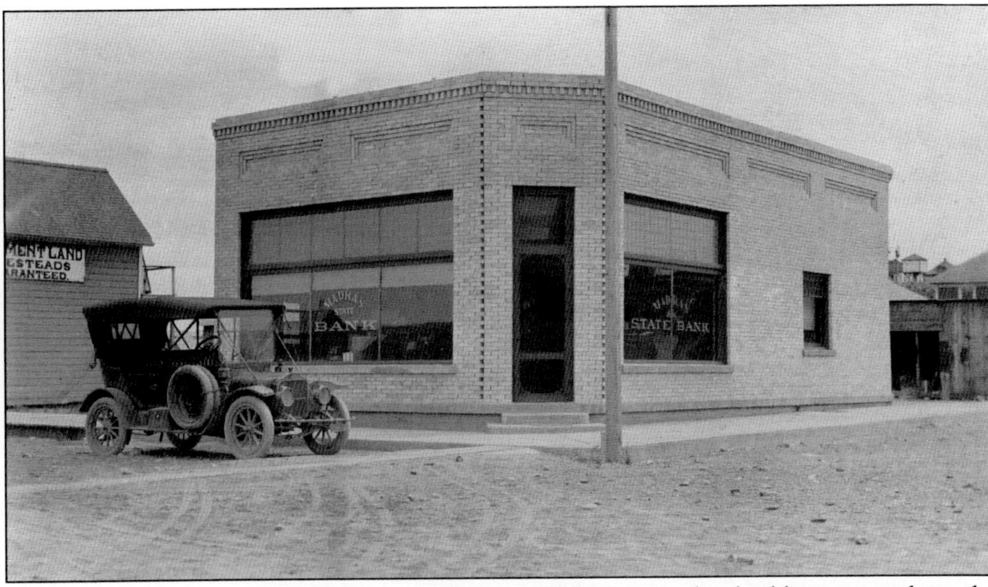

Madras State Bank was originally established in 1909 in a wooden building across from the Green Hotel, but this brick building was built in 1911 at the corner of Fifth and D Streets. The bank was forced out of business in 1926 after years of drought and crop failures forced farmers to default on their assistance loans.

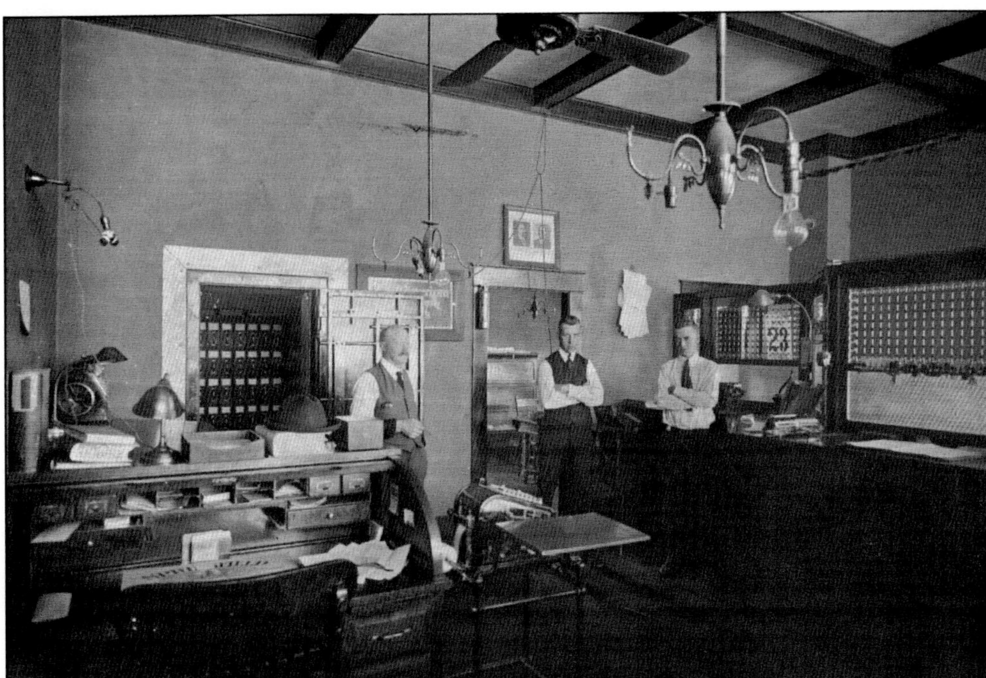

Richard Olson (left) and two other men stand inside the Madras State Bank around 1912. The bank became the First National Bank of Madras in 1926.

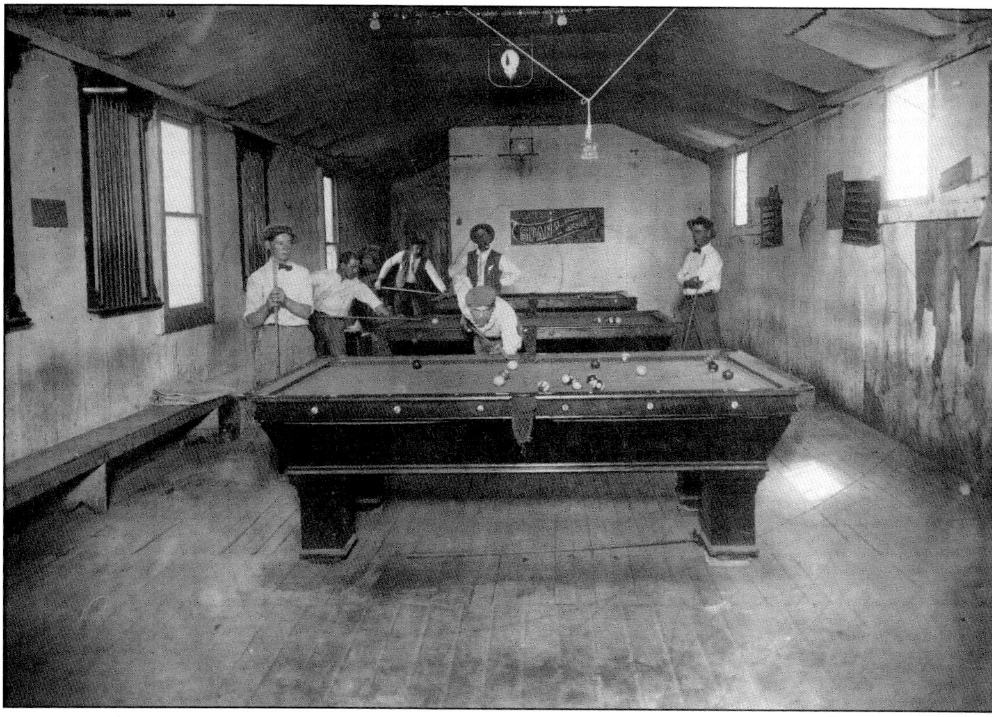

Austin Culp stands between the second and third pool table with his hands on his hips at the Culp Pool Hall around 1910. The business was located in the Sanford building.

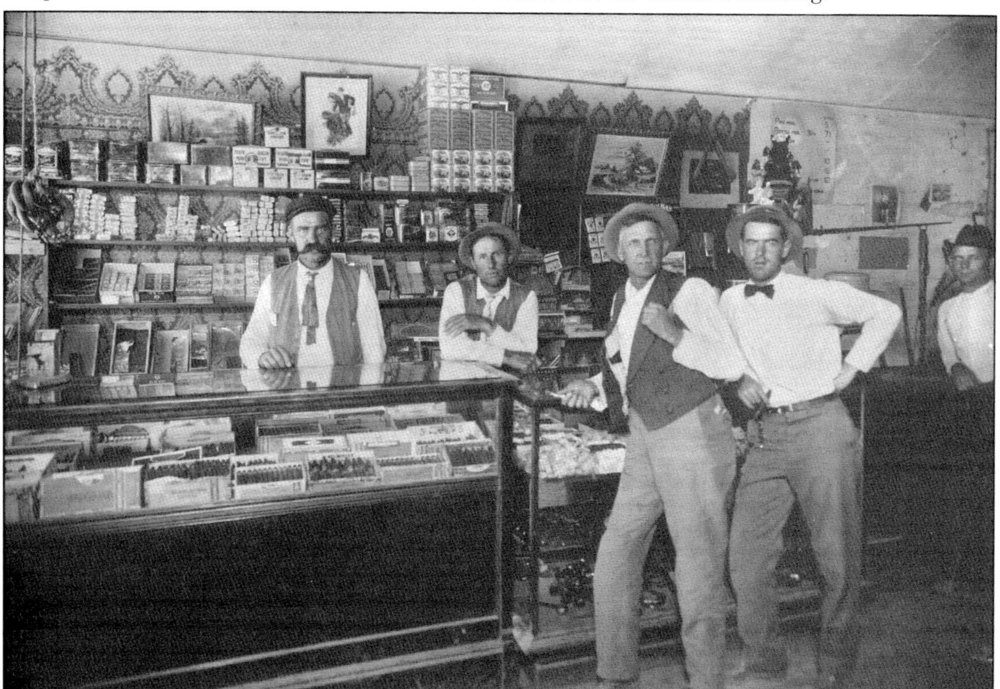

Cigars and other tobacco products were displayed for sale at the Culp Pool Hall around 1910. Austin Culp is second from the left behind the counter in this photograph.

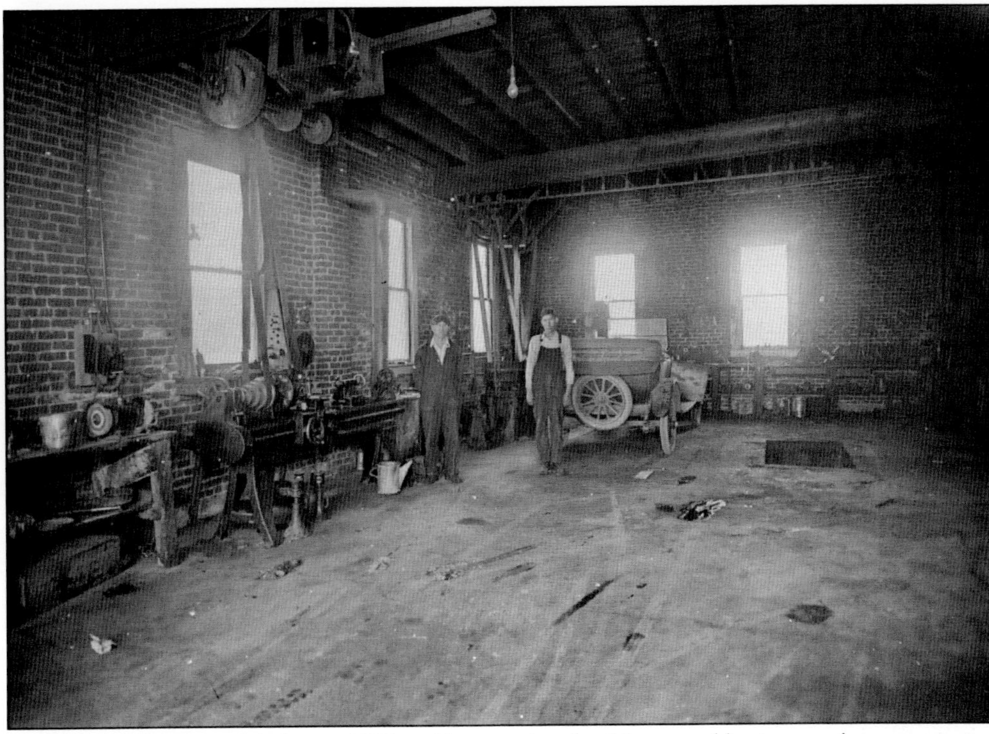

Douglas Hood came to Madras in 1906 and became involved in several businesses, later partnering with John Conroy to establish the Main Street Garage, seen here in 1915.

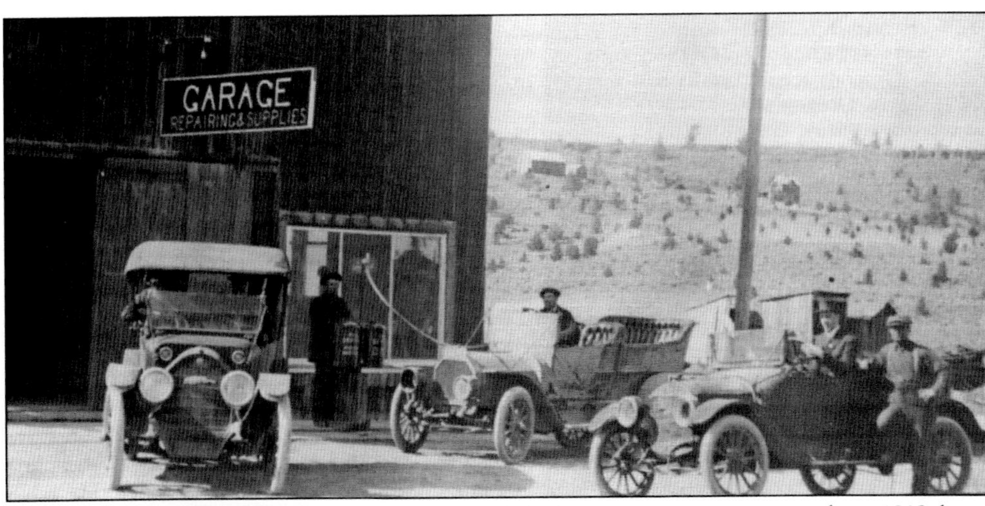

John Conroy and Roy Newell partnered to establish this automotive garage in about 1913, but it only operated for a short time.

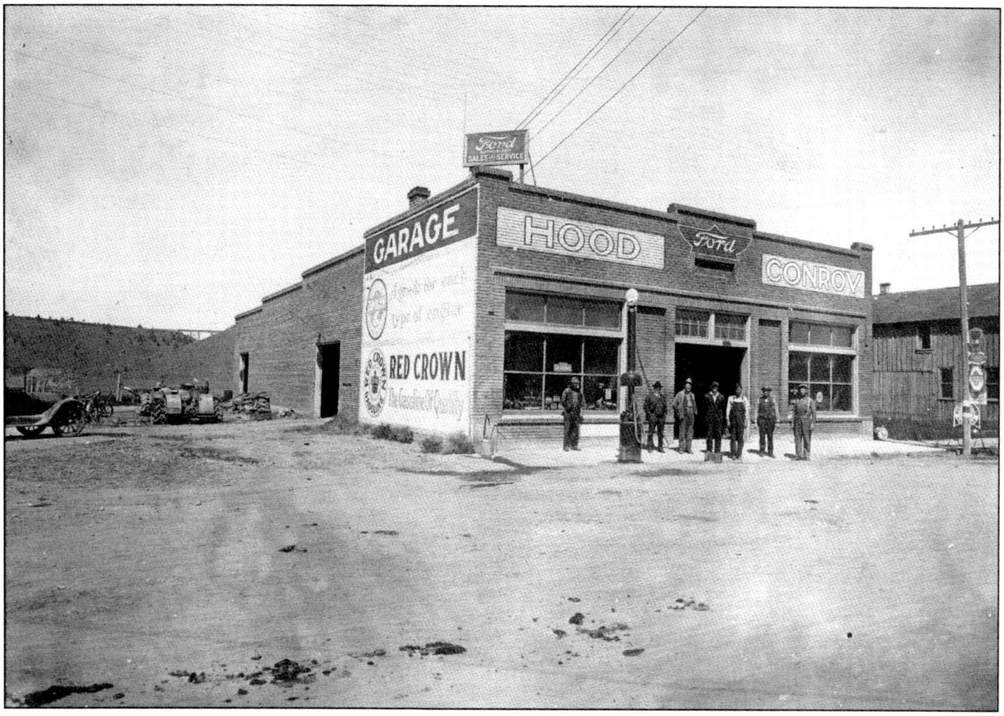

Employees of Hood and Conroy's Main Street Garage pose in 1916. Note the early gas pump in front of the structure. The men are unidentified but it is believed that John Conroy is second from left and Douglas Hood is second from right.

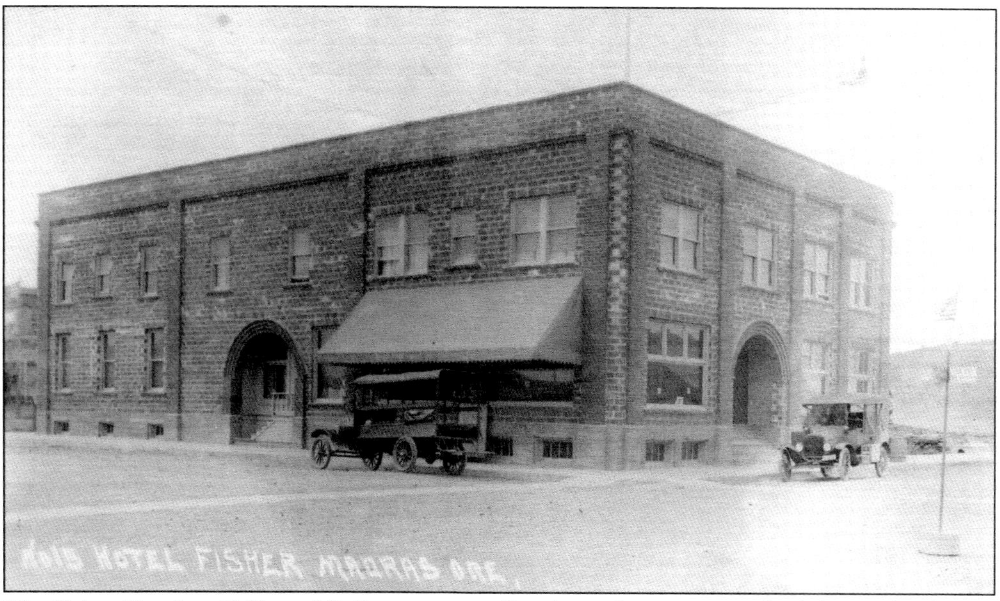

The Fisher Hotel, at Fifth and D Streets—now Sunshine Corners—was built by Fred Fisher in 1916. He sold the hotel in 1922, and it became known as the Hotel Jefferson. It had several owners over the next several years and was known as Bellamy House and the Hotel Madras before fire destroyed the building in 1957.

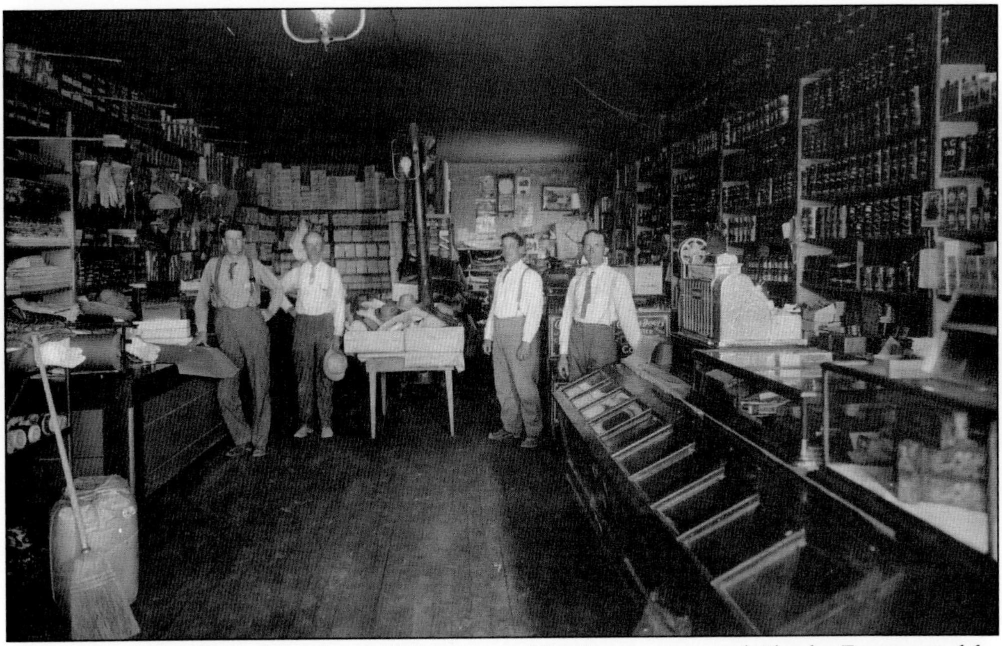

From left to right, Wade Silex, Louis Folkenhagen, Dan Rasmussen, and Charles Foote posed for this photograph at the Central Oregon Mercantile Company, previously Robinson Mercantile Store, around 1915.

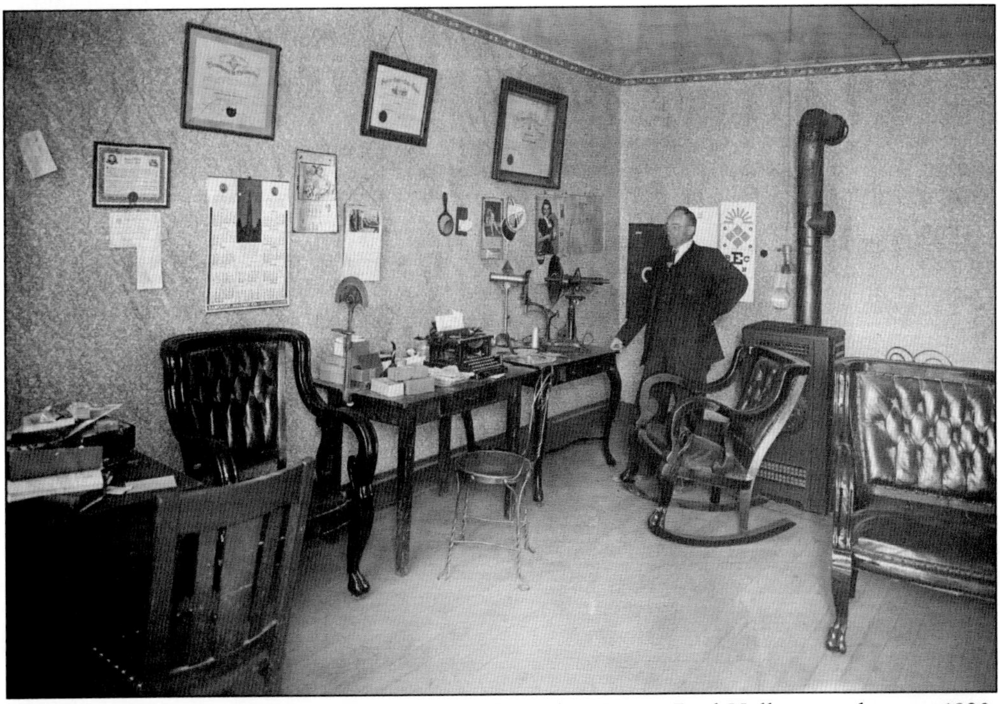

Dr. Victor Howard's optometry office upstairs from the Nugget Pool Hall is seen here in 1930. Dr. Howard was trained as an optometrist and also received a law degree from the University of Oregon. He served as Jefferson County district attorney from 1931 to 1935 and was active in several local social and service organizations.

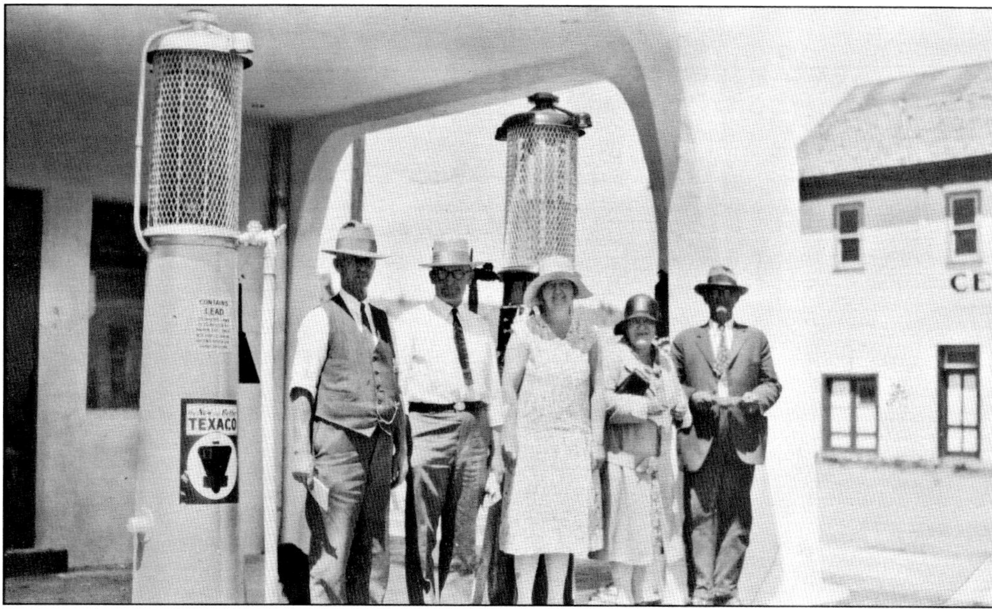

From left to right, Lewis "Turk" Irving, owner of Turk's Texaco, an unidentified couple, Lillie Turner, and Howard Turner stand in front of the station in 1935.

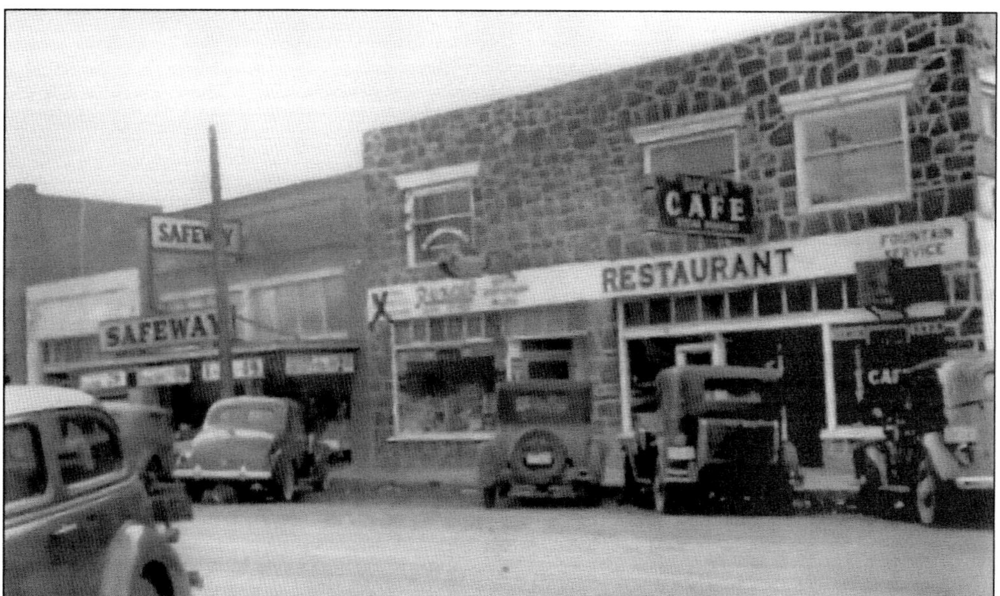

This view, looking toward the west side of Fifth Street between D and C Streets in 1947, shows Safeway Grocery on the left, with Rexall Drug Store just north of Safeway, and Dick's Café to the right.

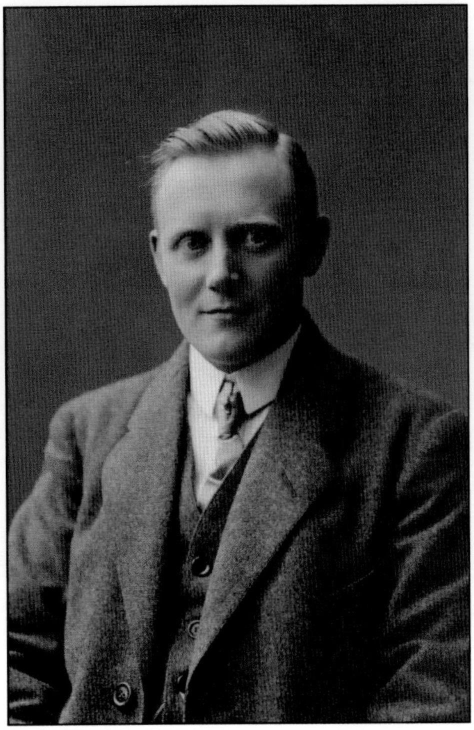

John Olaf "Ole" Hedlund was a photographer in central Oregon and ran a photography shop in Madras from 1909 until 1912. He specialized in postcard photographs, and he extensively photographed the arrival of the Oregon Trunk Railroad. Hedlund sold thousands of postcards to local homesteaders and provided a remarkable photographic history of the area, much of which is published in this book. Hedlund left Madras in 1913.

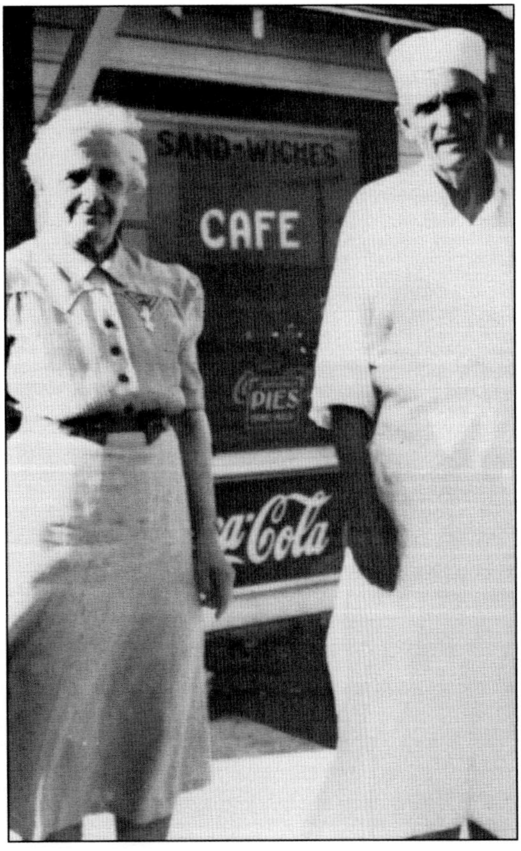

Edith and William Moore, in front of their Cactus Inn Café in 1942, had homesteaded north of Madras in 1904, and in 1912, William bought the Madras Hotel. They operated the Cactus Inn Café until William's death in 1942 and were both active in local affairs in Madras.

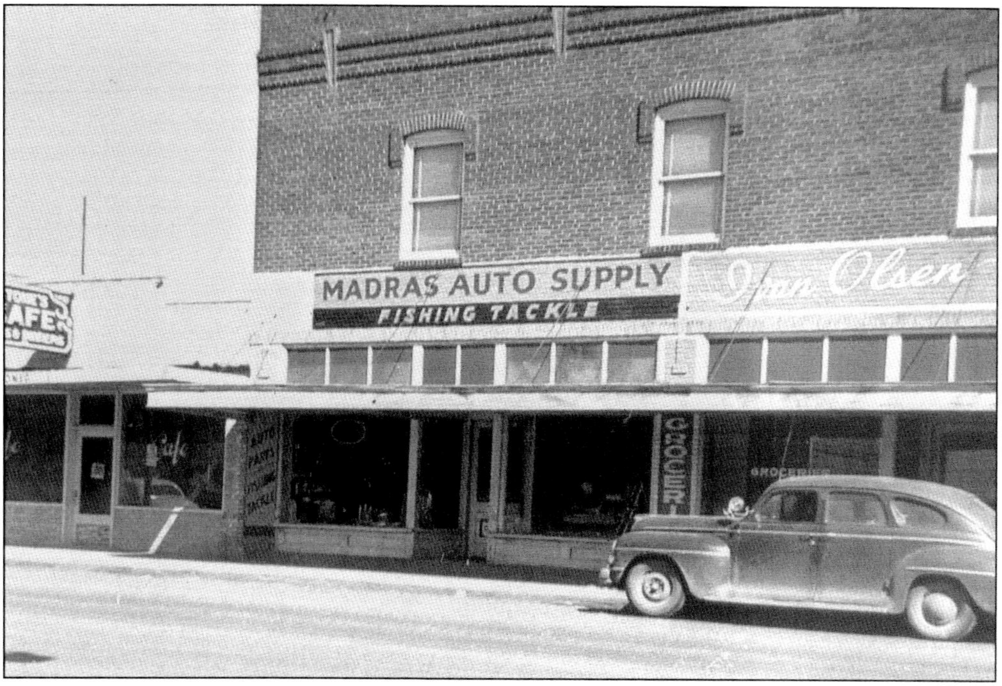

Stone Café is on the left in this view looking east on Fifth Street between C and D Streets in 1946. The brick building houses Madras Auto Supply and Sporting Goods Store, and to the right is Ivan Olsen's Grocery.

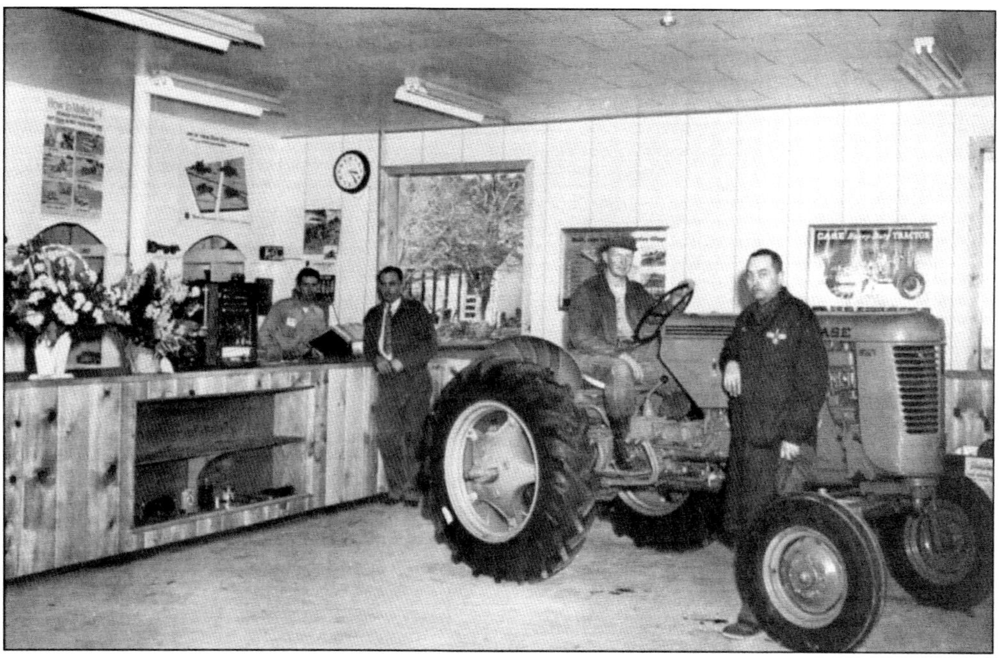

From left to right, Wayne Garren, Paul Jasa, Jewel Treanor, and Leland Otey are seen inside the Jasa Implement Company in 1949. Paul bought the Case Implement dealership in 1949 and moved to Madras. In the early 1950s, the business sold up to 50 combines a year for two years. He sold the business in 1957.

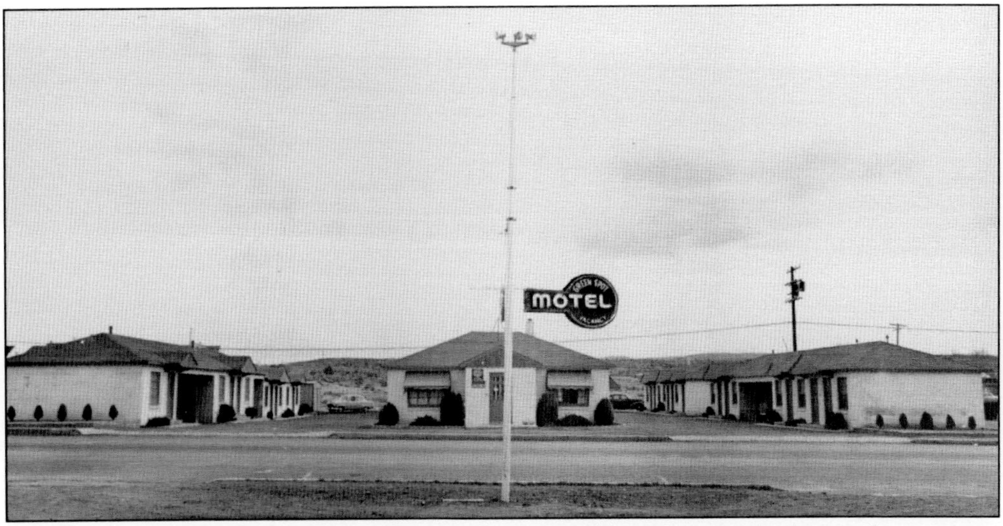

The Green Spot Motel in south Madras, seen here in 1955, was among the first in the region to be known as a motel. It provided a rest stop for travelers on The Dalles-California Highway (now Highway 97) and the Warm Springs Highway (now Highway 26).

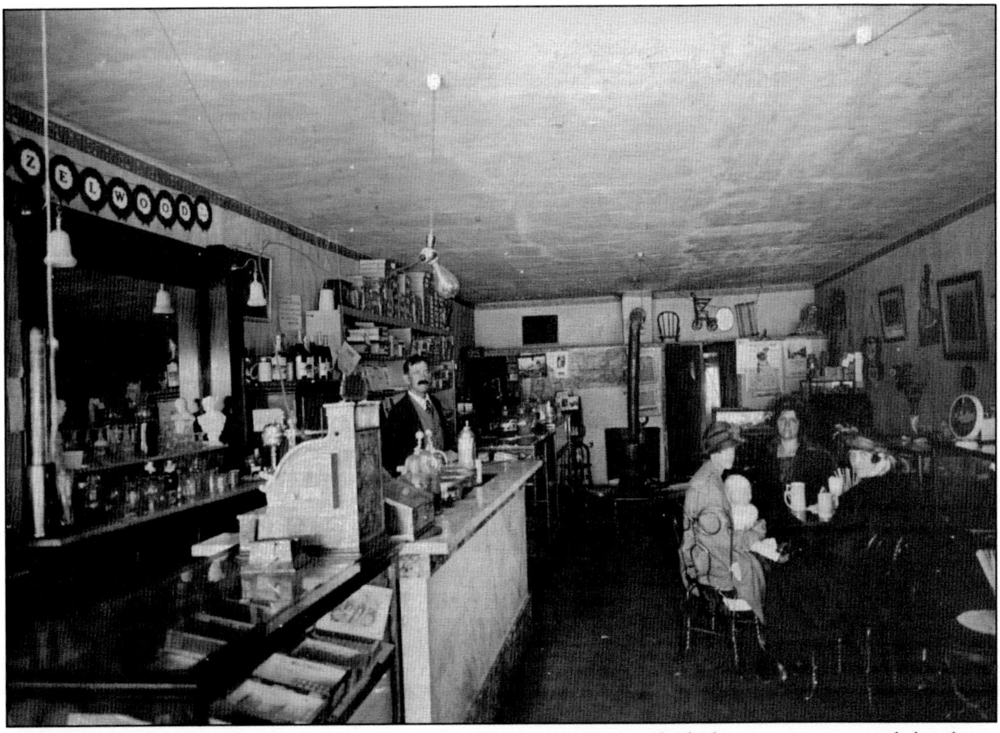

Pictured is the Sugar Bowl Café around 1933. Three women and a baby are visiting and drinking coffee as the proprietor looks on. Seated are Ella Campbell holding a baby, Eliza Oxburrow, and an unidentified woman. Horatio Jennings is behind the counter. He operated the café with his wife, Lillian.

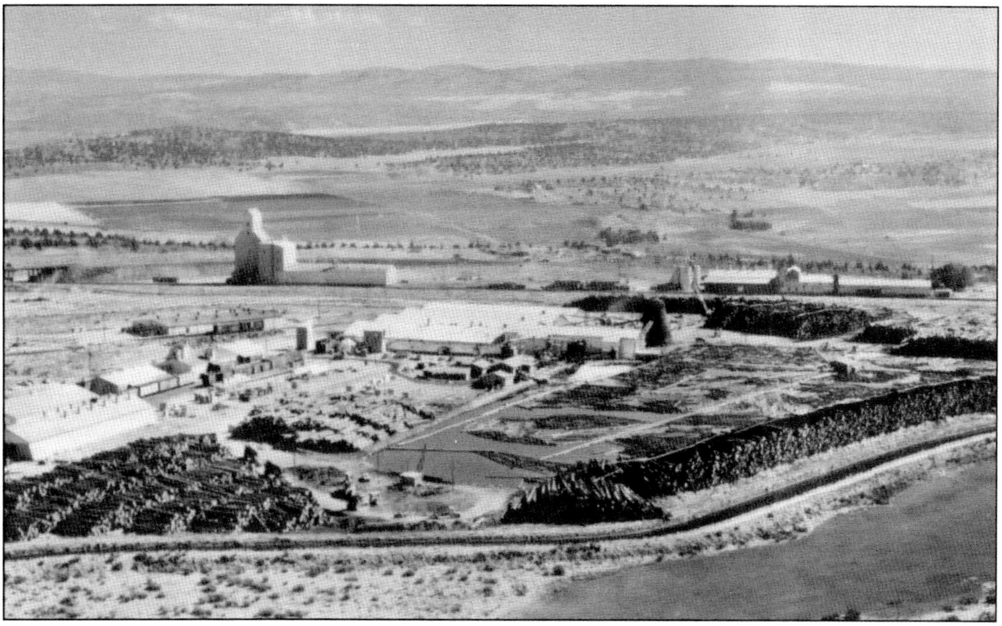

The Jefferson County Plywood Mill, seen here in 1960, was operated by Samuel Johnson and provided many jobs in Madras. The mill was on Agency Plains just north of Madras and west of Highway 26. Johnson sold the mill to the Confederated Tribes of Warm Springs in 1965. The mill equipment was moved to Warm Springs in 1979, and the facilities in Madras were used for lumber storage.

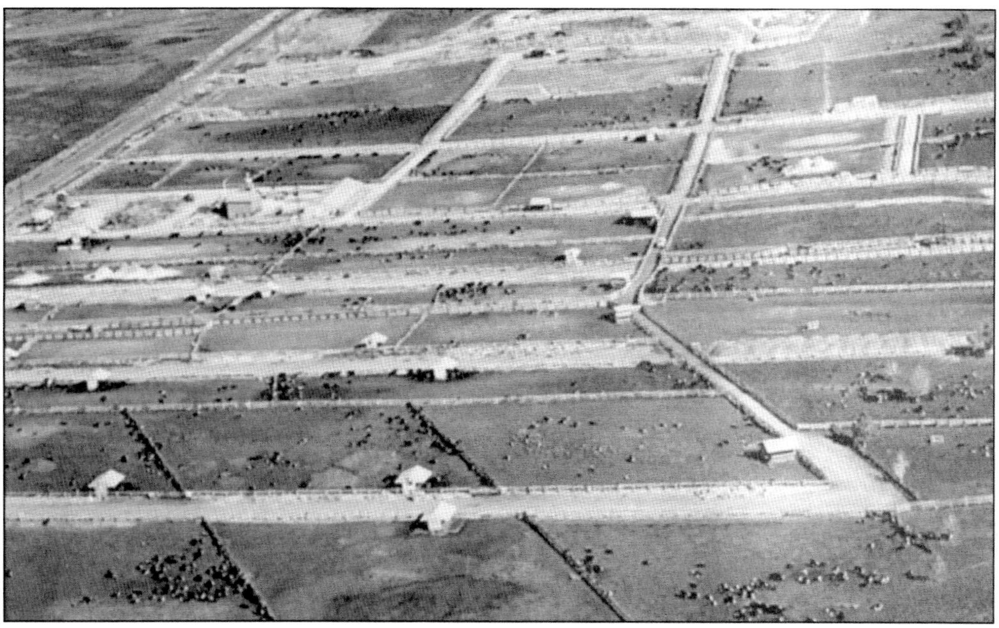

Madras Feed Lot, south of Madras and east of Highway 26, was operated by Earl John and Jack Rayburn and is seen here in 1965. Cattle were brought to the feed lot to fatten them for auction and sales. A livestock auction began in Madras and was a focal point for livestock sales for all of central Oregon. Livestock auctions continue to be a major activity in the community, although the location has changed.

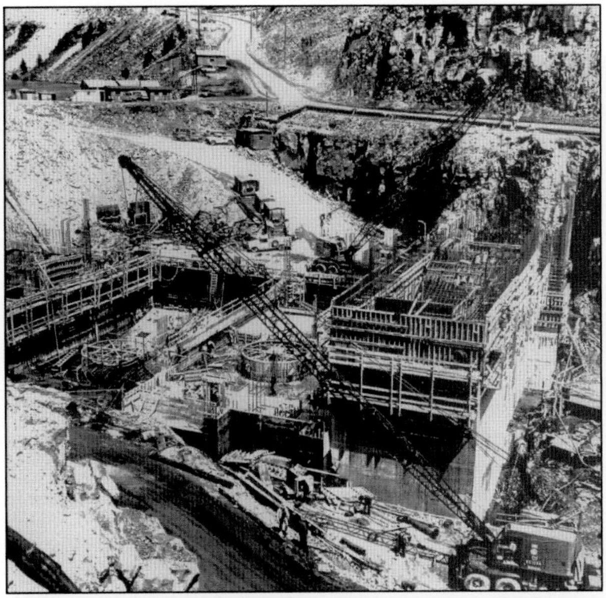

Round Butte Hydroelectric Dam was under construction in 1963, and Portland General Electric completed it a year later. The local economy was boosted by the construction work and there was a short boom in the Madras community. The hydroelectric dam originally produced 300,000 kilowatts of power. The reservoir behind the dam was named Lake Billy Chinook for an early Warm Springs tribal member. The reservoir has become one of the major recreation areas in Oregon and continues to attract tourism money to Madras and the surrounding area.

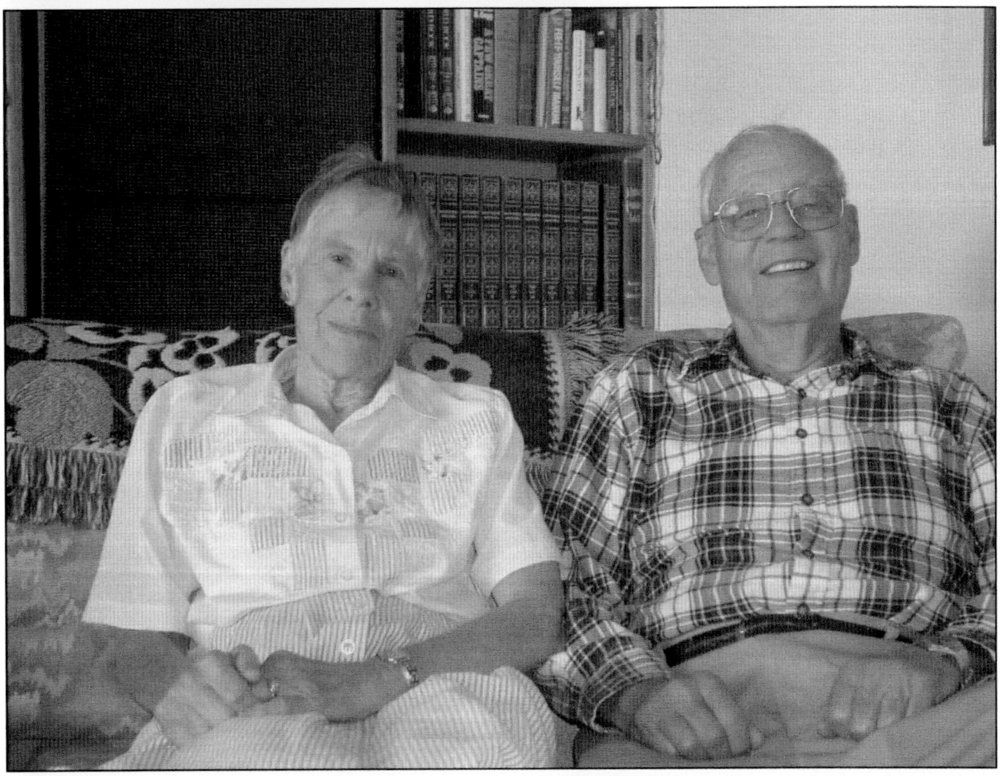

Adala and Sumner Rodriguez relax at their home around 1980. Sumner obtained a law degree from Stanford University in 1949 and established a law office in Madras shortly after his graduation. He became a successful lawyer in the county and was active in local affairs. He was also instrumental in creating the Mt. View Hospital District and helped integrate the Confederated Tribes of Warm Springs into the Jefferson County school district. He and Adala established a scholarship fund for local students to attend college.

Six

WATER FOR A THIRSTY LAND

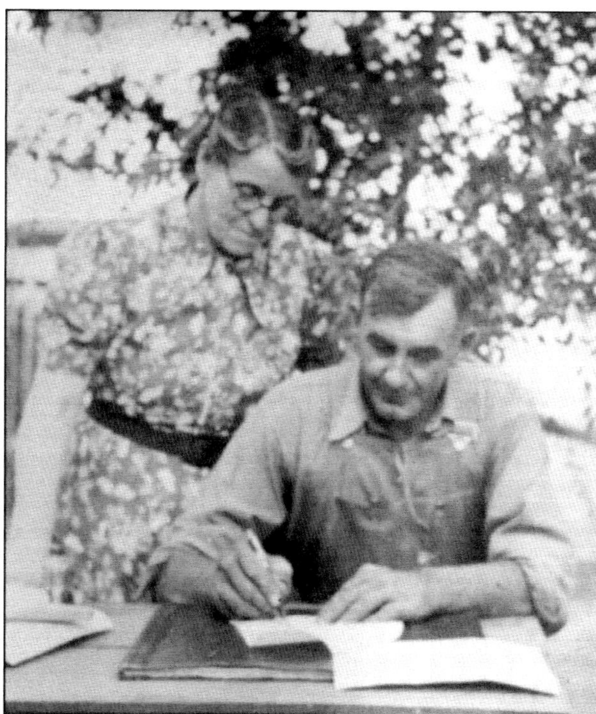

Dry land farming developed in the Basin and the areas surrounding Madras around 1900. Some farmers became prosperous and productive by growing dry land crops such as wheat and rye, but intensive agriculture was not possible without irrigation water. As early as 1913, unsuccessful attempts were made to divert water from the Deschutes River to the vicinity. Finally, after a long process, irrigation water arrived via the North Unit Project in 1946. Allie and Ward Farrell are seen here signing the first water contract for delivery of water in 1946.

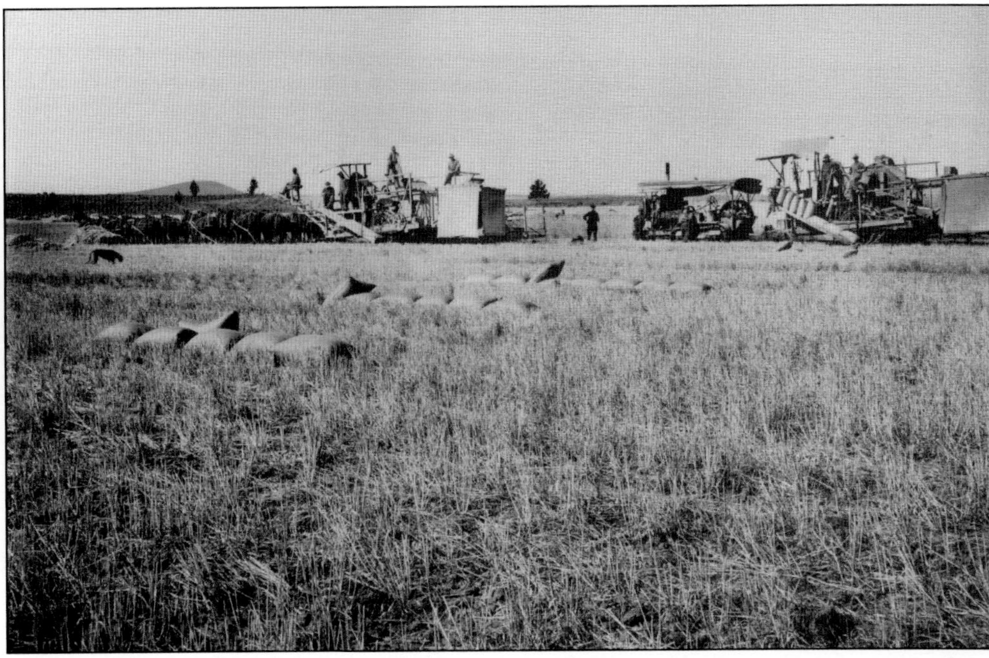

Since there was no irrigation in the Madras vicinity, the most common crop was winter wheat. Seed would be planted in the fall, and spring weather provided the necessary moisture to grow the wheat, which is seen here in 1910. Many acres of winter wheat were planted in the immediate area around Madras.

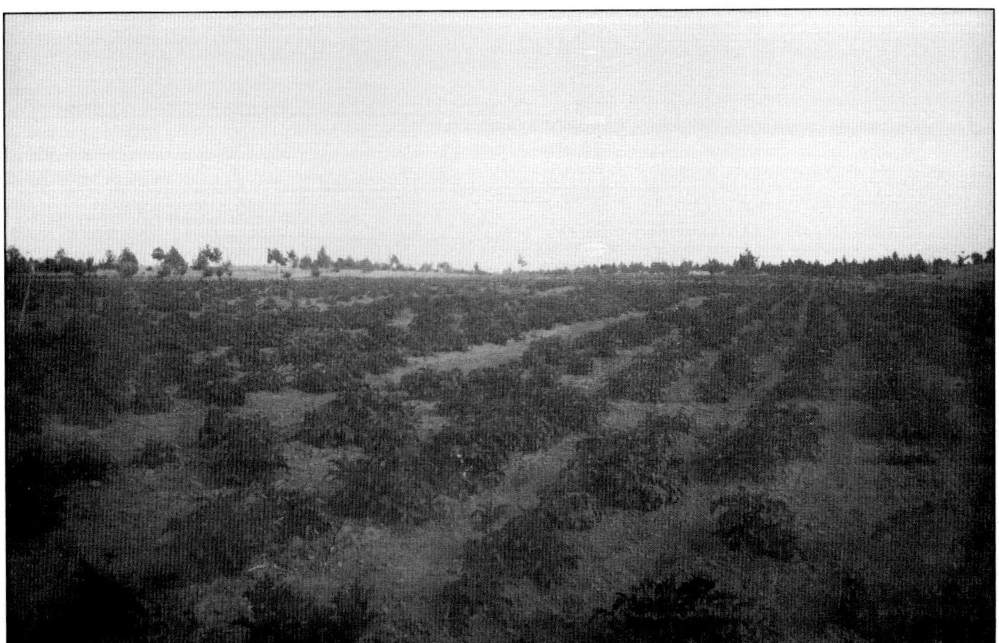

Another common crop in the arid land of central Oregon near Madras was dry crop peas. This field is on Agency Plains just north of Madras. Many farmers produced a variety of crops but were limited in what they could grow, and several years of drought in the early to mid-1930s forced many farmers to abandon their land claims and either find jobs in Madras or move on.

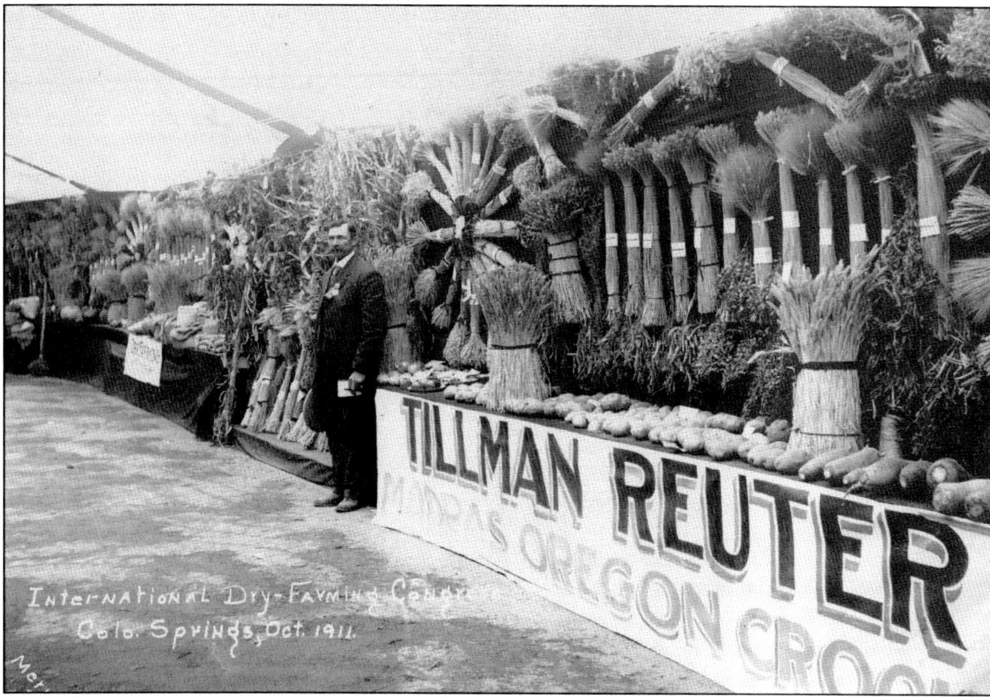

Tillman Reuter was one of the most productive dry land farmers in the Madras vicinity, raising a variety of crops and displaying his produce at fairs and exhibits around the country. He received many awards for his crops and is seen here exhibiting his crops at the International Dry Farming Congress in Colorado Springs, Colorado, in 1911. Other local farmers also contributed produce for his exhibits.

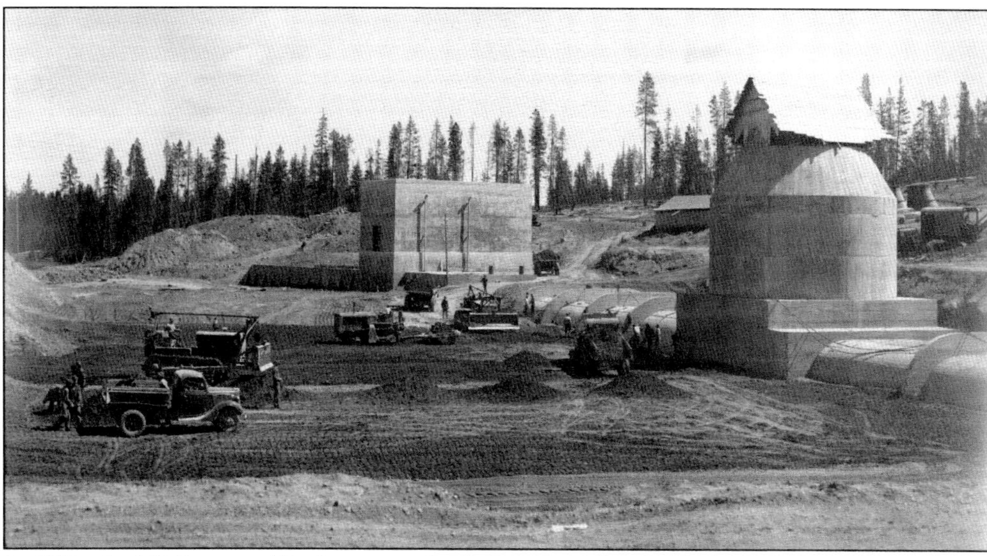

In 1938, the US Bureau of Reclamation finally began work on water storage for the North Unit Project to serve Madras. Construction of Wickiup Dam on the Upper Deschutes River near LaPine was key to securing a water supply for the project. In this photograph, the first stages of construction of the dam are seen. The North Unit Project was named for the delivery of water to the northern portion of central Oregon at Madras.

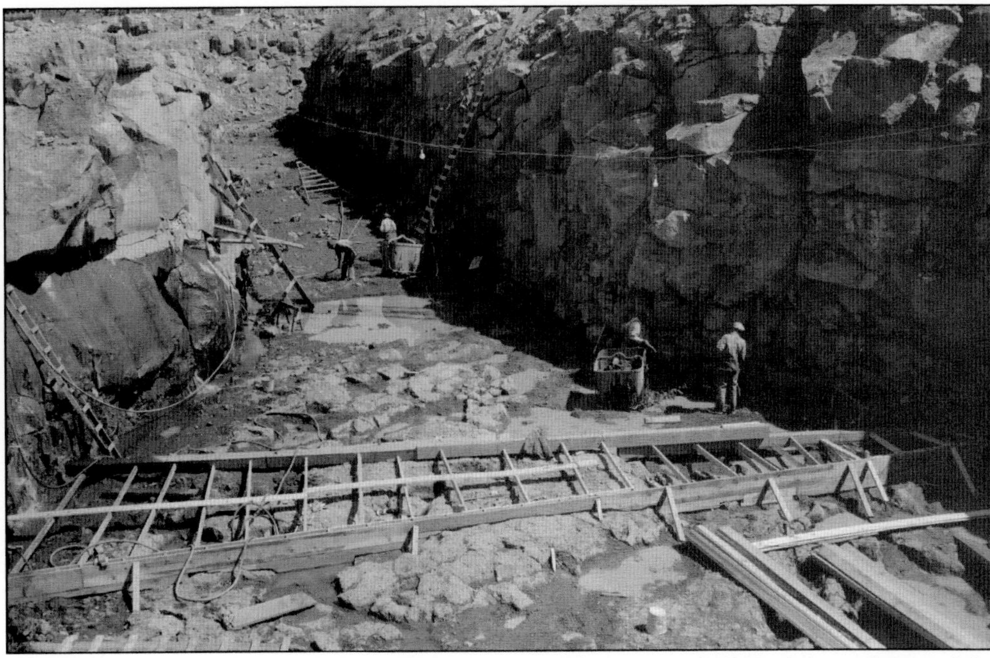

Construction of the North Unit Canal system is seen here around 1940. A critical part of the North Unit Project was the construction of canal feed lines to the farmland north of Redmond. Canal construction began on the north end of Bend on the Deschutes River and continued north. Civilian Conservation Corps (CCC) crews helped with the dam and canal construction.

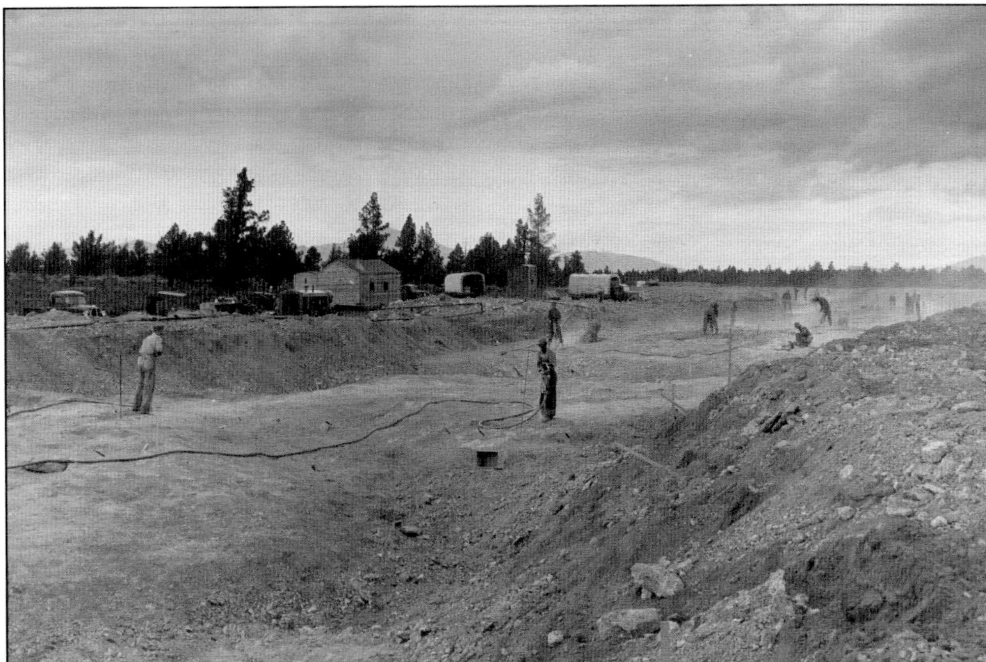

CCC personnel drill into lava bedrock for blasting on the North Unit Canal system just east of Redmond in 1941. Soil depth along the canal was only a few feet so it was a major undertaking to blast through the underlying lava to make a course for irrigation water.

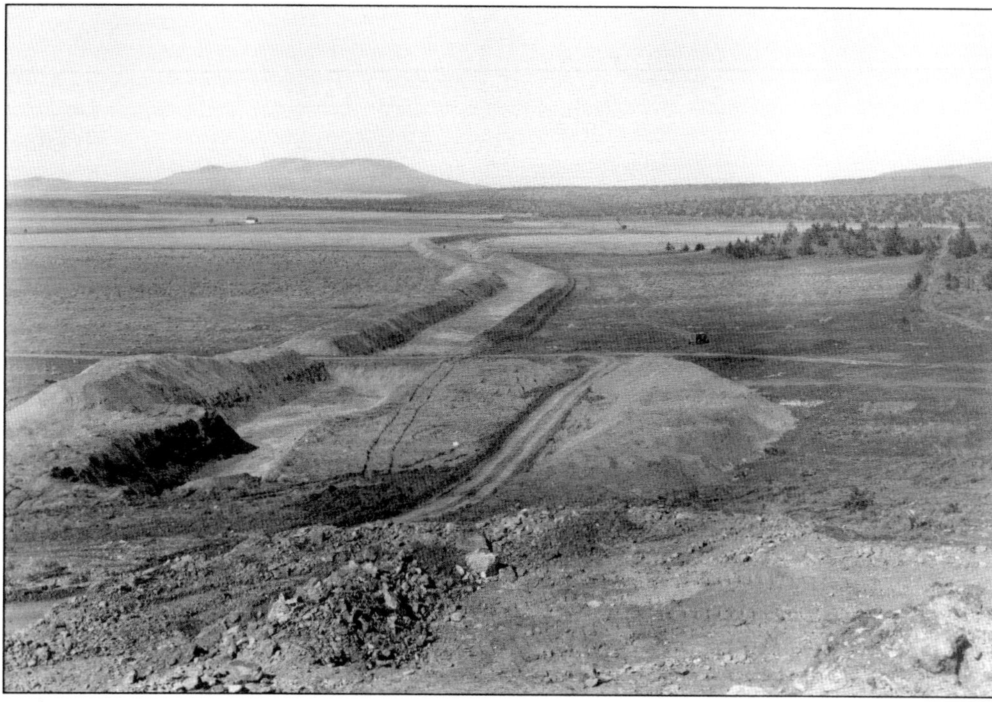

Preliminary construction began on the North Unit Canal south of Juniper Butte near present-day McPheeters Turf Farm east of Highway 97 and north of Crooked River Gorge.

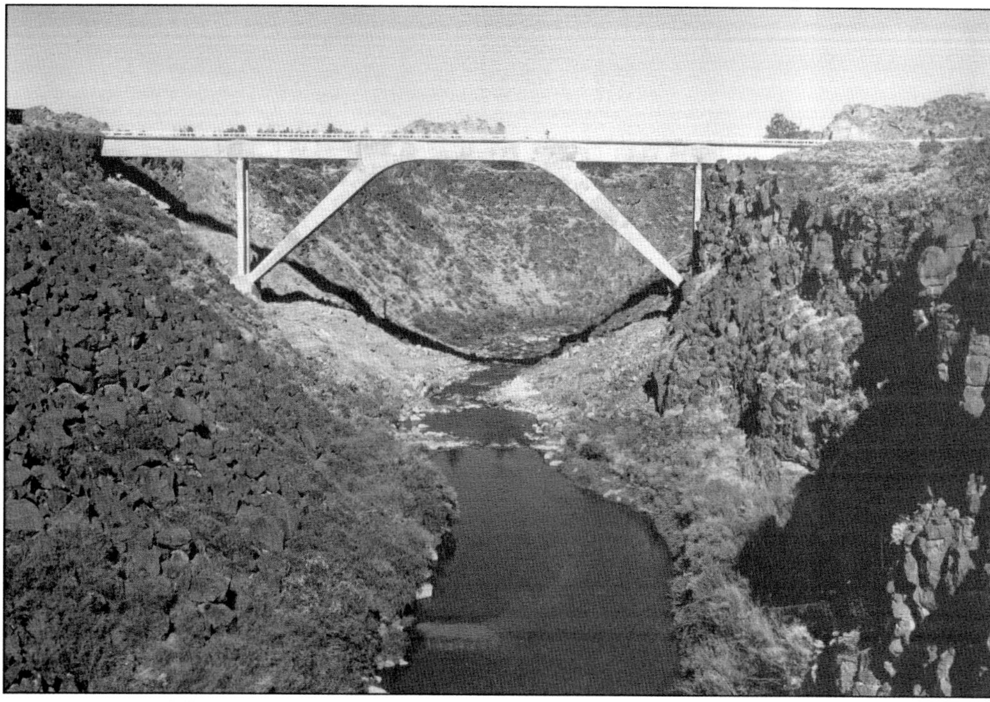

Construction of the flume across Crooked River Canyon just east of Smith Rocks was a major accomplishment, allowing the canal water to flow over the river and then traverse through two long tunnels, which had been one of the major obstacles along the canal route.

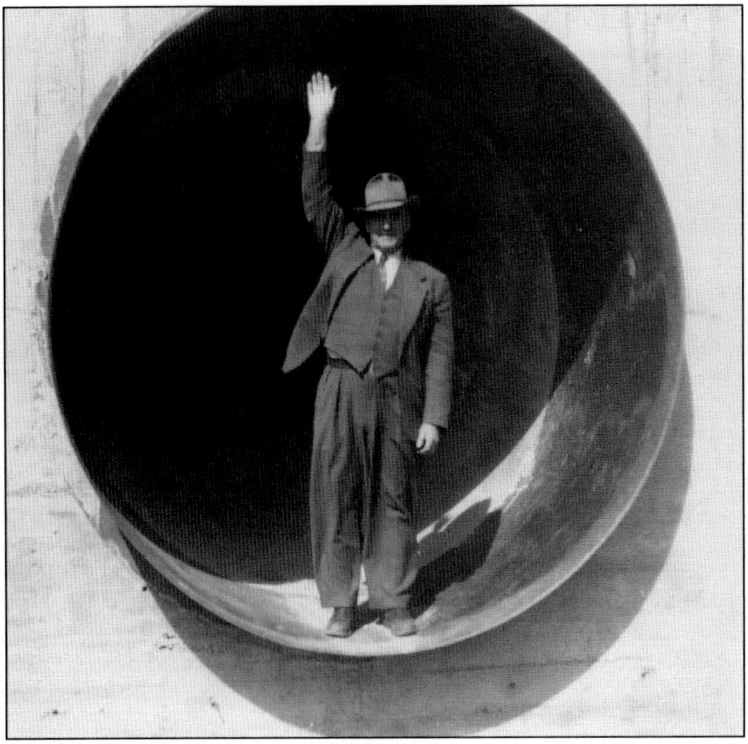

Prominent Madras official Howard Turner stands in the flume pipe of the North Unit Canal near Crooked River. Turner was active in promoting the canal construction and the water project.

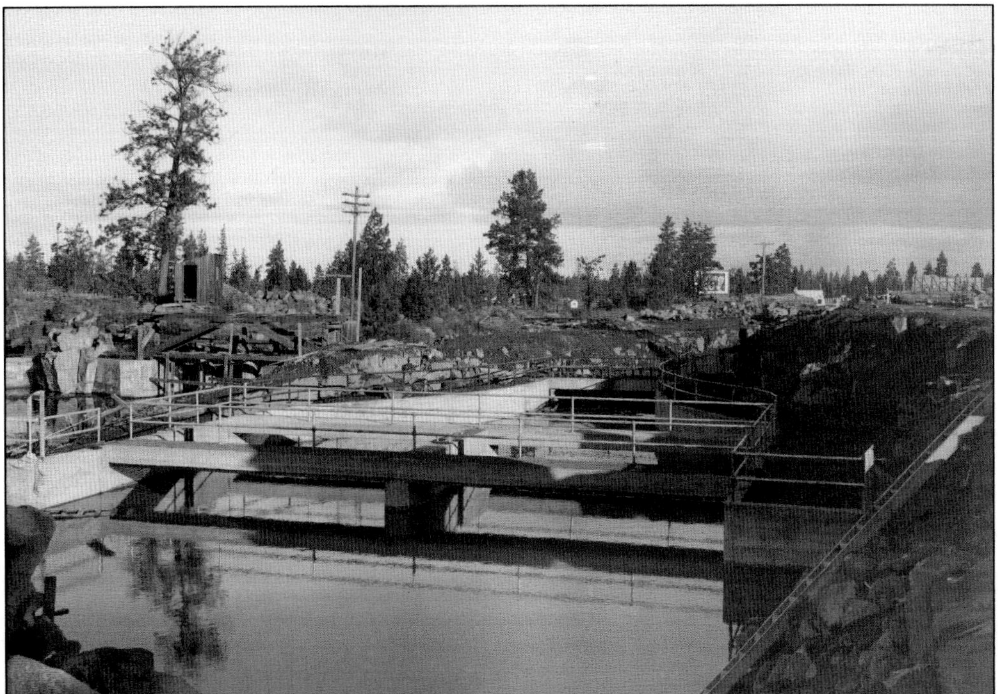

The head gate of the North Unit Canal just north of Bend is seen here shortly after its completion in 1942. Water storage at Wickiup Dam, 50 miles south, allowed water to be diverted from the Deschutes River near Bend to provide water flow along the North Unit Canal system.

George Rodman of Culver receives the first water delivery south of Madras in 1946. After several decades of frustration, irrigation water finally arrived to Jefferson County and the Madras vicinity and was followed by a period of more productive farming.

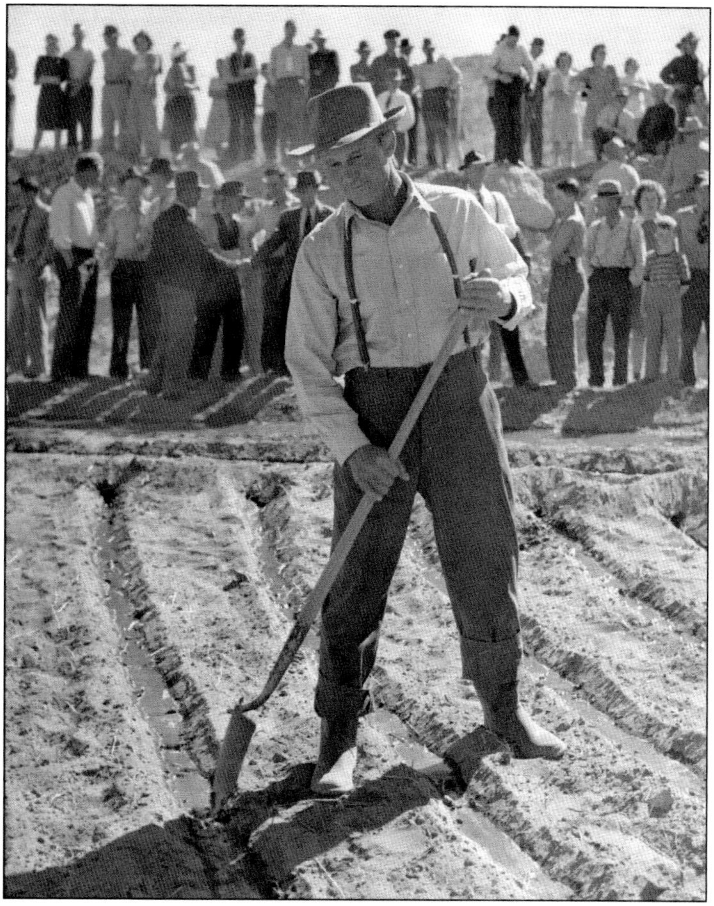

The first day of water delivery to the North Unit Project was May 20, 1946. A large crowd of local residents gathered for the Madras Water Festival to welcome the arrival of water. Here, the crowd is gathered to witness the first opening of gates, allowing water to flow through lateral ditches.

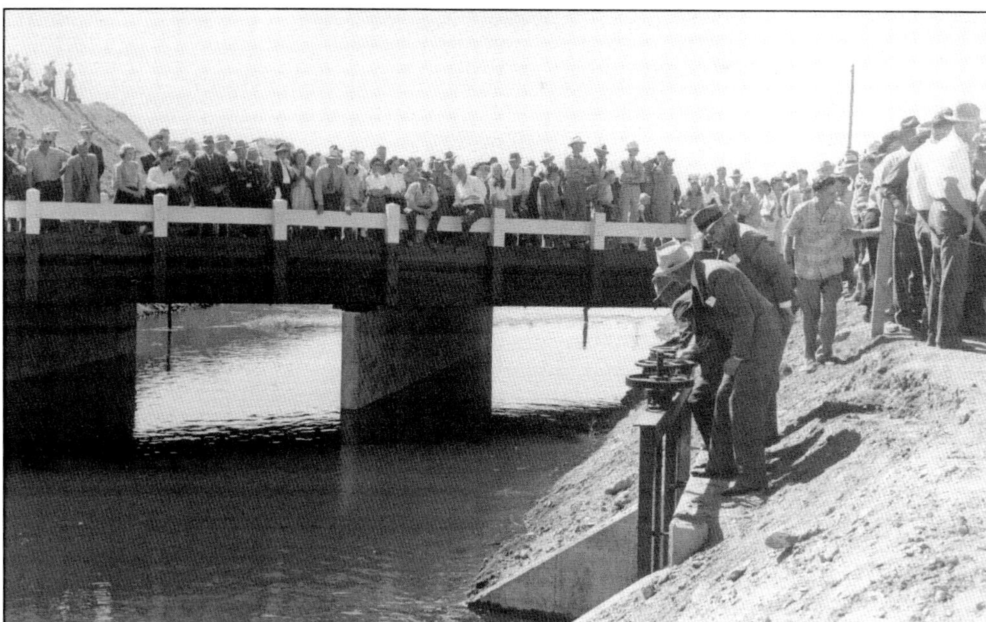

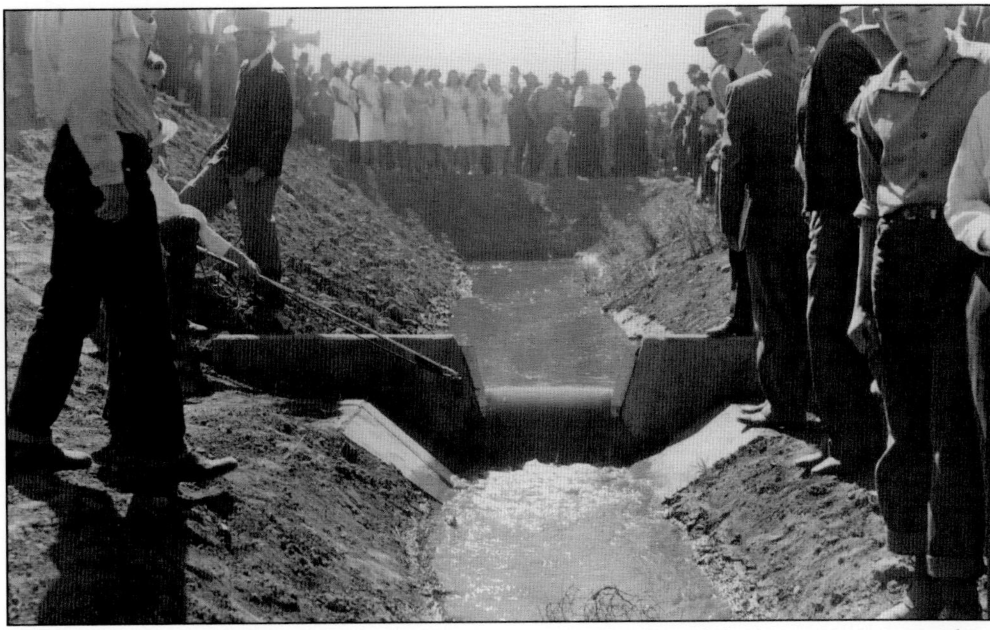

The Madras Water Festival crowd is gathered along the first lateral ditch to receive water from the main North Unit Canal on May 20, 1946. In the background is the Water Festival Court, wearing white dresses while observing the event. Howard Turner, who had proclaimed the arrival of the railroads as the greatest moment in Madras history, now proclaimed that the greatest day in Madras history was the arrival of irrigation water to the region.

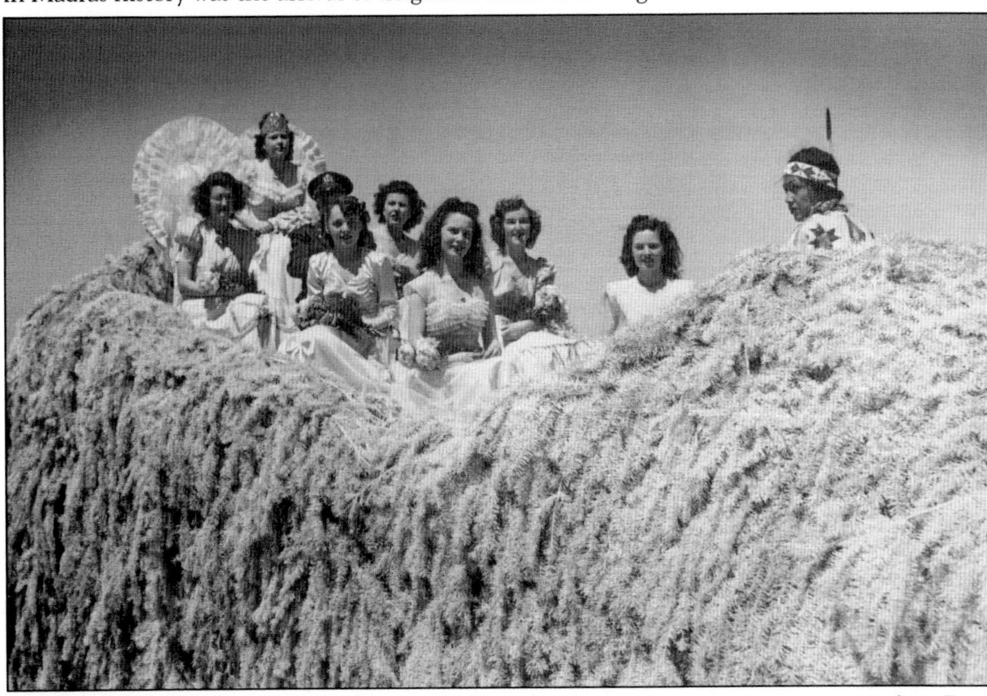

The Water Festival Court is on a float celebrating the arrival of irrigation water to Madras. From left to right are Bertie Ann McDonald, queen Evelyn Kelley, Donna Ramsey, Elna Degner, Phyllis Bolter, Kathryn Freeman, Shirley Bolter, and Thelma Davis. The gentleman is unidentified.

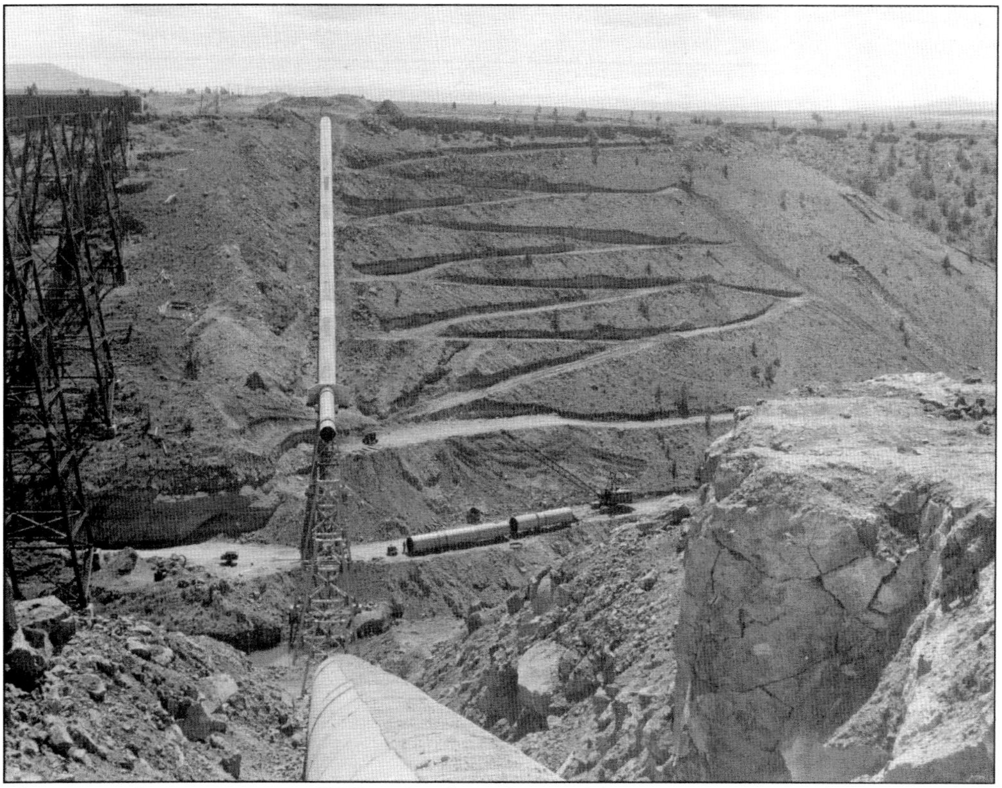

This pipe siphon went across Willow Creek to Agency Plains in 1948. Several major obstacles created engineering problems for completion of the canal water delivery, and the siphon was one of the last segments of the canal system to be completed. Water had been delivered to areas south of Madras in 1946, but it was not until 1948 that water was delivered to Agency Plains after the completion of the siphon.

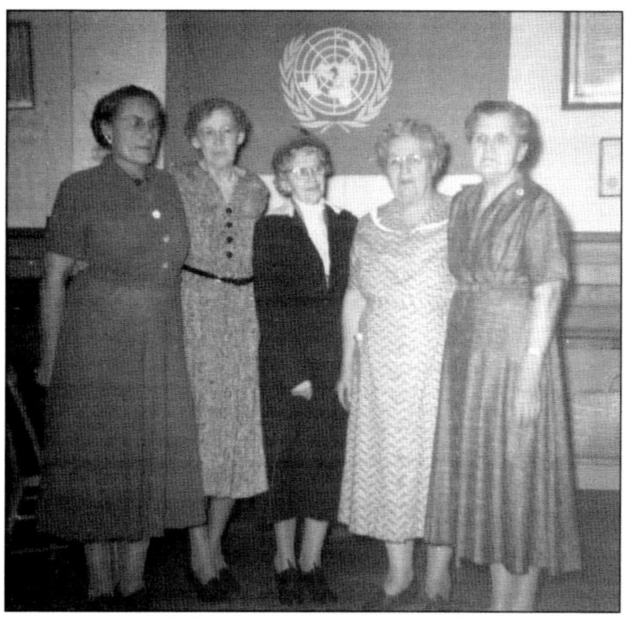

This 1950 photograph shows charter members of the Mud Springs Grange. From left to right are Leitha Richardson, Blanche Henderson, Eva Stebbins, Etta Lee, and Bertha Evick. Mud Springs Grange was first organized in 1923, and the first meetings were held in the Mud Springs school four miles north of Madras. In 1937, a building was moved from Metolius to Madras and used as the Grange Hall. Blanche Henderson, the first woman master for the Grange, presided over the first meeting at the new location.